Forgiveness in Conte

FORGIVENESS IN CONTEXT

Theology and Psychology in Creative Dialogue

Edited by

FRASER WATTS
AND
LIZ GULLIFORD

T&T CLARK INTERNATIONAL
A Continuum imprint
LONDON • NEW YORK

T&T CLARK INTERNATIONAL

A Continuum imprint

The Tower Building
11 York Road
London SE1 7NX, UK

15 East 26th St
New York, NY 10010
USA

www.tandtclark.com

British Library Cataloguing-in-Publication Data
A catalogue record for this book is available from the British Library

ISBN 0 567 08483 3 (Paperback)
ISBN 0 567 08493 0 (Hardback)

Typeset by Tradespools, Frome, Somerset.
Printed and bound in Great Britain by The Cromwell Press, Trowbridge, Wiltshire.

Contents

Preface

In this book, we have tried to bring the theology and psychology of forgiveness into dialogue with one another. Forgiveness has long been an important topic for theology, and recently it has become an active research area for psychology as well. We are not the first to have included theological and psychological contributions in the same book. However, we believe that this is the most truly interdisciplinary study of forgiveness so far, in that it brings the theology and psychology of forgiveness into a rich and creative dialogue.

We are conscious that acts of forgiveness are very diverse. The nature of forgiveness depends on the background and attitude of the individuals concerned, and on the social context. We hope that we have been sensitive to the diverse contexts in which forgiveness take place – hence our title. We have also tried to be sensitive to both the personal and social aspects of forgiveness.

Like all good edited books, this one arises out of collaborative activity. Most of us have links with Cambridge. The editors work there, and the contributors include former Cambridge students, a Visiting Fellow and a former College Chaplain. Though our contributions properly represent different approaches, we hope that on many issues we have forged a coherent and distinctive approach to this important subject.

Liz Gulliford
Fraser Watts

Contributors

Anthony Bash formerly practised law as a solicitor. He studied Theology at the University of Glasgow and gained his doctorate from the University of Cambridge. He is Honorary Director of New Testament Studies at the University of Hull and also vicar of a church outside Hull. Melanie Bash gained her doctorate in Psychology from Cambridge University, and is a clinical psychologist with Nottinghamshire Mental Health Trust.

The Revd Dr Stephen Burns is Tutor in Liturgy at the Queen's Foundation for Ecumenical Theological Education, Birmingham. His two masters degrees, including one in Cambridge supervised by Fraser Watts, considered aspects of forgiveness.

Stephen Cherry is rector of the parish of All Saints with Holy Trinity, Loughborough. He has degrees in both Psychology (Durham) and Theology (Cambridge) and in 1995 completed a PhD entitled 'The Coherence of Forgiveness' at King's College London. He has published in *Theology*, *Christian*, and written for *The Independent*. He was for five years chaplain of King's College Cambridge and recently spent time on study leave in South Africa.

Mary Anne Coate is a chartered clinical psychologist and a Fellow of the British Association for Counselling and Psychotherapy. She has worked both within the ministry of the Church of England – in parish work, university chaplaincy, adult education – and in the adult mental health services of the NHS. More recently she was Head of Training at WPF Counselling and Psychotherapy (Kensington), until her 'retirement' from a full-time post in 2000. She continues part-time, with work and projects at WPF and elsewhere. She has always been interested in atonement theology and in multidisciplinary work and thinking, particularly the interfaces between theological and psychological dimensions and between pastoral care and counselling and psychotherapy. She is the author of *Clergy Stress* (1989) and *Sin, Guilt and Forgiveness* (1994), both in the New Library of Pastoral Care, SPCK, and has recently contributed a chapter 'Beyond psychotherapy – beyond ethics?'

to *Values and Ethics and the Practice of Psychotherapy and Counselling*, edited by Fiona Palmer Barnes and Lesley Murdin (Buckingham: Open University Press, 2001).

Roger Grainger holds doctorates in Sociology, Theology and Implicit Religion. His books about liturgy – *The Language of the Rite* (1974), *The Message of the Rite* (1988) and *The Ritual Image* (1994) – gained him a Higher Doctorate at London University, and he has also written extensively about the interconnectedness of religion, healing and theatre, gaining a PhD from Leeds Metropolitan University for research into dramatherapy, which is one of his main interests. He is a chartered counselling psychologist, and a Professor Extraordinary of Potchefstroom University, South Africa. His latest book is *Health Care and Implicit Religion*, published by Middlesex University Press in 2002.

Liz Gulliford is a research assistant for the 'Psychology and Religion Research Programme' at Cambridge University. She first became interested in the interface between theology and psychology in Oxford whilst reading for a BA in Theology. From there she went on to gain an MPhil from Cambridge, where she studied various interdisciplinary topics, submitting her thesis on 'Theological and Psychological Aspects of Forgiveness' in 1999. Liz also holds a BSc in Psychology for which she studied whilst working for the Programme in Cambridge. She has published in *Ministry Today*.

Dr Solomon Schimmel, Professor of Jewish Education and Psychology at Hebrew College, Boston, is the author of *Wounds Not Healed by Time: The Power of Repentance and Forgiveness* and *The Seven Deadly Sins: Jewish, Christian and Classical Reflections on Human Psychology* (both published by Oxford University Press). He was a Fulbright Senior Research Scholar and Visiting Fellow at the Faculty of Divinity of Cambridge University, England for six months in 1998, has been a National Science Foundation Research Fellow at Harvard University, and a Visiting Professor at Brandeis University, University of Texas, Bar-Ilan University and the Hebrew University.

Fraser Watts, a former clinical psychologist and past President of the British Psychological Society, is now Starbridge Lecturer in Theology and Natural Science in the University of Cambridge and Director of the 'Psychology and Religion Research Programme' in CARTS (the Centre for Advanced Religious and Theological Studies). His recent books include *Theology and Psychology* (Ashgate, 2002) and *Psychology for Christian Ministry* (with Rebecca Nye and Sara Savage, Routledge, 2002). He is also a priest in the Church of England, and chaplain of St. Edward's Church in Cambridge.

Relating the Psychology and Theology of Forgiveness

Fraser Watts

No one can doubt the importance of forgiveness, both in human life generally, and in religious life and thought in particular. In this book we are concerned with both theological and psychological approaches to forgiveness, not only the purely human aspects of forgiveness elucidated by psychology, but also with the Judaeo-Christian tradition which places human forgiveness in the context of divine forgiveness.

Ruptures in human relationships of the kind that call for forgiveness occur very frequently in one-to-one relationships, in families and groups, and in wider society. In this volume we will draw on the resources of contemporary psychology to elucidate how forgiveness works at the human level. As will become clear, we do not imagine that forgiveness is easy or straightforward, or that it is a panacea for human problems. We particularly want to highlight how the context within which forgiveness occurs is a crucial factor to consider if we are to engage deeply with the questions forgiveness poses and avoid over-simplifying the concept.

While forgiveness works at the level of human relationships, it is also central to religious life and thought. The twin themes of repentance and forgiveness are central to the Hebrew Bible, and have continued to be important in Jewish thought. In the New Testament, Jesus frequently talks about forgiveness, and when Christianity is preached in the Acts of the Apostles it is the 'forgiveness of sins' that is proclaimed. Forgiveness has a double importance in the Judaeo-Christian tradition, in that people both believe that they are forgiven by God and also that they are called to forgive others. St Paul makes this link when he urges the Christians at Ephesus to 'be kind to one another, tender-hearted, forgiving one another, as God in Christ forgave you' (Eph. 4.32).

The centrality of forgiveness in Christianity is paralleled in other religious traditions. For example, in the Dhammapada, Gotama Buddha was reported to have said, 'Hatreds never cease through hatred in this world; through loving kindness alone they cease. This is the eternal Law.' Clearly, this has close ties with 'turning the other cheek' to those who would insult you. Other sayings in the Dhammapada highlight the cost of holding onto resentment, a concern echoed in recent psychological research on forgiveness: ' "He abused me, he beat me, he defeated me, he robbed me": in those who harbour such thoughts, hatred is not appeased.' Consider also: ' "He abused me, he beat me, he defeated me, he robbed me": in those who do not harbour such thoughts, hatred is quenched.'

Relating Theology and Psychology

Until relatively recently forgiveness was considered exclusively within a theological framework. Lately, there has been a widespread discovery of the value of forgiveness as therapy, and a secular psychology of forgiveness has begun to develop (see chapters 6 and 7). This is a development that has been welcomed by some, but deplored by others. It raises the question of what relationship a secular approach to forgiveness should have to religious traditions and practices. That can be seen as a specific example of the more general question of how to relate theology to a wide range of scientific disciplines, which Watts (2002, chapter 1) has discussed in connection with theology and psychology. Our general position is that:

(a)   it is valuable to have both a psychological and a religious approach to forgiveness;
(b)   these approaches are not completely separate from one another, but bear on different aspects of the same phenomenon of forgiveness;
(c)   the psychological and theological approaches are compatible with one another, and there is no necessary conflict between them.

There have been helpful discussions of the relationship between theology and psychology that have been oriented towards pastoral care and counselling (e.g. Hunsinger 1995). According to Hunsinger, there are three general principles for relating theology and psychology in this context. I am in complete agreement with her about the first two, which are:

(a)   that the two disciplines should be kept clear and distinct; but

(b)   that they should be brought into relationship with one another.

It is important to avoid the trap of confounding the psychological and theological approaches in a way that does justice to neither. We need to remember that we are dealing with two different disciplines, each with its own discourse and presuppositions. To ignore these differences and mix things together will only produce confusion. However, none of that means that there is no point of contact between them.

Hunsinger's third principle, that there should be a hierarchical relationship between theology and psychology, and that theology should take a determinative role in their relationship, needs more careful examination. In one sense, it is true that theology is a higher-order discipline: it includes a broader range of perspectives. Indeed, if it fulfils its potential, theology is perhaps the highest-order discipline possible. However, which is the superordinate discipline depends on context and purpose. Also, to imply that either discipline is more important than the other is not a good basis for a fruitful relationship. My position is that the theology and psychology of forgiveness are both valuable, but in different ways, and that it is not helpful to imply that one is more important than the other.

It is important to be clear that theology and psychology are not comparable disciplines. Psychology is a more focused and specific discipline that brackets out certain wider questions in order to focus on psychological processes. Theology, by its nature, takes a much broader, panoramic perspective on things. It sees everything within the framework of God, and that is the broadest possible perspective. In this sense, it is perhaps appropriate to think of a hierarchical relationship between theology and psychology, with theology being the broader discipline and psychology being the more specific one. However, that should not be confused with a primacy of importance, or lead to an attempt to subordinate psychology to theology.

It is possible, of course, to assume the primacy of one approach over the other. Either one can conceive of forgiveness primarily as a human phenomenon, admitting that there may be interesting historical background in religious traditions such as Judaism and Christianity, but being concerned with it only in so far as it bears upon current human experience and practice of forgiveness. Alternatively, one can take the theological approach to forgiveness as the primary one, claiming that the starting point for any proper understanding of forgiveness must be God's forgiveness of us, and that the out-working of that at the practical, human level can only be secondary to it. However, the problem with both these approaches is that they tend to marginalize the subordinate perspective, whether that is the religious or the psychological one.

In relating psychological and theological aspects of a topic such as forgiveness, the integrity of both disciplines should be respected. Neither discipline should be subordinated or assimilated into the other, nor be allowed to dictate what propositions are permissible in the other discipline. The coming-together of the two disciplines should be on the basis of each one respecting the autonomy and contribution of the other.

Too often, theological approaches to forgiveness have been abstract and rather disembodied, and not at all closely related to the human realities of forgiveness with which psychology is concerned. That is a sterile way of doing theology, and it is not how theology has to be done. On the other hand, many current psychological approaches to forgiveness have taken it entirely out of its theological context, resulting in a view of forgiveness that is at best impoverished, and at worst naïve. We hope that in this book we will not fall into either trap.

As this book explicitly includes a psychological approach, we need to emphasize that we are not trying to reduce forgiveness to a mere matter of psychology. On the contrary, we start from the assumption that forgiveness needs to be approached from complementary perspectives. There are human aspects of forgiveness that can best be elucidated by psychology, and broader aspects that require a theological perspective. Moreover, we believe that there can be fruitful dialogue between the two, and that this can go both ways. Religious teaching about forgiveness can be more effective if it takes account of the psychological realities of forgiveness. On the other hand, psychological approaches to forgiveness could be enriched by taking a fuller account of a theological approach.

Gregory Jones and Theological Primacy

Gregory Jones, in *Embodying Forgiveness*, protests against the replacement of Christian views of forgiveness with what he calls 'therapeutic forgiveness'. In many ways we would agree with his protest. Like him, we do not want to see religious approaches to forgiveness replaced by secular ones. We share his view that there is an important richness in the religious approach to forgiveness that should not be lost. However, we also think there is value in therapeutic forgiveness that he does not adequately recognize.

He argues that, as a result of our therapeutic culture, 'forgiveness has become an increasingly marginal notion' (p. 37). That claim is hard to reconcile with the facts. The development of a secular therapeutic forgiveness movement is, on the contrary, making forgiveness more central to the lives of many people. Jones also argues that there has been an impoverishment of religious understandings and practices of forgiveness, and we see more truth in that. However, the situation is perhaps not as clear-cut as he suggests.

As a result of the therapeutic forgiveness movement, our understanding of the process of forgiveness is probably now clearer and sharper than at any previous time in Christian history. Nevertheless, it may be true to say that some aspects of forgiveness are being clarified while others have been neglected. We do not see that as a necessary consequence of the therapeutic forgiveness movement, but rather as something that can be rectified by a more fruitful dialogue between the religious and secular approaches. Jones seems to have no interest in such a dialogue. In fact, the development of a more adequate therapeutic approach to forgiveness would represent a correction to some of the emphases in the personal therapy movement about which he complains. It would rebalance a focus on individual autonomy with one on reconciliation, and include the interpersonal dimension as well as the intrapersonal one. It is hard to resist the conclusion that Jones has so little awareness of the therapeutic movement that he criticizes that he is unaware of such subtleties, and of how it might develop.

To some people, like Jones, it will seem controversial to suggest that there is any valid approach to forgiveness apart from the theological one. They would argue that forgiveness cannot be removed from its context in the life and purposes of God, but an important distinction needs to be made between the idea of forgiveness without God, and conceptualisations of forgiveness outside theology. The two are not synonymous.

We would make the assumption that all human forgiveness occurs within the life of God. There is a general sense in which that is true of all human life. However, it is perhaps particularly true when human beings show qualities such as forgiveness, or love, which bring us more closely into union with the divine nature. We also assume that God makes a critical difference to the capacity of humanity to show forgiveness, even where that indebtedness is not fully acknowledged by those concerned. So, we would fully subscribe to the view that there is no forgiveness without God, though we would still submit that human activities, even those such as forgiveness that are central to the divine purpose, can be approached and conceptualized from different points of view. Of course, a non-theological perspective on forgiveness is inadequate in failing to state explicitly the importance of forgiveness in relation to the purposes of God. However, a theological approach to forgiveness is usually also inadequate in the different sense that it fails to engage in sufficient detail with the human context and processes by which acts of forgiveness take place. It is precisely this issue of the contextualization of forgiveness that concerns us in this volume. The assumption that there is no forgiveness without God does not lead to the conclusion that theology provides the only way of conceptualizing forgiveness.

Complementary Perspectives

The most appropriate way of conceptualizing the theological and psychological perspectives on forgiveness is in terms of complementary perspectives. Many human realities need to be described from more than one point of view, with no single description being able to capture the phenomenon completely. For example, depression is a multifaceted phenomenon with biological, social and experiential components. None of those aspects can be neglected if it is to be described satisfactorily. Similarly, going to sleep needs to be described from different perspectives: there is a place for descriptions of both what is happening to electrical rhythms in the brain, and the fragmentation of experience with the onset of sleep. In a similar way, we propose that forgiveness is a phenomenon that needs to be considered from more than one perspective if it is to be described adequately.

On the one hand, one can simply note the parallels, but welcome the development of a psychology of forgiveness that for many purposes supersedes the theological approach from which it has emerged. On the other hand, one can see both approaches as having continuing value, and welcome the development of a psychological approach as complementary to the theology of forgiveness. Much recent work on the psychology of forgiveness seems implicitly to take the first approach. In this book we assume that both theology and psychology have something valid and important to say about forgiveness, and we want to bring them into dialogue with one another. Forgiveness is now both religious and secular; it is not just one or the other.

William Meissner (1987) has provided a helpful example of how to see theology and psychology as complementary perspectives in connection with the subject of grace. Theologically, he sees grace as coming from God and arising from the relationship of people to God. However, he argues that there is also a psychological account to be given of how grace works itself out at the human level. The theology and psychology of grace can thus sit alongside one another, illuminating different aspects. We suggest that theology and psychology can combine to illuminate complementary aspects of forgiveness in a comparable way.

There is nothing very new or startling in this suggestion. There is widespread recognition that many phenomena considered within theology have both theological and human aspects. For example, from one perspective the Church is the body of Christ, while from another it is a human organisation (Dulles 1987). Also, Schillebeeckx (1965) indicates that marriage can be seen as both a 'saving mystery' and a 'secular reality'. In a similar way, there is scope for a theological account of forgiveness that emphasizes that human forgiveness is embedded in God's forgiveness of humanity. Alongside it, one can give a psychological account of the personal processes involved in giving and receiving forgiveness.

In approaching forgiveness from these two perspectives it is important to emphasize the diversity within each of the disciplines of theology and psychology. Within the Christian tradition, for example, there have been many different theological approaches to forgiveness, including an important debate in the early church about whether forgiveness preceded repentance or vice versa. Psychology is also a very diverse discipline that at one end shades into biology, and at the other comes close to sociology. Also, though the psychodynamic psychology of Freud is an important strand within the discipline of psychology, there are many other psychological approaches within which Freud has no place at all. We should therefore be clear that we are relating a range of theologies of forgiveness to a range of psychologies of forgiveness.

Yet another complication is that ideas and concepts tend to 'migrate' between theology and psychology. Broadly speaking, over the last few centuries we have moved out of a culture in which most issues were considered exclusively within a theological framework, and many theological ideas have reappeared in secular guises. For example, the Enlightenment idea that every human being has absolute human dignity seems to be a secular counterpart of the theological idea that we are all created in the image of God. The secular idea of emotion that came to prominence in the nineteenth century within materialistic psychology replaced an earlier theological approach to a similar phenomenon in terms of the 'passions and affections' (Dixon 2001). Even though theology and psychology are distinct disciplines, the relationship between them is made much more complex by the way in which ideas from each appear to have drifted into the intellectual terrain of the other.

Forgiveness is, of course, only one of a series of religious practices that have been raided by the contemporary consumerist world for their practical efficacy. Transcendental Meditation has similarly been taken out of its original context of yogic teaching and general lifestyle, and there have been widespread complaints from those familiar with that context that when meditation is reduced to a therapeutic technique a great deal is lost.

This raises the question of how far forgiveness can be taken out of its original moral and religious context and still be efficacious. It seems to be an empirical fact that people with no religious commitment can practise forgiveness, and to good effect. What is more doubtful is whether forgiveness remains equally helpful if it is practised out of deliberate self-interest. From one perspective, one can claim that forgiveness need not be a matter of principle, and does not need to be undertaken altruistically, but can be approached in a purely pragmatic way, simply out of self-interest. But what effect does it have on forgiveness if it is practised in this pragmatic way? It may well be that, if forgiveness is to be fully helpful to the person who practises it, that person may at least need to believe in the rightness of what they are doing.

There is a parallel issue about prayer. It has become increasingly clear that prayer is helpful, at least for people who practise it. It enables them to process experiences that might otherwise be difficult to assimilate and to develop attitudes that promote a healthy adjustment (Watts 2001). It may therefore be tempting for people with no religious faith to engage in prayer, simply because of its practical benefits. However, the question is whether it is advisable to take prayer out of the context of belief in this way. It may be that prayer is only psychologically beneficial for people who believe that they are practising it within the context of a relationship with God. There is a similar question about the secular practice of forgiveness. Part of the practical value of the religious approach to forgiveness may be lost by taking it out of its original religious context.

The Shape of the Book

Though we intend to be even-handed about the dialogue between the theology and psychology of forgiveness, any dialogue has to start somewhere, and we will start with theology. We look first at concepts of forgiveness in the Hebrew Bible and New Testament, and at how these have been developed respectively in the Jewish tradition and in the early Christian church. Next, we look at concepts of forgiveness in twentieth-century theology, focusing on debates about the nature of forgiveness such as the relationship between forgiveness and repentance.

In doing this, we are seeking not just to give an account of the theology of forgiveness, but to do so in a way that is attentive to the psychological resonance of Christian thinking about forgiveness. Theology often proceeds in an apparently abstract way that leaves people not fully aware of the human and personal significance of what is being said. To remedy that, it is helpful to use psychology to make the human significance of theology explicit (Watts has provided examples of how that can be done. See Watts *et al.* 2001: Chs 14–15; Watts 2002: Chs 7–11). The atonement is an area of theology that has lent itself particularly well to psychological explication, and we hope that the present study of the psychological significance of the theology of forgiveness will make a similar contribution.

We then look at forgiveness in the liturgical life of the church. Our concern is not specifically with liturgies of forgiveness, but with the broader question of how the experience of forgiveness is mediated through liturgical life. Liturgy provides a very interesting arena in which theoretical and practical issues intersect, and provides a point of transition in the book between chapters that start from theology and those that start from psychology.

We then turn more explicitly to the psychology of forgiveness. In these chapters we take a multifaceted approach to forgiveness as a human phenomenon, looking first at what forgiveness requires of the individual (chapter 6), and then at more interpersonal and systemic aspects of forgiveness (chapter 7). We also want to emphasize that forgiveness involves various different facets of human functioning, and in this it is rather like an emotion such as anxiety. There are several important aspects of anxiety (leaving aside the bodily processes that need not concern us here). First there is the subjective experience of anxiety. Next, there is the framework of cognitive assumptions and thought processes within which that is embedded. There is also the pattern of behaviour which arises from anxiety, such as flight or avoidance. Finally, there is the interpersonal context in which anxiety arises.

All these are apparent with forgiveness as well, and this emphasizes what a psychologically rich phenomenon forgiveness is. The sense of estrangement that arises prior to forgiveness involves a set of cognitive assumptions; equally, forgiveness involves a degree of cognitive reframing of the sources of this estrangement. The social context is also important, as forgiveness is by definition an interpersonal phenomenon, even though it may sometimes be undertaken privately: the need for forgiveness arises at the rupture of relationships, and the act of forgiveness is normally instrumental in restoring them. Usually, forgiveness involves observable personal behaviour, one person talking to another and expressing their forgiveness, though on occasions forgiveness is private and intentional rather than spoken and observable. Finally, there are components of subjective experience in forgiveness, often in the form of an empathic reaching out to the other person. Moreover, an act of forgiveness often involves personal transformation, in the sense that people feel different after giving or receiving forgiveness. In what follows, we hope we have been faithful to the complex multifaceted nature of forgiveness, as it is embedded in a range of different contexts.

It has sometimes been supposed that psychology assumes that forgiveness is easy. On the contrary, psychology provides the resources for understanding why forgiveness is so difficult for many people, and this is explored in chapter 8. Where people have not reached the necessary level of psychological maturity it is very difficult for them to rise to the challenge of forgiveness, though the religious hope must be that the resources of God's grace can in some way compensate for insufficient personal resources.

There are also circumstances in which forgiveness is particularly difficult, and the principal one that we explore in chapter 9 is forgiveness following child abuse. It is not just that forgiveness is psychologically difficult in such a context; there are also serious issues about how far forgiveness is even appropriate, and about the consequences of forgiveness in the context of abuse. At the very least, it is evident that it is counter-productive to press people to forgive their abuser when they are not ready or able to do so.

At one end of the spectrum, forgiveness raises very personal issues for the individual, such as whether they have the resources to give or receive forgiveness, what is required of them in doing so and what benefits it brings them. At the other end of the spectrum, forgiveness raises broad societal issues, and the main example we take in chapter 10 is the role of forgiveness in societies such as South Africa, where there is a clear need to seek reconciliation against a background of previous division. With forgiveness there is always a to and fro between the individual and the societal level. It is surely a mistake to regard either the individual or society as primary. The patterns of forgiveness within a society are obviously dependent on what individuals are capable of. However, it is equally true that the character of a society shapes the way individuals function. This is an issue to which we will return in the final chapter.

2

Interpersonal Forgiveness and Repentance in Judaism

Solomon Schimmel

The central theme of this book is how theology and psychology interact constructively to provide a deeper understanding of forgiveness and how it can be applied in interpersonal relationships. As a psychologist, my emphasis will be on human relationships, with a realization that Judaism's views on interpersonal encounters are significantly shaped by its theological ideas. Hence, I begin with a brief discussion of the relationship between divine forgiveness and human repentance in the Hebrew Bible before turning to Jewish teachings about the relationship between forgiveness and repentance in the interpersonal sphere.

Any consideration of forgiveness in a Jewish context must assign to repentance a central role. In Judaism there is, for the most part, an inextricable link, both theologically and psychologically, between forgiveness and repentance. Indeed, in the interpersonal sphere, repentance is more central to Jewish thought than is forgiveness, although forgiveness is important. Even in the theology of Judaism, divine forgiveness is, for the most part contingent upon human repentance, albeit with some exceptions.

Divine Forgiveness and Human Repentance in the Hebrew Bible

The Hebrew Bible is replete with divine calls to the people of Israel, and to other nations (e.g. the Ninevites in the Book of Jonah), to repent of their sins against God (which include crimes against humans), and promises that, if they do so, God will forgive them and not punish them

11

as he otherwise would have done. This divine call for repentance is especially developed in the prophetic books of the Hebrew Bible.

The Hebrew word for repentance, *teshuva*, is derived from *shuv* which means to return, turn back or turn away. Israel as a nation, and individual Israelites, are beseeched by prophets speaking in the name of God to return to him, by turning away or turning back from the sinful, disobedient direction in which they are going. He wants the sinner to return because he does not want the sinner to die, but rather to return and live. In other texts it is the person praying who confesses guilt, promises to change his ways and 'return', and pleads that she or he be forgiven: 'Return, faithless Israel, says the Lord. I will not look on you in anger, for I am merciful, says the Lord; I will not be angry forever.' (Jeremiah 3.12).

> But if the wicked turn away from all their sins that they have committed and keep all my statutes and do what is lawful and right, they shall surely live, they shall not die. None of the transgressions that they have committed shall be remembered against them; for the righteousness that they have done they shall live. Have I any pleasure in the death of the wicked, says the Lord God, and not rather that they should turn from their ways and live? (Ezekiel 18.21–23)

In these and other passages (see Jonah 3.1–10; 1 Kings 8.46–52; Psalm 51.1–4) God is described as merciful, compassionate and forgiving in response to the repentant sinner who acknowledges his or her sins, expresses remorse and makes an effort to change his or her behaviours. However, none of these passages depict God forgiving a non-repentant sinner who, having been warned and given time to repent, fails to do so.

Jeremiah 31 depicts God as deeply pained by the suffering that Israel experiences as punishment for her sins. He is not only willing to forgive Israel in response to her repentance but, like a loving and compassionate parent, yearns for his child to return to him. He wants to forgive so that their earlier relationship of love and companionship can be re-established. Because of his recollection of that earlier love, he will be responsive to initial, if not yet complete, demonstrations of repentance. God had punished the tribes of Israel (symbolized by Ephraim) by exiling them from the Holy Land. When the Lord saw the depths of Ephraim's suffering and recalled Israel's love and devotion in the early phase of their covenantal relationship, his compassion and mercy were aroused. He saw that Ephraim (Israel) was remorseful for his sins although he found it difficult to break away from them on his own initiative. The Lord's mercy in response to Ephraim's shame will result in a new covenant between God and Israel, one in which Israel's commitment to the Lord will be more resilient and more deeply internalized than before.

Although divine forgiveness is largely contingent upon human repentance, some biblical passages seem to suggest that there are times when God might forgive the remnant of Israel even if they have not fully repented:

> Who is a God like you, pardoning iniquity and passing over the transgression of the remnant of your possession? He does not retain his anger forever, because he delights in showing clemency. He will again have compassion upon us; he will tread our iniquities under foot. You will cast all our sins into the depths of the sea. You will show faithfulness to Abraham, as you have sworn to our ancestors from the days of old. (Micah 7.18–20)

In addition to appealing to God's merciful nature there is also an appeal to the commitment God had made to the patriarchs: Israel appeals to God for mercy and forgiveness not on its own merit, but because of the promise God made to Abraham of siring a great nation. If Israel will not be forgiven God will, in effect, renege on his commitment to the patriarchs.

Other grounds for requesting divine forgiveness of Israel, while acknowledging Israel does not deserve it, is that it is in God's 'selfish' interest. God's reputation among the nations depends on Israel's flourishing, and if she is destroyed or exiled this would reflect poorly on God. This argument was used by Moses when he successfully appeased God's wrath after the sin of the golden calf, convincing him not to destroy Israel (Exodus 32.9–14). In a similar vein Ezekiel (36.22–31) says:

> It is not for your sake, O house of Israel, that I am about to act, but for the sake of my holy name, which you have profaned among the nations to which you came...the nations shall know that I am the Lord...when through you I display my holiness before their eyes...I will sprinkle clean water upon you, and you shall be clean from all your uncleannesses...A new heart I will give you...and make you follow my statutes and be careful to observe my ordinances...and I will summon the grain and make it abundant...so that you may never again suffer the disgrace of famine among the nations. Then you shall remember your evil ways, and your dealings that were not good; and you shall loathe yourselves for your iniquities and your abominable deeds.

This passage suggests that forgiveness, or rather remission of punishment (but not necessarily divine love), will come first, *for God's sake*. In response to this divine redemptive action Israel will eventually experience remorse and self-loathing for her sins.

I have surely not done justice to the full range and depth of the theology of repentance and forgiveness in the Hebrew Bible, but have selected those elements which I think bear most directly on subsequent developments in Judaism and that relate to repentance and forgiveness in the interpersonal sphere.

In post-biblical Judaic ethics the notion of imitating God is central. Jewish thinkers looked at how God dealt with repentance and forgiveness, and modelled their ideas on how humans should behave based upon God's ways. What they saw was that, for the most part, God called upon sinners to repent, and forgave them when they did, and did not forgive them when they did not. We too have to forgive those who repent of their sins against us. That said, there were times when God forgave unrepentant, or not fully repentant, sinners, which left open the possibility that in some situations people can be asked or expected to forgive a perpetrator who had not repented. We will now turn directly to what Judaism has to say about repentance and forgiveness in interpersonal relationships, beginning with the Hebrew Bible.

Interpersonal Repentance and Forgiveness in the Hebrew Bible

There is very little in the Hebrew Bible about interpersonal repentance and forgiveness. A few narratives describe forgiveness and reconciliation. Esau does not exact revenge on his brother Jacob, who took advantage of Esau's thirst to pressure him to sell his birthright, and who fooled their blind and aged father Isaac into giving him the superior blessing that Isaac had intended for Esau. When Jacob, who fled from Canaan out of fear that Esau would kill him, returns, he offers magnanimous gifts and an implicit apology to Esau, who had come to meet him with four hundred men. Esau is moved and reconciled with Jacob.

Joseph, who was sold into slavery by his brothers and is now vice-regent of Egypt, forgives his brothers when they plead for mercy. They had by then demonstrated some elements of repentance: confession, apology, and a willingness to resist a temptation similar to the one they faced and had succumbed to when they sold Joseph. They had offered to sacrifice themselves to protect their father's 'favoured' son, Benjamin. This offer contrasts with their behaviour in selling Joseph into slavery because they envied him for being Jacob's favourite (and for insensitively flaunting his favoured status).

In a few stories David is depicted as forgoing revenge and controlling his anger, at Nabal, and perhaps at Saul and Absalom, all three of whom had tried to kill him. In these stories the forgiver is someone in power who shows mercy towards an offender whom he could have put to death. There are no instances of a powerful offender requesting forgiveness from, or being forgiven by, a weak victim of his, or of someone forgiving an offender no more, or less, powerful than the victim. These narratives enhance the reputation of the powerful party who 'pardons' and acts mercifully towards an offender who is in a temporary or permanent position of weakness.

The motives for the forgiveness differ in each case. Joseph seems to forgive out of brotherly affection, respect for his father, and a belief that his brothers had been God's instrument for good, even though they had intended evil. We are not informed of Esau's motive for forgiving and reconciling with Jacob. David does not kill Nabal because he is moved by the pleas of Nabal's wife, Abigail, who appealed to his magnanimity and self-interest, and whom he desires, and indeed takes as a wife when Nabal later drops dead. There is no indication that he is in any way less resentful towards Nabal or 'loves his enemy'. David spares Saul's life because of his reverence for one anointed by God, his deep and loving friendship with Saul's son Jonathan (who would be pained were his father killed) and perhaps out of appreciation for the love that Saul had once shown him. In each of these cases the forgiveness or mercy is not a 'free gift of love'. It is grounded in self-interest or in natural emotions that are more powerful than the desire for revenge. However, on his death bed David instructs Solomon to exact revenge on Joab and on Shimei son of Gera (1 Kings 2.5–9).

Many Psalms are replete with requests that God punish and destroy the pray-er's enemies or are expressions of gratitude to God for having done so. The supplicant does not beseech God to forgive his enemies, nor does he himself forgive them.

Just as there is a paucity of stories and prayers advocating interpersonal forgiveness in the Hebrew Bible, there are no explicit laws or commandments to forgive someone who has injured you. The one closest to it is the admonition, 'You shall not hate in your heart anyone of your kin; you shall reprove your neighbour, or you will incur guilt yourself. You shall not take vengeance or bear a grudge against any of your people, but you shall love your neighbour as yourself: I am the Lord' (Leviticus 19.17–18).

This admonition prohibits concealed hatred and revenge. It does not prohibit resentment expressed openly and channelled legitimately and fairly through the justice system. The prohibition is with respect to your 'kin' and 'neighbour'. If 'Love your neighbour' is the coda to verses 9–17 in their entirety (as some suggest), then 'love' refers primarily to compassion for the poor, honesty and integrity in matters of money, truth and objectivity in legal judgment, and sensitive and ethical behaviour. To 'love' is to act properly. It is not necessarily to forgive injuries. Later rabbinic teachers broadened the meaning of 'love your neighbour as yourself' beyond its original sense.

The Ethos of Forgiveness in Post Biblical Judaism and in the New Testament

Reimer (1996) demonstrates that Jesus' teaching on forgiveness is not a sudden and radical break from post-biblical Jewish views. It can be traced back to some books of the Apocrypha and other intertestamental Jewish works. For example, we read in the Wisdom of Ben Sira, 'Forgive your neighbour the wrong he has done, and then your sins will be pardoned when you pray' (Wisdom of Ben Sira 28.2). In The Testament of Gad Joseph's brother Gad offers ethical instruction to his children before he dies. He had hated Joseph, but repented of that hatred and learned how important it is to overcome it:

> Love one another from the heart, therefore, and if anyone sins against you, speak to him in peace. Expel the venom of hatred, and do not harbor deceit in your heart. If anyone confesses and repents, forgive him...Even if he denies it and acts disgracefully out of a sense of guilt, be quiet and do not become upset. For he who denies will repent and avoid offending you again...But even if he is devoid of shame and persists in his wickedness, forgive him from the heart and leave vengeance to God. (Testament of Gad 6.3, 6–7)

Not all Jewish sages of the rabbinic period taught that repentance must be a prerequisite for forgiveness. We find several teachings that call for forgiving even the non-repentant offender. A story is told of the renowned Rabbi Meir (second century CE) who had been offended by villains in his neighbourhood. He prayed that the perpetrators should die. Meir, it seemed, justified his prayer by appealing to the verse 'Let *htm* be consumed from the earth, and let the wicked be no more' (Psalm 104.35). The Hebrew consonants *htm* in this verse can be vocalized as *hotim* (which means sinners), or *hataim* (which usually mean sins). Rabbi Meir understood the passage to refer to sinners, so he prayed that the sinners would die. On hearing this his wife, Beruria, criticized and corrected him: 'You should vocalize *htm* as *hataim*, referring to sins, not sinners. The verse should be interpreted that if sins would be removed, there would no longer be sinners. Rather than pray for the sinners to die, pray that they should repent and no longer sin.' Meir followed his wise wife's advice, and prayed on behalf of the sinners, that they should repent, which eventually they did (*Talmud Berakhot* 10a). This is the idea that God loves sinners even though he hates their sins.

This idea can be understood in several ways, but one common one is that almost every sinner also has the potential to do good, which is what God wants of him. God, in his patience, sets aside punishment so that the sinner can reform himself. We should treat sinners who hurt us similarly. One way of understanding Joseph's benevolent and forgiving behaviour towards his brothers (for whom he engineered an opportunity to repent) is that he was more concerned with their spiritual well-being than with revenge or strict justice. If we did not love the perpetrator or have compassion for him we would not *want* him to repent, just as Jonah did not want the Ninevites to repent. This is not precisely the same as forgiveness as a pure act of grace (because repentance is still the focus of concern) but it comes close to it.

Although the predominant theme in traditional Jewish teaching about forgiveness is that you need not forgive someone who has sinned against you who does not express remorse, compensate you and request forgiveness (the victim, if he or she chooses, may forgive the offender, as long as there will not be any adverse consequences for others as a result of this voluntary forgiveness), there appears to have been a debate about this which is reflected in two closely related texts from the second and third centuries CE. The first is from the *Mishnah*. The context of this teaching is the law of torts, which specified the fines that a person who shamed another was required to pay. After having specified the monetary penalties the *Mishnah* states: 'Even though he (the perpetrator) pays (the victim of his insult), he is not forgiven until he requests from him [forgiveness]' (*Mishnah Bava Kamma* 8.7). It continues with an admonition that it would be cruel for the victim not to grant forgiveness once the perpetrator has paid the fine and requested forgiveness. This teaching reflects the predominant attitude of the tradition. However, another rabbinic text takes a different approach. It teaches that the victim of an assault should pray to God to have mercy on his assailant even if the assailant has not requested that he do so (*Toseftah Bava Kamma* 9.1). Later commentators who juxtaposed these two passages either accepted that there were two different views, or tried to harmonize the texts by explaining the latter to mean that if the perpetrator has requested forgiveness, the victim should not only forgive him himself, but also pray to God on his behalf, even though he did not request that from the victim.

Repentance and Forgiveness in Mediaeval and Modern Jewish Thought

When you commit an offence against someone (whether by an act of commission or of omission) you usually produce three deleterious effects. First, in doing evil you lessen your own moral status: you are a less worthy individual than you were before your offence. Second, you have caused pain, humiliation or injury to your victim. Third, beyond the specific pain or suffering which you inflicted, you have breached a human relationship. Consequently, there is now a net increase in the level of bitterness, hatred and ill will in your familial or social setting. Not only does your victim bear you a grudge but usually friends and family are affected by what you have done, so many human relationships which were amicable, or neutral, have now become infected with negative affect. Repentance is the process whereby you rectify the harm you have caused. What does repentance entail and how might it repair the deleterious consequences of interpersonal sins or offences? Ideally, repentance includes four elements. First, you must recognize and acknowledge your sin, and feel guilt and remorse for having committed it. Second, you must repair the injury you caused. Third, you must apologise to your victim. Fourth, you should be able to face again a situation similar in its pressures and temptations to the situation in which your offence was committed, and not succumb.

Recognition, acknowledgment of your sin and remorse, constitute guilt. Justifiable, or warranted, guilt (unlike neurotic or irrational guilt) is an emotion that is necessary and desirable as a stage in the process of repentance.

After the Second World War, Jewish philosopher Martin Buber (1957) addressed a group of theologians and psychologists on 'The Genesis of Guilt'. He distinguished between guilt, in the sense of full acknowledgment that you did something morally wrong, and painful guilt feelings. There are too many of us who have committed sins or offences, and are thus objectively guilty, yet who do not experience guilt feelings as we should. Sometimes we may feel unease (a vague or repressed sense that we have done something wrong), but we need to be prodded, by our own consciences or by others, to examine ourselves, experience remorse and repent. If we do not, we will be morally at fault forever and, if not totally in denial, continuously gnawed at by this sense that we have violated a moral norm.

Buber had in mind, among others, German theologians and other 'respectable' Germans who remained 'neutral' during the period of Nazi atrocities against Jews and others. They did not protest and sometimes silently or indirectly collaborated. After the war some denied their dereliction of moral responsibility, others felt an uneasy anxiety, and some experienced actual guilt feelings, even as they denied their objective guilt. Is it the responsibility of the therapist, asks Buber, to help these people assuage their anxiety and guilt feelings, without pointing them to the way of remorse and repentance? No. Each one of us has to live up to our responsibilities and hold ourselves accountable for our misdeeds. Deserved guilt feelings (deserved because we are actually morally guilty) should not, and often cannot, be severed from the objective evils we did, and 'therapeutically treated' independently of their source in our actions or failure to act. The therapeutically and morally correct approach is to undergo repentance, either in its religious form for those who are religious, or a secular equivalent. For Buber, the therapist's role is at times to point the guilt-ridden or guilt-deserving patient in the direction of three demands of conscience and repentance:

> ...first, to illuminate the darkness that still weaves itself about the guilt...with a broad and enduring light; second...to persevere in that newly won humble knowledge of the identity of the present person with the person of that time, and third, in his place and according to his capacity...to restore the order-of-being injured by him through active devotion to the world – for the wounds of the order-of-being can be healed in infinitely many other places than those at which they were inflicted. (Buber 1957b: 122)

The concept of the 'self' is paradoxical in the context of thinking about repentance. To be truly penitent one must acknowledge that he who I am today is continuous with he who I was when I sinned, last week, last year, or decades ago. Only by acknowledging the continuity between my past, my present and my future can I regret my past, feel contrite about it, try to remedy to the extent possible its continuous effects on the present, and hope for future purification and reconciliation. On the other hand, when we repent we request that we be judged not only or primarily by what we were, but by who we are now, and now we believe that we would no longer commit such a wrong. We want our victim or society to see us as discontinuous with the self of our past. Only then can we hope for mercy, forgiveness and reconciliation. The paradox of true repentance is in its assuming responsibility for the past while hoping that one will be freed of that past to start anew.

For Buber an offence against a single human being is also an offence against 'the order-of-being' – analogous in religious thought to an offence against God. Since one often cannot repair the damage caused to a specific individual, does that mean that there is no hope for the truly remorseful offender to assuage his guilt? Jewish moralists such as Buber suggest that there are other pathways to repair and healing.

The teaching that the obligation of a victim to forgive an offender is contingent upon the offender's sincere repentance is summarized in Maimonides' Laws of Repentance. Maimonides, for the most part, based his formulations on the Hebrew Bible and on rabbinic literature such as the *Talmud* and the midrashic collections.

> A man is forbidden to be cruel and must be conciliatory; he should be easily appeased, hard to make angry, and when a wrongdoer begs his forgiveness, he ought to forgive with a whole heart and willing spirit. Even if he was persecuted and much wronged, he ought not to be vengeful and bear a grudge, because such is the way of the upright hearts of the children of Israel...

> One who sins against his friend and his friend dies before forgiveness is sought should bring ten men and stand at his grave and say to them: 'I have sinned against the God of Israel and my friend and have done thus to him.' If he owed money it should be returned to the inheritors; if they are not known it should be left with the Beth Din (court) with a confession. (Maimonides, Laws of Repentance, 2.9–11)

Elsewhere in his *Code*, in the context of injuries and humiliation caused by an assault, Maimonides writes:

> The offended person is prohibited from being cruel in not offering forgiveness [Heb. *mehilah*], for this is not the way of the seed of Israel. Rather, if the offender has [resolved all material claims and has] asked and begged for forgiveness once, even twice, and if the offended person knows that the other has done repentance for sin and feels remorse for what he has done, the offended person should offer the sinner forgiveness [*mehilah*]. (*Mishneh Torah*, Laws of Assault, 5.10)

The Jewish theologian, David Blumenthal (1998), distinguishes between two aspects or types of forgiveness, *mehilah*, (a forgoing of indebtedness) and *selihah*:

> The principle that *mehilah* ought to be granted only if deserved is the great Jewish 'No' to easy forgiveness. It is core to the Jewish view of forgiveness, just as desisting from sin is the core to the Jewish view of repentance. Without good grounds, the offended person should not forgo the [moral] indebtedness of the sinner; otherwise, the sinner may never truly repent and evil will be perpetuated. And, conversely, if there are good grounds to waive the [moral] debt or relinquish the [moral] claim, the offended person is morally bound to do so. This is the great Jewish 'Yes' to the possibility of repentance for every sinner.
>
> The second kind of forgiveness is ... *selihah*. It is an act of the heart. It is reaching a deeper understanding of the sinner. It is achieving an empathy for the troubledness of the other. *Selihah*, too, is not a reconciliation or an embracing of the offender; it is simply reaching the conclusion that the offender too, is human, frail, and deserving of sympathy. It is closer to an act of mercy than to an act of grace. (pp. 79–80)

In Judaism repentance, justice and forgiveness are central values. However, for the most part, and especially for egregious crimes, repentance and justice are prioritised over forgiveness. Repentance is related to justice in various ways, but especially in so far as it includes reparation or, where that is not possible, some substitute. To forgive an unrepentant criminal or sinner could lead to injustice. Yet to forgive a repentant sinner, especially where the harm he has caused continues to have an effect on the victim and his family, is no easy matter. Aware of the natural resistance of a victim or his or her family to forgiving even the sinner who has sincerely repented, Jewish sages of the rabbinic and mediaeval period emphasized in a variety of teachings and laws how important it was to do so.

Most of the Jewish respondents to Simon Wiesenthal's question about whether he should have forgiven a dying Nazi soldier who had committed atrocities against Jews agreed that he need not – indeed, even should not or could not – do so. It is the victims of a crime or injury who are 'authorized' to forgive the offender, and they are under no obligation to do so in the absence of as sincere and as full a repentance as is feasible for him. Where the victim is dead no human can forgive the perpetrator (Wiesenthal 1976, 1997).

Repentance and Reintegration Into the Community

Judaism took it for granted that society should do what it could to encourage sinners to repent, and that if they sincerely repented they should be reintegrated into the community. Can a criminal or sinner who has repented and who has paid whatever penalty the law requires be trusted and restored to his pre-criminal social status and rights? The question is debated by Jewish jurists. Maimonides states that various sinners (including thieves and others who take money illegally) are disqualified to be witnesses. The thief is barred from testifying in any judicial proceeding even if he returned that which he stole. Some jurists maintain that if he returned the money on his own initiative (rather than because he was compelled to do so by a court) he is assumed to have repented and can now serve as a witness. Others, however, maintain that even in the latter case he remains disqualified. Perhaps this stricter view reflects a deep suspicion of the sincerity of an ostensible penitent's repentance, or a gnawing suspicion that even a sincere penitent is in danger of relapsing. Since testimony in court affects the fate and fortune of others it is necessary to be especially careful with respect to who is permitted to testify.

Is there anything a repentant sinner can or must do to convince society that he is sincere and deserves to be restored to full and trusted membership in it? Since only God 'knows the thoughts of man', mortals have to rely on behaviours they observe in others when they assess whether repentance is feigned or authentic.

Addressing this issue, the *Talmud* tells of a *shohet*, a ritual slaughterer and butcher, who sold meat that the *shohet* knew was non-kosher to a Jew, because the *shohet* did not want to sustain the financial loss of discarding the meat. The *shohet* had (for the sake of money) committed the sin of causing a fellow Jew to unknowingly eat forbidden food. When the communal leader, Rabbi Nahman, found out he declared that the *shohet* could no longer be trusted, depriving him of his occupation and income. The *shohet* let his hair and nails grow long, making himself disgusting – traditional acts of self-humiliation that penitents were accustomed to perform as signs of their repentance. Rabbi Nahman was prepared to reinstate him in his position. However, Rava objected on the grounds that he might be feigning repentance to get his job back. Was there anything, then, that he could do to convince Rava that he was sincere, and that he could now be trusted to be willing to sustain a financial loss rather than sell to an unknowing public non-kosher meat as if it were kosher? Yes, says the *Talmud*, as Rabbi Idi the son of Avin taught:

> One who is suspected of selling non-kosher food as kosher has no remedy [that will restore his trustworthiness] until he goes to a place where no one knows who he is and having found a valuable lost object returns it to its rightful owner, or who having slaughtered an expensive animal of his own and then found it [by examining its innards] to be non-kosher, declares it to be so. (*Babylonian Talmud Sanhedrin* 25a)

In other words, the litmus test has to be some behaviour which unambiguously suggests that the sinner, having faced a situation of temptation similar to the one in which he initially succumbed, will not repeat the offence. In both of these 'test' situations the slaughterer could have gotten away with violating the law for the sake of monetary gain or to prevent monetary loss, without detection, and yet he chose to follow the law and sustain a loss. The reason he has to do this in a locale where he is not known is because that lessens the probability that he is doing what he does in order to regain his original job as slaughterer. In this new locale he would have no such motive. Although this test of probity and sincerity is very demanding, it does enable a sincere penitent to regain his good reputation, and reclaim his social status and rights.

A responsum by the tenth-century jurist Rabbenu Gershom deals with the restoration of ritual privileges to a *kohen*, a member of the priestly family. After the destruction of the Temple in Jerusalem in 70 CE, priests retained a few vestigial ritual obligations and privileges. One of these is to publicly bless the congregants in the synagogue in a special ceremony conducted on certain festivals. All the priests in the congregation stand in the front of the synagogue where the Ark and its Torah Scroll are kept and chant the blessings. Priests are also called up to recite the first of the blessings when the Torah is read in public during a service. These honours are accorded to priests in recognition of their lineage, and as signs that the priests have maintained their sanctity notwithstanding the loss of the Temple and its worship service.

A certain priest had committed one of the gravest sins imaginable to a mediaeval Jew: conversion to Christianity. The priest had now repented of this sin and wanted to participate again in the privileged priestly blessings. Rabbenu Gershom ruled that since he had repented he could do so. In supporting his ruling he cited several biblical and rabbinic texts which testify to the great concern (as well as respect) for the repentant sinner that permeates the Jewish ethos. For example, the rabbis expand the meaning of the biblical prohibition against monetarily oppressing one's fellow to refer to verbal oppression as well. They give as one example that it is forbidden to say to a repentant sinner 'remember your previous [sinful] deeds'. There is no greater oppression of this repentant priest, says Rabbenu Gershom, than to deny him his original privileges. Since these privileges are manifested in public settings, the very fact that the priest would be publicly denied the right to perform them would be a recurring public reminder to him, in the presence of the congregation, that he had once been a sinner. Moreover, says Rabbenu Gershom, if you do not allow the priest to begin his life anew as a purified penitent you will discourage him (and others) from repenting in the first place. These rabbinic teachings and rulings are sensitive to the fact that repentance does not take place in a social vacuum. Repentance is not exclusively a personal experience between man and God, or between man and his conscience, uninfluenced by social forces.

As further support for his ruling, Rabbenu Gershom cites the talmudic statement that 'anyone who asserts that [King] Manasseh has no share in the world to come is weakening the hands of penitents' (*Babylonian Talmud, Tractate Sanhedrin*, 103a). What were Manasseh's sins? We read in 2 Chronicles 33 that Manasseh (who assumed the throne after the death of his God-fearing father Hezekiah) 'did what was evil in the sight of the Lord...erected altars to the Baals...worshipped the host of heaven and served them. He built altars [to foreign deities] in the house of the Lord...' (vv. 2–4). The list of Manasseh's abominations goes on and on. His sins were not just personal, but corrupted the entire nation.

In the rabbinic world-view, a leader who causes others to sin typically forfeits any right to the rewards of the hereafter, notwithstanding positive deeds he may have done. But Manasseh had a saving grace. Eventually he was bound in fetters and brought to Babylon where, we are told, 'While he was in distress he entreated the favour of the Lord his God and humbled himself greatly before the God of his ancestors. He prayed to him, and God received his entreaty, heard his plea, and restored him again to Jerusalem, and to his kingdom. Then Manasseh knew that the Lord indeed was God' (vv. 12–13).

The rabbis saw the profound psychological and theological implications of this story. Here was a man who had committed a catalogue of sins so evil that one would expect no mercy or forgiveness for him. Yet because he repented he was reinstated. It seems that there were people in talmudic times who, quite understandably, found it difficult to imagine that such a sinner could ever merit reward in the eternal hereafter. They might have felt that his reward for his repentance was given him in this world, with his reinstatement as king, but surely such an ex-sinner cannot have a share in the world to come. To this, the rabbis responded that even Manasseh can rehabilitate himself to the point of eternal reward.

If Manasseh can be purified then almost any sinner can. Those who would deny this possibility are sending a message to sinners that repentance does not pay: there is no hope. This is not the message the rabbis wanted to convey, even to the worst of sinners. On the contrary, repent sincerely and you will be accepted, no matter how far you have deviated from the path of righteousness.

Rabbenu Gershom teaches that it is not only God who accepts the repentant sinner. We, as individuals and as a community, have to reintegrate him as well. If we do not we will have lost an opportunity to save a soul that is groping for redemption and needs helping hands to draw it back into the sphere of virtue. The rabbis and Rabbenu Gershom want us to overcome our natural inclination to shun the sinner even after he has repented.

Repentance, Forgiveness and Reconciliation in Conflicts Involving Jews as a Group

In recent years there have been voices calling for the introduction of the concepts, and more importantly, the practices, of repentance and forgiveness at a group level and in the political sphere (e.g. Gopin 2000, Muller-Farenholz 1997, Shriver 1995). They maintain that the practices of repentance and forgiveness are useful (or even necessary) for effecting reconciliation between groups in conflict in which injustice has been perpetrated by one group against another, or by two groups against each other. When two national groups are locked in long and painful conflict in which both suffer and hurt, the practice of 'individual' repentance and forgiveness and 'group' or 'political' repentance and forgiveness should nurture and reinforce each other.

If repentance and forgiveness are to play constructive roles in the resolution of conflicts between groups or nations then, from a Jewish perspective, the question of the *degree* of moral blame of the antagonists cannot be shunted aside for the ostensible sake of peace. This does not, however, mean that reconciliation between groups should always be made contingent upon both parties eventually adopting a shared interpretation of their painful interactions, since that will rarely happen.

Reconciliation also cannot be made contingent upon *full* repentance and *full* forgiveness, or on the rectification of *all* the injustices perpetrated during the protracted conflict, because that too can rarely happen. However, if each side comes to better understand and empathize with the other side, and some elements of repentance and forgiveness are employed at the individual and the 'political' level, there is a chance for the cessation of the conflict and for peaceful coexistence. In some cases a deeper reconciliation, with the development of positive attitudes and feelings between the antagonists, may emerge over time. Conflict resolution and reconciliation do not require that the antagonists deny or ignore the terrible wrongs of the past. On the contrary, the more honest an acceptance of the past and acknowledgment of wrongs committed in the past, with expressions of regret, efforts at reparation, and forgiveness, the greater the probability of an enduring peaceful relationship between the two groups in the future.

Jews as a group, and the State of Israel, are often called upon (especially by Christians) to forgive their enemies, such as Palestinian terrorists who have massacred innocent Jews, and Arab nations who have initiated wars against Israel with the intent of eliminating its existence as a sovereign state with a Jewish majority. Others appeal to both Israeli Jews and Palestinian Arabs to forgive one another for past injuries and move towards reconciliation. Some Israeli and non-Israeli Jews call upon Israeli Jews as embodied in the State of Israel to repent for the suffering that they have inflicted on Palestinian Arabs. I believe that the Jewish, Muslim and Christian concepts of repentance, forgiveness and gestures of reconciliation can contribute to a peaceful resolution of this conflict. Their role, however, would be one of supporting and shaping the contours of broader diplomatic, economic and political measures that are being brought to bear in the efforts of recent years to resolve the Israeli-Palestinian conflict.

Group reconciliation and conflict resolution can take place directly between small groups of individuals who are members of the groups in conflict. At the grass roots level there are several groups of Israeli Jews and Palestinians, of different ages, who meet for the purpose of working towards peaceful reconciliation. Where the individuals who meet for the purpose of reconciliation have themselves suffered directly from the actions of their antagonist, the attempt has greater legitimacy and credibility in the eyes of the group than when the conciliators have not suffered directly from the conflict. If Jews who were injured by Palestinian bombs and Palestinians who were injured by Israeli soldiers (or if parents of Jews and of Palestinians who died in the conflict) can meet in a serious endeavour to overcome antagonisms and hatreds, other Jews and Palestinians, whose sufferings have been less direct, will find it easier to accept the possibility of reconciliation. One such group, *Parents Circle*, of parents and relatives of Israelis and Palestinians killed in the conflict, has been meeting to see if steps towards reconciliation can be taken. Since both groups believe that justice is on their side it is difficult to think of reconciliation in terms of repentance, which implies admission of guilt, or of forgiveness, since who should be forgiving whom? The focus is more on the pragmatic and mutually beneficial goal of overcoming the enmity on the person-to-person level in the hopes that this will reinforce political attempts to negotiate peace (Sennott 1999).

However, to be willing to make peace with an enemy when under no duress suggests a measure of empathy for him and perhaps a willingness to concede that there is some justification for his animosity, if not for his behaviour. It may also suggest a willingness to be sufficiently critical of one's own position to concede that what one's own group has done has not always been justifiable. These are early stages of repentance.

There are many similarities between Judaic, Islamic and Christian understandings of repentance as a religious value and as a psychological process. To the extent that the antagonists in the Israeli–Palestinian conflict identify with the religious values of Judaism, Islam and Christianity respectively (some Palestinians are Christian), calls for repentance can be meaningful to both sides. Appeals to religious values are most effective when made by spiritual leaders to their own adherents, rather than when made by the antagonist. For a rabbi to preach repentance to a Muslim, or for an Imam to preach repentance to Jews, will engender indignation, resistance and hostility rather than a move towards the difficult, emotionally wrenching process of repentance which, as we have seen, includes self-criticism, overcoming the denial of one's wrongdoing, remorse, empathy for the 'other', apology and restitution.

Perhaps the most effective approach to harnessing religious values such as remorse, repentance and forgiveness to group conflict resolution would be for clergy of the different faiths in conflict to try to better understand how their own religious traditions can enhance peace-making. If they can arrive at a consensus (for example, that sinful behaviours have been engaged in by members of their group in the context of the conflict) they can work towards educating their followers towards the process of self-transformation that is repentance. Religious leaders have to condemn vociferously and unambiguously those who murder innocents. They have to condemn also those who support the murderers, calling upon supporters of the murderers to reassess and change their attitudes and behaviours in light of their own religious teachings – in other words, to call them to repentance. Religious leaders regularly admonish their flock to repent for personal sins. They have to be willing to do so for sins committed under the aegis of political acts.

Repentance and Forgiveness in Kabbalistic Ethics

A more elaborate and radical Jewish version of an ethos of forgiveness can be found in the sixteenth-century book *The Palm Tree of Deborah* (translated by Louis Jacobs 1960). This brief but influential ethical-mystical treatise by the great kabbalist (Jewish mystic), Rabbi Moses Cordovero of Safed in the Galilee, applies in detail the notion of the obligation to imitate God as a vehicle for teaching values that relate to how one should respond to insult and injury. Cordovero cites biblical verses that describe how God behaves towards the people of Israel as a model for how Jews should respond to one another. The book, being meant as a spiritual guide for the Jews in their Jewish communities, focuses on interpersonal Jewish behaviours, alluding only briefly to mankind in general. It is possible that the ethos Cordovero advocates might not be expected by him to apply in all contexts, since the demands he makes, as we shall see, are emotionally and ethically daunting. Cordovero cites the passage from Micah 7.18–20, which we quoted earlier:

Who is a God like You,
Forgiving iniquity
And remitting transgression;
Who has not maintained His wrath forever
Against the remnant of His own people,
Because He loves graciousness!
He will take us back in love;
He will cover up our iniquities,
You will hurl all our sins
Into the depths of the sea.
You will keep faith with Jacob,
Loyalty to Abraham,
As You promised on oath to our fathers
In days gone by.

Cordovero analyses each phrase for the message it teaches about forgiveness. The Jew is to act towards his fellow Jew in the same way that God is described (in these passages) as acting towards the people of Israel as a collective. Here are a few of the teachings which Cordovero derives regarding interpersonal forgiveness.

Forgiving iniquity (or bearing sins)

... a man should learn the degree of patience in bearing his neighbor's yoke and the evils done by his neighbor even when those evils still exist. So that even if his neighbor offends he bears with him until the wrong is righted or until it vanishes of its own accord... (p. 50)

Because He loves graciousness

Even when he is offended or provoked, if the offender has his good points in that he is kind to others or he possesses some other good quality this should be sufficient to soothe his anger so that his heart is pleased with him and delights in the kindness he does. And he should say: 'It is enough for me that he possesses this good quality.'... So he should say with regard to all men: 'It is enough for me that he has shown me or another man kindness or that he possesses this particular good quality.' And he should delight in mercy. (pp. 56–57)

In days gone by

Even when he cannot discover any plea [on behalf of the sinner]... he should still say: 'Behold there was a time when they had not sinned. And in that time or in former days they were worthy.'... In this way no man will be found an unworthy recipient of goodness nor unworthy to be prayed for and to have mercy shown on him. (pp. 68–69)

[Man] is to bring the love of his fellow-men into his heart, even loving the wicked as if they were his brothers and more so until the love of his fellow-men becomes firmly fixed in his heart... (p. 79)

The overall perspective garnered from Cordovero's teachings is similar to the Christian approaches that many Jews have found to be inappropriate responses to insult and injury. Be that as it may, Cordovero is solidly within the Jewish tradition of ethical teachings even though his view is a minority one. Cordovero is aware that it would be unrealistic and even inappropriate to demand such forbearance, love and compassion all the time. There are times, he says, when other emotions and reactions, more in line with justice than with compassion, are necessary. However, the Jew, he says, should at least try to respond with compassion, mercy, love and forgiveness towards evildoers on Sabbaths and other holy days and occasions, where aspirations for holiness are particularly called for.

Substantial sections of this chapter have appeared in, or are slightly modified versions of material that appears in my book, *Wounds Not Healed by Time: The Power of Repentance and Forgiveness* (Oxford University Press, 2002). Appreciation to Oxford University Press is hereby expressed for permission to use this material.

3

Early Christian Thinking

Anthony Bash and Melanie Bash

Christianity is a religion that emphasizes forgiveness, and Jesus Christ, on whose teachings Christianity is based, spoke about and practised forgiveness. Perhaps the most famous words on forgiveness that Jesus is thought to have said are his prayer on the cross, 'Father, forgive them, for they do not know what they are doing' (Luke 23.34). And certainly the most often quoted words of Jesus on forgiveness are in the Lord's Prayer in its traditional form, 'Forgive us our trespasses, as we forgive them that trespass against us'. Forgiveness is part of what it means to love, and Christianity is, above all, a religion of love.

If we were to ask a person who was reasonably familiar with the New Testament – perhaps a person who regularly attended a church, for example – about who wrote the most, and the most passionately, about forgiveness in the New Testament, the answer we would almost certainly receive is, 'The Apostle Paul'. And if that were the answer, it would be wrong. For the New Testament writer who has written most about forgiveness is Luke, even if we take into account that he wrote the largest portion of the New Testament (the Gospel of Luke and Acts). For example, Jesus' prayer on the cross (Luke 23.34, quoted above) is, surprisingly, in Luke's gospel alone.

Luke's theology of forgiveness is the most thorough and extensive of any New Testament writer. In Luke's gospel and in Acts, forgiveness of sins is at the heart of the message of the kingdom of God. It is part of a cluster of ideas that explicate what the gospel meant for Jesus' hearers, both then and in the life to come. Other New Testament writers have, as we shall see, a contribution to make on the subject, but theirs is a much less self-consciously systematic and thorough approach.

The Gospels and Acts

Since Luke's theology of forgiveness is the best developed, Luke and Acts will be used as the basis of the discussion in this section. Where there are points of difference with the other gospel writers, these will be explored. In the following discussion, we assume the widely held view that Mark was written first and that both Luke and Matthew knew and used Mark's gospel or a version similar to it.

Luke's Language

The most frequent words that Luke and the other gospel writers use to express the idea 'forgive' and 'forgiveness' are the Greek verb *aphiemi* and its cognate noun *aphesis*. The usual meaning of the verb is 'to leave, abandon'. So, for example, in Luke 4.38f. Jesus healed Peter's mother-in-law and as a result the fever from which she had been suffering left her. In pre-Christian secular Greek, the word does not refer to forgiveness in a religious sense, but in biblical and biblically influenced Greek (such as in the Septuagint, the Greek translation of the Hebrew Scriptures, and in the writings of Josephus) it does. Luke uses these words when referring to the actions of Jesus in relation to a person's sin (*hamartia*) to explain what it is to have a part in the kingdom of God.

When Luke uses *aphiemi* or *aphesis* referring to sin, what does he mean has been 'left' or 'abandoned'? We might say with our modern perspective – and conflating the synoptic gospels with other parts of the New Testament – that by the sacrifice of the cross it is the guilt that comes from sinning, and perhaps even the penalty for sin itself, that have been left, and as a result the person becomes free of the guilt of sin and its penalty. The Levitical priests atoned for sin through the sin offerings (Leviticus 4.1–5.13) and the popular impression is that in a similar way Jesus atoned for sin through his sacrificial death. This view of the cross is reinforced by the fact that the words *aphiemi* and *aphesis* in secular Greek often carry a juridical sense, meaning (in the case of the verb) to discharge someone from a legal relationship, such as a marriage, debt or punishment. So some say that it is by the sacrifice of the cross that the legal debt that sin creates is waived.

A juridical use of *aphesis* and *aphiemi* does occur in some parts of the New Testament – in 1 Corinthians 7.11–13, for example – but not in relation to forgiveness. Seeing a sacrificial sense in texts on forgiveness in the synoptic gospels is reading what is not there. Mark, for example, sees the cross as being about ransom, a word most often used in relation to the ransom of slaves, not sacrifice (10.45//Matthew 20.28), and he sees the shedding of Jesus' blood (14.24//Matthew 26.28, Luke 22.20) as being about establishing a new covenant and so new communities. Those who are forgiven – and here Mark might say those ransomed from their sins – are the ones who enter the kingdom of God. They have been released from their sins and so from the present age. The cross is central to this, but not as sacrifice (but cf. Hebrews 9.22). Sin and its consequences are characteristic of the 'present evil age'; in the age to come, they will have been dealt with and their presence and consequences banished by Jesus.

Luke also uses another word to express the idea of 'forgiveness' in Luke 6.37 and this is the verb *apoluo*. The verb means 'to release', in the sense that Pilate released Barrabas from custody (Luke 23.16–25). Here the idea of being released explicates the nature of forgiveness. Once again, the same idea is present as with the verb *aphiemi*: those whose sins are forgiven have been released from sin and have become part of the kingdom of God.

Luke's language has its roots in the Hebrew Scriptures and the Greek translation of them in the Septuagint. Two Hebrew words express the idea of forgiveness: *ns'* (e.g. Exodus 32.32; Psalm 25.18 and 31.5) and *slḥ* (e.g. Leviticus 4.20; 5.10, 13; Numbers 14.19; 15.25f.; Isaiah 55.7). These are translated by *aphiemi* in the Septuagint. *Slḥ* means to forgive – whereas the basic idea of *ns'* is to remove, lift away or carry away, and so (in some contexts) to forgive. The removal of sin through forgiveness is also expressed in Psalm 51.1; 85.2; 103.12; Isaiah 43.25; 44.22; Jeremiah 31.34; and Micah 7.19. Luke's contribution is to retain the basic meaning of these Hebrew words when they refer to sin and to put them into an eschatological context, that is, into a context to do with what will take place at the end of human history and time when God will transform the world into something different. For Luke forgiveness means release from the present evil age into the age to come.

John the Baptist

Forgiveness was central to John the Baptist's preaching (Luke 3.3 – and see Luke 1.77). He called people to a 'baptism of repentance for the forgiveness of sins' (Luke 3.3; Mark 1.4). The forgiveness that John promised was an eschatological forgiveness, to come with the kingdom of God. Since judgment of sins was also integral to the future kingdom, repentance was essential preparation for John's hearers.

But in John's message it was not repentance that *led* to forgiveness, in the sense that one thing causes another. Rather, baptism signified repentance (see Acts 2.38) and the *purpose* of the baptism signified that the people were ready to receive God's forgiveness and to be spared his judgment when the kingdom came.

The washing that is part of baptism is a figure of the washing away of sin in forgiveness. In this sense, the baptism of John was akin to the baptism of the Qumran community where only those whose lives had already attained an adequate level of achievement were permitted to undergo washing in the community's purificatory bath.

Jesus

Forgiveness as an aspect of Jesus' ministry, practice and teaching is evident at most of the significant points in the life of Jesus. Forgiveness was not just a promise for the age to come: it could be enjoyed in the present as well (Luke 5.17–26; 7.47) in a proleptic sense, as a foretaste of future realities, during the time of Jesus' ministry.

Jesus says that the Son of Man has authority to forgive sins (Luke 5.24//Matthew 9.6; Mark 2.10), but he forgives on only two occasions (Luke 7.48 and Luke 5.20//Matthew 9.2; Mark 2.5 – and see Hooker 1991: 86). John's baptism signified repentance (and so being ready to receive forgiveness and the kingdom of God), but it was possible to receive forgiveness without first being baptised. In the story of the man let down through a roof (Luke 5.17–26//Matthew 9.2–8), for example, there is no indication that the man was baptised *before* he was forgiven.

The word that is usually translated 'forgiveness' (*aphesis*) occurs in Luke's gospel at the start of Jesus' ministry when Jesus preached in the synagogue in Nazareth. Then, Jesus set out the good news of the gospel to the world, promising 'release' or 'liberty' (in both cases the word is *aphesis*) to the captives and the oppressed (Luke 4.18). This reflects the use of the word in the Septuagint which in the NRSV is also translated 'jubilee' (Leviticus 25.10–54), 'release' (Deuteronomy 15.1f.) and 'liberty' (Isaiah 58.6; 61.1). When Luke uses this word, he has in mind more than sins: the word encapsulates an idea at the centre of the good news of the kingdom. It points to a whole new order that God was to introduce, in which people would be released from living in the present order of reality alone and would be made part of God's eternal community. Forgiveness and release are one and the same, and both are part of the hope of the kingdom of God.

Forgiveness is also evidently what Jesus practised in relation to his killers – and he was even able to pray for them when dying (Luke 23.34), and forgiveness is an essential constituent of the gospel that the risen Jesus commanded the disciples to preach to the world (Luke 24.47).

Omissions in Luke's Gospel

Given these observations, there are two surprising omissions in Luke's gospel. The first is in Luke's record of the institution of the Eucharist (Luke 22.15–20//Matthew 26.26–29; Mark 14.22–25) when he does *not* say that the blood of new covenant, symbolically represented in the cup of wine, has been given 'for the forgiveness of sins'. Matthew *does* use these words (Matthew 26.28 – and this is the only place where Matthew uses the word *aphesis* in relation to sin), expanding his likely source, the Gospel of Mark (Mark 14.24) that, like Luke, does not have the words. The reason may become apparent if we also note that Matthew omits to record what is in Mark 1.4 (// Luke 3.3) that John's baptism was for 'the forgiveness of sins' (see Matthew 3.1f.). Matthew seems to want to highlight that the death of Jesus establishes a new covenant with humanity that brings about the forgiveness of sins. It is Jesus, in the words of Matthew 1.21, who will 'save his people from their sins' and Matthew's focus for this is the covenant made through the cross. Luke, on the other hand, does not see forgiveness of sins as coming through a covenant made with humanity by the cross: for Luke, forgiveness comes from believing the message of the kingdom and being released from sin.

The second surprising omission is in Luke 8.10. This is part of a quotation in Mark 4.12 from Isaiah 6.9f. which says that Jesus taught in parables to those outside God's kingdom 'so that they may not turn again, and be forgiven'. Luke omits the words 'so that they may not turn again, and be forgiven' for two reasons. First, because he did not want to suggest that God hid the gospel in parables to prevent repentance and forgiveness. Second, because he wants to emphasize that it is not repenting or turning to God that bring forgiveness (as the passage from Mark seems to imply): rather, forgiveness would come as a gift from God to those who were ready for the kingdom when it came.

Acts

Acts, written by Luke as the second of a two-volume work, develops and reinforces what Luke's gospel explains. Jesus and his ministry were central to the eschatological gift of forgiveness and did what the Old Testament law could not do (Acts 13.38f.). Forgiveness came to people, according to 5.31, when the work of Jesus was completed and Jesus had been exalted to God's right hand. If the people repented and were baptised, they would be forgiven and, as evidence, they would receive God's gift of the Holy Spirit, one of the authenticating experiences of those who had a part in the kingdom of God (2.38 with 5.32). Believing

Jesus to be the eschatological prophet ensures God's forgiveness (10.42f.), whether the person was a Jew (2.38) or a Gentile (26.17f.).

In short, whether in the Gospel of Luke or in Acts, forgiveness is one of the words that best explains why Jesus came, what he sought to teach and what he offers the world. At every significant point in Luke's gospel in particular, forgiveness is highlighted, modelled and proclaimed. In Acts, it is central to the message of the kingdom of God and the fulfilment of a long-awaited promise.

Is Forgiveness Conditional?

In each of the synoptic gospels Jesus says that God's forgiveness is linked with the forgiveness that human beings extend towards one another. So in Luke 6.37, those who forgive will be forgiven (and see also Mark 11.25 and Matthew 6.14f.).

Does this mean that God's forgiveness is conditional upon a person practising forgiveness first? In one sense this is unlikely, given that forgiveness is what a hardened, unforgiving human being needs. So in Luke 5.17–26 (//Mark 2.1–12; Matthew 9.1–8), the paralysed man who was let down through a roof was forgiven his sins (without a prior pre-condition that he should forgive others) – and this was on the basis of the faith of those who had let him down through the roof.

What Luke means is that those who experience God's love and mercy should themselves be able to mediate and practise them (see, for example, 2 Corinthians 1.3–6 and 1 John 4.7–12, 19) and, unless they do so, it is questionable whether they have in fact experienced that love and mercy. A true experience of God's forgiveness will imprint itself onto the character of the recipient and enable the recipient to forgive others. A forgiven person should be a forgiving person. So the friends of the paralysed man could extend love and grace to their disabled friend because they themselves had first received God's love and grace. Unforgiveness in the human heart – as well as lack of love or mercy or grace or any other Christian virtue – may well indicate that the person concerned has never truly experienced God and his forgiveness first hand.

These observations may also explain Luke 11.4, part of the Lord's Prayer. People are to pray 'Forgive us our sins, for we ourselves forgive everyone indebted to us.' The word 'indebted' in this petition is from the verb *opheilo*, and refers to obligation or debt, usually in relation to financial matters. Here Luke seems to be saying that when people experience God's lavish forgiveness of sins – that is, when they experience God's release through forgiveness – they will be transformed and should model the same release towards others. Matthew 6.12 has 'Forgive us our debts (*opheilemata*) as we also have forgiven our debtors (*opheiletais*)'. Matthew's intended audience was almost certainly Jewish and they, unlike Luke's Gentile audience, would have understood the idea of 'debt' here as being a religious term meaning 'sin' because sin made a person indebted to God: see Davies and Allison 1988–1997: I, 611f.). If God has forgiven a person their sins, it should be easy for the forgiven person to waive a mere debt. Mercy received in one area of life should spill out in mercy demonstrated in other areas of life towards others. The same idea is found in the parable of the unforgiving servant in Matthew 18.21–35 and in the story of the forgiven prostitute in Luke 7.41–43, 47.

The forgiveness people are to extend to one another is, according to Matthew, not to be exercised to a limited and measurable extent (and so conceived of in quantitative terms) but to be limitless, practised as often as needed. In the kingdom of God, forgiveness is not to be limited to seven occasions for one offence (as Peter mistakenly thought – though even this seems more generous than popular opinion at the time: see Davies and Allison 1988–1997: II, 793) but it is to be unbounded and lavish (Matthew 18.21f.), sincerely and without limitation or restriction by law and casuistry (and so 'from the heart' – Matthew 18.35).

Though there are similar passages warning about unforgiveness in both Luke and Matthew (e.g. Luke 11.4 – cf. Matthew 6.12), Matthew's overall intention is different from Luke's. Matthew's gospel, when read as a whole, does say that forgiveness is conditional. In 5.7, it is the merciful (those who show mercy to others) who will receive mercy; and in 6.14f. (//Mark 11.25f.), those who forgive others their trespasses will be forgiven – but those who do not forgive will not be forgiven.

In part, the context of Matthew's gospel explains this difference between Matthew and Luke: Matthew's gospel was written principally for Jewish Christians, that is, for those who had received and experienced the love and grace of God both under the 'old covenant' as Jews and then under the 'new covenant' as Jewish Christians. Whether under the old covenant or the new, forgiveness demonstrates that the one who forgives is a recipient of grace through the covenant. Lack of forgiveness casts doubt on that, and may mean that the person is outside the covenant and so also outside the community.

But we cannot avoid the fact that there are some people who have received forgiveness and yet who do not practise it. If Luke's distinctive contribution to the theology of forgiveness is to point to the fact that forgiveness of sins is at the heart of the message of the kingdom of God, it is also important to recognize what Matthew's distinctive – and different – contribution is. That contribution is in tension with what much else of the New Testament implies. Davies and Allison (1988–1997: I, 89f.) state Matthew's contribution succinctly in relation to those who would claim to be part of the Christian worshipping community: 'Matthew's most characteristic contribution to the theological idea of forgiveness is his emphasis upon its pre-conditions. Divine forgiveness cannot be appropriated unless one forgives others ... God's forgiveness depends upon man's forgiveness.' And the sober warning to explain the Parable of the Unforgiving Servant (Matthew 18.23–35) should not go unheeded: those who have received forgiveness but do not practise it await judgment and condemnation (v. 35). That there are unforgiving Christians is not merely conjectural or hypothetical. They do exist, according to Matthew, and Matthew cautions that a grim future awaits them.

In addition, in Matthew 5.23f., a saying found only in Matthew, we are told that it is the responsibility of the person who stands in need of forgiveness from another to take the initiative and to seek reconciliation. So it is not just the case that a person who has been wronged should forgive the wrongdoer: it is also the case that the wrongdoer should actively seek the wronged person to promote an opportunity for forgiveness. One reason, presumably, is because of the grave danger, alluded to in 6.14f., facing the person who has been wronged: for unforgiveness on their part could lead to destruction. To seek reconciliation is a priority, according to Matthew, and takes precedence over one's religious duties, such as to offer a sacrifice for sin.

Unforgivable Sins

Lastly, are there sins of which forgiveness is not possible? Some interpret Luke 12.10 (// Matthew 12.31–37, Mark 3.28–30), the sin of blasphemy against the Holy Spirit, in that way. Anxious Christians through the years have wondered whether they had committed this blasphemy so as to exclude themselves from the possibility of forgiveness and of salvation.

This interpretation is mistaken. Jesus is referring to those who denied that God had come to save his people and that Jesus was empowered by the Holy Spirit to demonstrate this. So, for example, some regarded the exorcisms of Jesus as being empowered by demons, not God who acted through Jesus by the Spirit (Luke 11.14–23 with Luke 4.18f.). Mark makes the point in 3.30. Today those who look at what is good and ascribe it to Satan deny the Holy Spirit and cut themselves off from the one who can forgive their sins. In contrast, the early church regarded blasphemy against the Holy Spirit as opposition to the Spirit's inspiration: see *Didache* 11. 7; Ambrose *De Spiritu Sancto* 1. 3. 54 and Irenaeus, *Adv. Haer.* 3. 11. 9.

The Pauline and Deutero-Pauline Letters

Paul is regarded as having written at least seven of the letters that appear in his name in the New Testament (Romans, 1 and 2 Corinthians, Galatians, Philippians, 1 Thessalonians and Philemon). The other six letters that bear his name (Ephesians, Colossians, 2 Thessalonians, 1 and 2 Timothy and Titus) are generally thought to have been written by an admirer, probably after Paul's death, with the intention of carrying on and developing the tradition of Paul's thought. (Many think that Paul did write Colossians, but the argument cannot be regarded as settled.) These six letters are called 'the Deutero-Pauline letters'.

In his thought, Paul is more concerned with dealing with sin (an alien force or power to which all human beings are subject) than with sins (particular expressions of wrongdoing). He certainly lists the sins into which humanity has fallen (e.g. Romans 1.29–31; Galatians 5.19–21) and acknowledges that Christ died for – and so dealt with – the sins of human beings (Galatians 1.4 and 1 Corinthians 15.3). Paul also says that in Christ the power of sin has been broken: Christian living is being dead to one sort of life and beginning another, new life (2 Corinthians 5.17).

Paul describes through a variety of metaphors the way that God has addressed the problem of sin. The most common metaphor is 'justification', a juridical concept. Justification and forgiveness go together. To be justified means to be acquitted: as Romans 4.7f. shows, it means that a person's sins are covered over (because properly dealt with in a juridical sense), forgiven, and hence God 'does not book the sin in the ledger of life against a person' (Fitzmyer 1993: 376, and see also Romans 6.7–11, 18, 22 referring to people who are 'set free' from sin). We see here a clear parallel with the idea of forgiveness in both the Hebrew Scriptures and in the Synoptic Gospels. While Paul does not say this in Romans 5.1f., one could imagine him saying that since we are justified by faith, not only do we have peace with God and access to grace but also we have received the gift of forgiveness. Taylor (1946: 3) makes the important point that forgiveness of sins means that sins are remitted (that is cancelled or covered), not that the penalty for sins is paid.

In the genuinely Pauline letters, Paul uses *aphiemi* only once, in Romans 4.7, in a quotation from Psalm 32.1. It is significant that the one idea (sins forgiven) is expressed in two examples of synonymous parallelism, that is, examples where the equivalent ideas are expressed in parallel but different ways. So Paul refers in the quotation to lawless deeds that have been forgiven, to sins that have been covered over and to those against whom their sins are not counted or reckoned by God. The three verbs – forgive, cover over and not count/reckon – all express the same basic idea and are important for understanding what Paul means is true of someone who is, in his words, 'righteous' and 'justified' before God.

An entirely different word that is translated 'forgive' is also used by Paul in 2 Corinthians 2.7, 10 and 12.13. This is the word *charizomai*. In 2 Corinthians 2.7, 10 it refers to the forgiveness that the Christian community in Corinth was to exercise towards a repentant offender and which Paul also would exercise towards that person. Perhaps there are echoes of the dominical saying in Matthew 6.14f. here. In 2 Corinthians 12.13 it is used with biting irony by Paul against the Corinthians, begging for forgiveness for a supposed wrong that he had done. When Paul uses the verb *charizomai* generally, he uses it to refer to the gracious gifts of God to his undeserving people who have been justified (e.g. 1 Corinthians 2.12 and Romans 8.32). The grace (or capacity) to forgive one another is one such gift, according to Paul – and see Colossians 2.13.

There is another instance of a word that may mean 'forgiveness', and this is in Romans 3.25. The word used is the noun *paresis*, a rare word that does not occur in the Septuagint and in biblical Greek occurs only here in the New Testament. If the word does mean 'forgiveness' in the same sense as *aphesis*, Paul means in this verse that as a result of the cross, God has forgiven sins committed in the period before Christ. The noun *paresis* is from the cognate verb *parienai* that means 'to pass over, let go'. If the noun is understood as having the same meaning as the verb, then Paul may mean here that God has passed over (rather than forgiven) the sins in the period before Christ.

The paucity of references to forgiveness indicates that forgiveness is not a central category of Paul's thought – though justification, which implicitly assumes forgiveness, is. Dunn (1998: 327) suggests that the reason for the absence of terms such as 'repentance' and 'forgiveness' 'may possibly be because such terms were so characteristic of [Paul's] own former theology and practice' in Judaism that he 'preferred not to talk in these terms'.

Some comment should also be made about reconciliation. In Romans 5.9–11 Paul treats justification and reconciliation as parallel concepts. But in 2 Corinthians 5.18–20, the metaphor of reconciliation is not synonymous with justification (justification or forgiveness is referred to in the phrase in v. 19, 'not counting their trespasses against them') but is used to explicate the significance of Christ's death. Justification (or forgiveness) comes first; reconciliation follows.

The Deutero-Pauline letters emphasize that forgiveness should characterize the corporate life of Christian communities (Ephesians 4.32, Colossians 3.13). Members of those communities should consciously model the forgiveness that they themselves have experienced and received from God (Colossians 3.13). This perspective perhaps reflects difficulties with communal relationships that the more settled and established post-Pauline churches faced.

Finally, though there are substantial differences of language in Paul's writings and the synoptic gospels on the subject of forgiveness, there is substantial congruence of thought. In both, sin is not counted against human beings. In both, as a result of sins being forgiven, people enter into a new order of experience. In both, forgiveness is to characterize the corporate and personal lives of those who are in that new order of experience. In Paul's writings, and implicitly in the synoptic gospels, Christ's death brings reconciliation between God and humanity.

The Remainder of the New Testament

In only five other places in the New Testament is forgiveness referred to, in every case expressed by *aphiemi* or *aphesis*. In two of the references, Hebrews 9.22 and 10.18, the death of Jesus and the ensuing forgiveness are understood in sacrificial terms. These have to do with interpreting the mechanism of how God effected salvation, and are not further relevant to this chapter. The other three references are James 5.15 and 1 John 1.9; 2.12. In these places forgiveness is explored in the context of how communal relationships were to be regulated. The emphasis is on *confessing* sins, rather than repentance, as part of the religious practices of the Christian community. In James it appears that confession should be in the presence of elders. In addition, James understands illness in part to be the result of sin, and confession and further prayer to be part of the process that leads to healing. In 1 John 1.9 and James 5.15f., forgiveness is assured for those who confess their sins.

But what sort of forgiveness? 1 John 2.12 assures the members of John's community that their sins *have* been forgiven, a perfect tense, indicating a once-for-all completed action in the past with consequences continuing into the present. (The same idea is also strongly affirmed in Hebrews 10.18 where the writer says that because sins have been forgiven effectually through the sacrifice of Christ there need be no further offering for sin.) If so, why should there be further confessions of sin? Presumably because, though justification and forgiveness in an eschatological sense occur at a point in time for someone who enters the kingdom of God, nevertheless justification and forgiveness need to go on being actualized and realized on a day-to-day basis. Continued confession of sin involves an acknowledgment that one is not living the way one should in the kingdom of God; the forgiveness that follows is a reminder that one stands as a forgiven sinner, able to go on seeking to live God's way.

Who, then, absolves sins in such a confession? Most likely it is the leaders of the early church, perhaps, for example, the elders who are referred to in James 5.14. If it is some of the leaders in the early church, this may explain John 20.23, where the eleven are given power to forgive or retain sins. It may also help explain Matthew 16.19 and 18.18 where Jesus refers to 'loosing' sins: this may be a reference to forgiveness (Davies and Allison 1988–1997: II, 636). Certainly the passages in both John and Matthew are almost certainly later additions, reflecting the interests of the respective communities to which these Gospels were addressed.

There seems, therefore, to be a development in early theology that understood forgiveness to be not only a once-for-all experience but also an ongoing experience for the Christian. This latter forgiveness seems to have been mediated through the eleven and perhaps the elders in James' church. Perhaps it is in this period of the life of the church that Matthew's severe warnings to unforgiving Christians have their place and origin, reflecting the interests of Matthew's own, late first-century, community. There will be, he may be saying, no forgiveness as an *ongoing* experience for the Christian if that Christian is unforgiving. Perhaps the strictures about unforgiving Christians in Matthew's gospel are intended to promote the good order of the church and carry with them the threat of discipline (withheld forgiveness) for those who were contumacious.

The Early Church after the New Testament

In the early church, confession of sin was an important element of baptism. Baptism was usually administered by a bishop and was followed by laying on of hands, anointing and participation in the eucharist (e.g. Tertullian, *De Baptismo* and *De Corona*). From an early date it was believed that baptism could remit sins committed by an individual up to the moment of baptism.

What of sins committed after baptism (see Telfer 1959: 33–60, 75–83)? The early church was divided on the question whether those who committed deliberate sins after baptism could be forgiven. The *Didache,*

Clement of Rome and Polycarp held out the possibility of forgiveness; Justin denied it. In the third century, Clement of Alexandria and Origen accepted that some sins could be forgiven (but not serious ones like murder, adultery and idolatry). A third-century document from Syria, the *Didascalia Apostolorum*, urged bishops to forgive all sinners who were truly penitent, and this was the position that the church as a whole eventually adopted.

Some believed that sins committed after baptism must be atoned for in part by the punishment of the sinner. To this end, a system of public penance emerged. Penance is different from repentance. Repentance refers to a person's acknowledgment that they have sinned and is coupled with a turning from sin; penance emphasises sorrow for the sins committed, confession of guilt and punishment of the sinner in satisfaction (payment of a penalty due to God) for the sins: see di Berardino (1992) s. v. Penitence: II, 667–69.

Public penance involved, first, the excommunication of the sinner, and then the eventual readmission of the sinner – but only after a period of penitential discipline (by way of reparation), the severity of which depended on the gravity of the sins. Penance involved confession of sins to a bishop in front of the whole church congregation. The system of penance was by no means uniformly practised.

As for confession of sin, there were no priests in the modern understanding of the term in the early church. The term 'priest' (etymologically derived from the Greek word that is translated 'presbyter' or 'elder') does not seem to have been applied to Christian ministers before the end of the second century, and this term at first referred to the ministry exercised by bishops (who, in the period of the New Testament, were sometimes interchangeably also called 'presbyters' or 'elders' – see Titus 1.5,7). It was only when the church spread to the countryside and parish churches were established that some of the bishops' tasks were delegated to those who became known as priests.

The idea that bishops could absolve people of their sins (that is, pronounce the forgiveness of sins by Christ) has its origins in John 20.23 and Matthew 16.19 and 18.18. Clement of Rome, before the end of the first century, emphasized that there was a succession of ministry from Christ to the apostles and from the apostles to bishops. This line of succession is generally given as the reason why bishops may pronounce absolution: through their consecration to the episcopate, they succeed to the privileges, enabling and authorization given by Jesus in the gospels.

Psychological Significance

While Christianity is not the only religion to promote the idea and practice of forgiveness, Christianity has probably the most developed theology of forgiveness of all faiths. What is the significance today of forgiveness in the New Testament and the early church for psychological practice and therapeutic understanding? The remainder of this chapter explores issues to do with forgiveness in therapy and does so in dialogue with the New Testament's theology of forgiveness.

Subjectivity and Objectivity

It is important to note at the outset that modern psychology does not work with the dogmatic, and perhaps sometimes even simplistic, view of right and wrong that the New Testament offers. Wrongdoing in the New Testament arises from the fact that certain forms of human action, inaction and sometimes even motive are regarded as inherently wrong and that it is God who declares them to be wrong. Consequently, in the New Testament and beyond, forgiveness has to do with actual wrongdoing in an objective sense, whether or not the parties recognize it to be wrongdoing and however they may *feel* about it. It also has to do with the wrongdoer's guilt (the juridical declaration that God makes about the wrongdoing), whether or not the wrongdoer acknowledges – or feels – the guilt. Three assumptions are made: that 'right' and 'wrong' exist in an objective sense, that 'right' and 'wrong' can be known and that human conduct is to be measured according to whether it is 'right' or 'wrong'. The New Testament and the early church are not concerned with the psychological effects of wrongdoing. As the following discussion illustrates, a modern psychological view of wrongdoing is more nuanced and developed, and explores degrees of responsibility and culpability, and works with how a person perceives an action rather than only with the nature of the action itself.

Forgiveness and Therapy

Although the New Testament was written in the 'pre-psychological era', parts of the New Testament show some considerable psychological insight. For example, Jesus recognized that sin is not only what a person does in terms of outward actions (i.e. behavioural) but also what a person thinks and feels (i.e. cognition and affect) – see Matthew 5.21–48. Similarly, in the story of the woman taken in adultery (John 8.3–11), Jesus exposed the judgmentalism and hypocrisy of those who wished to condemn the woman adulterer – but he showed empathy and compassion for the woman herself. But on the whole, the New Testament in general (and Paul in particular – see Bash 2001: 59–67) does not show what we call 'psychological awareness' as we understand this today.

Despite some limitations of the outlook of the New Testament from the point of view of contemporary psychology, ideas on forgiveness from the New Testament have many parallels with modern psychological practice and therapeutic understanding. Forgiveness in the New Testament is when God lets go of or abandons the sin that stands between the wrongdoer and God. It is God's voluntary, unilateral action. In relation to wrongs that people do to one another, forgiveness in the New Testament is the wronged person's unilateral choice to pass over, disregard or remove from focus another's wrongdoing. As we shall see, forgiveness in therapy is the same as both of these, and the aim of the therapist is to help the client, by a voluntary and unilateral act of the will, to let go of the past, experience inner healing and then move on.

In addition, the New Testament, and especially the Jesus and Pauline traditions in the New Testament, can affirm four very significant insights that a modern therapeutic approach to forgiveness offers. First, the New Testament recognizes that forgiveness is not the same as reconciliation. Second, reconciliation *follows* forgiveness and has to do with a restored or renewed relationship. The Parable of the Prodigal Son (Luke 15.11–32) illustrates this clearly: the father of the Prodigal had already forgiven the son before he returned. This is forgiveness – or, to express it theologically, justification in the Pauline sense (and reconciliation as Paul uses the term in Romans 5.10f.). When the son acknowledged his wrongdoing, he was reconciled to his father. This is reconciliation in the 2 Corinthians 5.18–20 sense. Third, the New Testament marks a further development of what had begun in the Hebrew Scriptures, namely, a recognition that motives (that is, the workings of the inner life) are as important as outward actions. So, for example, in the Hebrew Scriptures the last of the Ten Commandments (Exodus 20.1–17) deals with covetousness, an aspect of the inner life. This recognition accelerated in the nineteenth century and beyond, and is now an axiom of modern psychology. Lastly, as we have seen, though God's forgiveness is for all people, only those who forgive others will be forgiven. In contrast, the forgiveness that human beings are to extend to one another is to be unconditional. Not surprisingly, modern psychological practice parallels the approach that the New Testament says human beings are to take towards one another.

Forgiveness as an aspect of therapy is now increasingly accepted (see, for example, McCullough *et al.* 2000 and West 2001). Some of the therapeutic models that are being developed substantially conform to the pattern of forgiveness that the New Testament sets out. From the point of view of the wronged person, one therapeutic model of forgiveness (adapted from Enright & Coyle 1998) includes, for example:

(a) the recognition of wrong done;
(b) a voluntary decision not to enforce justifiable retribution or retaliation;
(c) a voluntary decision to respond unconditionally with mercy;
(d) an outcome intended to restore and promote good relations.

We now explore the points of difference and similarity with the New Testament and the psychological and theological implications.

Recognizing Wrongdoing

The therapeutic model stipulates that there must be recognition that wrong has been done. In some cases, this is easy to define. An example of wrongdoing that is easy to recognize is a bogus caller who preys on a vulnerable older adult to gain access to the adult's home in order to steal. In other cases, a person may consider that they have been wronged, but upon closer examination it may be that the wronged person has some degree of responsibility for having been wronged and/or mitigating circumstances that help explain why the perceived wrongdoing occurred. The recent case involving Tony Martin illustrates the point: in 1999, Martin, who was found to be suffering from a paranoid personality disorder and was acting under diminished responsibility at the time of the crime, shot two burglars who had entered his house to steal, killed one (Fred Barras, aged 16) and injured the other (Brendan Fearon). Martin was imprisoned for manslaughter and, at the time of writing this chapter, Brendan Fearon, the surviving burglar, is suing Martin for compensation for the injuries Martin inflicted on him. Of Martin and the injured burglar, who committed the more wrong and which of the two was the more culpable? One of the reasons why Martin was not released early on parole was because he denied that he had done wrong. Perhaps the only clear issue in these events is that defining wrongdoing in clear terms is very difficult.

A person may have difficulty accepting that they have been wronged. In one case, a young teenager who had been gang raped returned to the weekly youth club where the perpetrators had initiated contact and was, some months after returning, gang raped a second time. The client blamed herself and had difficulty in acknowledging that wrongdoing had taken place. The only forgiveness that she was trying to deal with was, inappropriately, to forgive herself. The first step in therapy was to help the client realise that she had been wronged and that she was not to blame.

The Response of the Wronged Person

The therapeutic model aims for the wronged person to respond unconditionally with mercy. This is probably the hardest part of the therapeutic process for many people.

Why do people find it hard to forgive others? Perhaps one of the reasons has to do with power. A person who has been wronged may feel powerless because abused. In forgiving, the wronged person gives up their defences against the abuse, such as anger or self-pity. Forgiveness may mean the wronged person acknowledges their powerlessness, and the pain and suffering of being wronged. It may also mean that the wronged person gives up the hope of having the pain and suffering acknowledged in some way.

The pattern of acknowledging one's own powerlessness (and the pain and suffering that go with it) is, according to Paul's understanding, central to what the cross is about. For in Paul's understanding, human powerlessness was the platform on which God would demonstrate divine power. For as Jesus was voluntarily powerless on the cross, so he was raised to new life by God's power. This pattern of human powerlessness followed by an experience of God's power will be replicated in the Christian's own experience of life, according to Paul. So the Christian who forgives – that is, the Christian who faces his or her own powerlessness – will also experience God's power (Barrett 1973: 136–48, 335). Expressed in psychological terms, a person who acknowledges their powerlessness and who also forgives, whether or not they are a Christian, may experience healing and restoration in relation to the hurt and damage that the wrongdoing has caused. The practice of forgiveness is therefore central not only to living as a Christian, for it is imitative of the cross, but also it is one of the routes to good psychological health.

Patton (2000: 287) gives another psychological reason to point to the psychological benefits of forgiveness. He says: '... not forgiving functions as a way to hold on to an old and familiar relationship through maintaining an incomplete transaction, a debit on ... "the ledger of justice".' As long as there is unforgiveness, he continues, the unforgiving person is 'still owed something ... If the forgiveness is offered, and the debit removed, [the] relationship ... may be lost.' In promoting forgiveness, the New Testament is promoting good psychological health and growth, encouraging people to let go of the past and to move on.

Sayings from the later New Testament period indicate that the failure of people to forgive one another could jeopardise their own forgiveness before God. Clinical practice quickly confirms the harmful and destructive effect – not only psychologically but also sometimes physically (Thoresen *et al.* 2000) – on those who are unforgiving. What the sayings fail to recognize, however, is that forgiveness may be part of a lengthy process of healing and growth. They also fail to recognize that precipitately insisting that a person forgive before the necessary psychological groundwork has been completed may some-times reinforce the trauma.

It is certainly easier to forgive where the wrongdoer acknowledges wrongdoing. For those who are victims of serious crimes or who suffer serious physical and/or sexual violence, completing the process of forgiveness can sometimes occur fully only when the wrongdoer acknowledges the wrongdoing. Until then, it can be extremely difficult for the person who has been wronged to forgive. In the case of the teenager who had been gang raped twice, the client disclosed in therapy that one of the perpetrators had defended himself in court by saying, 'She went back. She knew what would happen. She wanted it.' This perpetrator's refusal to recognize that wrongdoing had occurred reinforced the client's tendency to blame herself, and so complicated her capacity to forgive herself for her gullibility and (ultimately) to forgive the perpetrators of the rape.

The question remains: how *can* human beings forgive one another unconditionally when the wrongdoer does not acknowledge wrong-doing? The process by which a client lets go and eventually moves on has many parallels with the stages that a person goes through in bereavement. There may be at times denial, anger, depression and eventually acceptance, leading to hope and investment in new things (Kübler-Ross 1970). But many clients remain 'stuck' and are unable to forgive those who do not acknowledge or recognize that they have done wrong.

This question about how human beings can forgive is really a question about justice. A wronged person often longs for justice, or at least an acknowledgment that they have been wronged. Such longing for justice lies deep within human beings. Perhaps unconditional forgiveness is only truly possible if a client knows that, with God, there is ultimately justice and that, unless wrongdoers repent, God will judge the wrongdoers. To know that there is accountability and judgment in an eschatological sense may then make it possible to forgive those who do not acknowledge their wrongdoing. Romans 12.19 implicitly acknowl-edges this point: people are not to avenge themselves, but to leave it to God for, says God, 'Vengeance is mine, I will repay' (and see also

Hebrews 10.30 where the same words are quoted in the context of eschatological judgment). Even so, for some the inability to forgive in such circumstances causes a crisis of faith because they are unable (for psychological reasons) to practise what they profess: see, for example, the moving story of Marie McNeice, a religious sister in Belfast, who faced such a crisis when in her anger she could not forgive the killers of a friend of hers (McNeice 1996).

Related to the question of justice, it is noteworthy that the therapeutic model of forgiveness includes a voluntary decision not to enforce justifiable retribution or retaliation. In the New Testament model of forgiveness, this is the way people are to behave towards one another. But there is an important qualification: though God always forgives, God waives the retribution or retaliation *only* if the wrongdoer acknowledges – and repents of – wrongdoing. If a person is not reconciled to God, God's retributive justice will ultimately follow. If the Prodigal Son had not returned, he would have lived with the folly of his actions and remained at odds with his father. The belief that ultimately there will be retributive justice may well help a client to forgive unconditionally and not to seek retribution or retaliation.

The Intended Outcome

In the therapeutic model, the intended outcome of forgiveness is to promote and restore good relations. In some cases it is possible to forgive but without this intended outcome. For example, forgiving an anonymous terrorist is possible without also intending to promote a good relationship. Similarly, an adult may forgive a deceased parent who abused him or her as a child, when there is no possibility of restored relations. In one case, a very young woman who had undergone what later transpired to be an unnecessary double mastectomy due to a negligent misdiagnosis did, after lengthy therapy, forgive those who had (mis)treated her. After therapy she continued to regard it as inappropriate to receive treatment from the medical staff who had misdiagnosed her, and so continued with further treatment in another hospital from different staff.

In the New Testament, the intended outcome of God's once-for-all forgiveness is always to *create* (rather than promote and restore) good relations, but such relations will not exist if the wrongdoer has not repented. In the case of the concept of ongoing forgiveness developed in the later period of the New Testament and in the early church, forgiveness through the confession of sin is intended to promote and restore good relations with God (but see Acts 15.36–40, the disagreement between Barnabas and Paul, the result of which was that Paul and Barnabas went separate ways).

Release from Guilt

In the earlier period of the New Testament, release from guilt in a juridical sense came by accepting God's unconditional and voluntary offer of release. Human beings were to model that release by unconditionally forgiving others. This is the pattern that the therapeutic model follows.

Later, in the early church period, release from guilt became conditional. Release could come through the leaders of the church, who were regarded as having power delegated to them by God to release people from their guilt before God. They also had power to withhold this release. Making forgiveness dependent upon a broker's consent detracts from the idea that forgiveness should be freely offered to people.

In a still later period, release from the guilt of sin was in some circumstances (such as post-baptismal sin) also made dependent upon a person enduring punishment for the sin. This is a further derogation from the model of forgiveness of Jesus and the early church. Both these deviations from the earliest model of forgiveness would now be regarded as psychologically unhelpful in therapy.

Seeking Forgiveness

A significant principle in the New Testament that is not in the therapeutic model of forgiveness is that it is the duty of *all* people – whether they committed wrong or were wronged – to seek forgiveness and reconciliation. In the case of someone who has done wrong, there is a duty to put right what they can. Zacchaeus, for example, a tax collector who had defrauded his constituents, made fourfold restitution (Luke 19.1–10). A therapeutic model for those who have done wrong could involve:

(a) the recognition of having done wrong;
(b) a voluntary decision to ask for the forgiveness of the person wronged;
(c) an outcome intended to restore and promote good relations;
(d) a commitment, where possible, to right the wrongs.

Concluding Reflections

Whatever one's faith position, it is undeniable that there are many parallels between what the New Testament says about forgiveness and the practice of forgiveness in psychological therapy. It is also undeniable that practices to do with forgiveness that are in the late New Testament in inchoate form (such as we see in John 20.23), and subsequently developed in the early church, detract from and even undermine the teaching of Jesus on forgiveness. Therapeutic practice accords with the model of forgiveness that Jesus set out, not the practices of the later church.

There are three areas where modern psychology can – and often does – make a significant contribution to areas not addressed by the New Testament. First, the New Testament is not concerned with the question of forgiving oneself for having done wrong. One senses that some of Paul's 'drivenness' was in part due to his unresolved guilt that he had formerly been a persecutor of the church (1 Corinthians 15.9f. and, from a later period, see 1 Timothy 1.12–16). Second, the New Testament does not offer people who are wronged and who need to forgive others help in how to deal with their own unresolved anger, resentment, fear and hurt. Third, this question remains: *how* do we forgive? Most people cannot forgive as swiftly and unconditionally as Jesus did on the cross. Common experience, as well as therapeutic understanding, indicate that almost always forgiveness is a process, and that forgiveness begins to occur when personal growth takes place both in relation to the wrong done (and its effect on the wronged person) and in relation to the person who has committed the wrong. In this process the wronged person may also realize that they are, to some extent, also like those who have caused the hurt rather than wholly different from them (Patton 1985: 16).

The discussion of forgiveness in the New Testament raises at least two questions for the therapist. First, forgiveness in the New Testament is predicated on the assumption that people are able to forgive if they themselves have experienced forgiveness (see 1 John 4.7, 19 and the discussion above). Is it a realistic therapeutic goal to expect a wronged person to forgive if the wronged person has not at some point experienced a good model of forgiveness that can be replicated? Second, a Christian may be enabled to forgive another who does not acknowledge their wrongdoing in the confidence that there will be eschatological justice, if not justice before then. Can a client who does not have this confidence truly have the capacity to forgive – and, if the client does forgive, where is justice for such a client?

The creative dialogue between psychology and early Christian thinking that puts forgiveness in its therapeutic and theological context continues to enrich both theologian and therapist.

4

Christian Theology

Fraser Watts

The focus of this chapter will be on theological concepts of forgiveness. However, the intention is to approach that in a way that attends to, and elucidates, the psychological significance of the theology of forgiveness. The recurrent theme of the chapter will be that theology has a broader understanding of forgiveness than that found in contemporary psychological literature, and that there is much in this broader theological approach that future psychological research on forgiveness would benefit from paying attention to.

This chapter is selective in its treatment of the theology of forgiveness, and I need to indicate at the outset the boundaries of the study. First, I confine myself to the theology of forgiveness of my own religious tradition, the Christian one, though much of what is said would also be applicable in other faith traditions. Second, I largely confine myself to contemporary literature, though with two exceptions of particular psychological interest, Bishop Joseph Butler, and R. C. Moberly. I also do not attempt to present a comprehensive Christian theology of forgiveness. Indeed, it is more a Christian theological anthropology of forgiveness. My focus is on what Christian theology has to say about the nature of human forgiveness, rather than on God's forgiveness of humanity. I also make little reference to the philosophical literature (e.g. Haber 1991; Murphy and Hampton 1988), and postpone to the close of the chapter the political literature of forgiveness (Shriver 1995). For those who want a broader survey, there is an excellent one by Biggar (2001).

There has been a curious neglect of the theology of forgiveness in recent years. The most significant recent theological study has been Gregory Jones' *Embodying Forgiveness* (Jones 1995), though Adams (1991), McFadyen and Sarot (2001) and Volf (1996) are also helpful. I fully share the widespread appreciation that has been expressed for Jones' work, and it makes a good starting point for this chapter. That may seem surprising in a book such as this that is explicitly concerned with the interface between the theology and psychology of forgiveness. As we saw in the first chapter, Jones himself offers a trenchant critique of what he calls 'therapeutic forgiveness'. However, there is actually much psychological sophistication in Jones' theology of forgiveness, even though the psychological significance of what he is saying is not explicitly acknowledged. Jones complains about an approach to forgiveness that he calls 'therapeutic forgiveness' on the grounds that it is bad theology. I would want to add that it is also bad psychology. There are psychological as much as the theological reasons for moving beyond the superficial and unbalanced approach to forgiveness that Jones castigates. This reinforces my conviction that there is no tension between theological and psychological approaches to forgiveness. I submit that good theology and good psychology do not point in opposite directions, though there may be tension between bad theology and bad psychology. There can be a fruitful convergence between the disciplines, both in general (Watts 2002) and on the specific topic of forgiveness. I thus want to escape a polarisation between a theology of forgiveness that denigrates psychology, and a psychology of forgiveness that ignores theology.

Positive and Negative Aspects

One of Jones' key points is about the importance of the context of forgiveness. For example, pressing people to forgive in contexts where forgiveness is deeply problematic can be counter-productive. The title of this book, *Forgiveness in Context*, signals agreement with the general point about the importance of context where forgiveness is concerned. Later chapters are explicitly devoted to the issues about forgiveness that arise in problematic contexts.

There are various aspects of context that are important, both theologically and psychologically. For one thing, it is important to experience life in a balanced way. Life has its light and dark sides. It is as unhealthy psychologically as it is unsound theologically to distort this balance. The approach to forgiveness that Jones castigates is one that takes an unremittingly positive approach and refuses to recognize the dark side of life. Pushed to its extreme, that becomes a 'manic defence' rather than psychologically healthy.

As Jones says, we need 'to attend to the dynamic relations between judgment and grace, repentance and forgiveness. For it is all too easy to have either grace without judgment or judgment without grace, to have forgiveness without repentance or repentance without forgiveness' (p. 135). In similar vein he says later, 'God's forgiveness requires us to confront the tendencies to see the world either as lighter than it is (hence engaging in cheap forgiveness) or as darker than it is (hence believing that forgiveness is impossible or ineffective)' (p. 165). Similarly, we need to avoid both 'cheap grace' and 'harbouring unjustified anger or desires for vengeance' (p. 226).

Theologically, the question of seeing God's creation in balanced terms is fundamental. All creation arises from God and, at root, reflects his goodness. However, as Christians have always said, the world as it is falls short of that goodness and stands in need of redemption. It is God's promise, and the Christian hope, that creation will eventually reflect the goodness of God more clearly and fully. It is important to keep in balance on the one hand the essential goodness of creation and the promise to which it is called, and on the other hand how at present it falls short of that.

Psychologically, it seems extraordinarily difficult for people to keep the positive and negative aspects of their experience in balance. Which is seen as the predominant element depends on a person's mood state. Many people see only the positive, and hide their eyes from negative aspects of their experience. There is much psychological evidence that testifies to that 'rosy glow' mind-set. On the other hand, when people become depressed, the balance swings round, so that they can see only the negative; for example, negative memories predominate in their recollection of the past. Neither is psychologically healthy.

It is also important for there to be both positive and negative strands in relationships. People flourish best in the context of relationships that are both challenging and nurturing. There is psychological evidence for this in a variety of contexts (see Watts and Williams 1988). For example, leadership is most effective when it fulfils both functions. Also, parental upbringing is most effective when it is both challenging and supportive. Forgiveness should find its place in a socialising relationship that is balanced from this point of view. Forgiveness is perhaps most helpful when it is neither reduced to indulgent and uncritical exoneration, nor given in a grudging spirit that lacks all warmth and positive regard. That desirable balance in forgiveness can perhaps be seen most clearly in divine forgiveness. Indeed, it is part of the psychological value of divine forgiveness that God is able to maintain the balance between support and challenge more perfectly than any human being could. The forgiveness of God integrates love and judgment in a unique way.

Forgiveness and Repentance

The balance between positive and negative aspects of forgiveness comes into clear focus with the question of the relationship between repentance and forgiveness. To emphasize forgiveness and minimize the need for repentance is too positive, and amounts to what Dietrich Bonhoeffer (1971) in *The Cost of Discipleship* disparagingly called 'cheap grace'. As chapter 2 made clear, the Jewish tradition has always been careful to avoid that mistake. On the other hand, to emphasize the need for repentance almost to the exclusion of forgiveness is too negative. As chapter 3 described, the relationship between repentance and forgiveness was a subject of vigorous debate in the early Christian church.

There are two separate questions here. One is about whether there can be forgiveness without any repentance at all. The other is about sequence, whether repentance needs to precede forgiveness, or whether it is acceptable sometimes for forgiveness to come first and for repentance to follow later.

On the first question, there is surely a need to hold repentance and forgiveness together in some way. Jones is undoubtedly right to be critical of forgiveness without any repentance, though he is very strong in his assertion of the primacy of forgiveness over repentance At a human level, forgiveness that is not linked to repentance is likely to be superficial and of little enduring value. The case for holding together repentance and forgiveness is both a theological and a psychological one.

However, the question of sequence is a different matter. Some of the early church Fathers made a serious theological case for forgiveness preceding repentance. The testimony of the Gospels on this issue is mixed. Though Jesus is certainly sometimes seen as being stern in his demands on people, there is also a sense in the Gospels that the kingdom extends super-abundant and unconditional forgiveness to all. That does not remove the call to repentance, but the unconditional grace associated with the kingdom seems to be primary.

My own view is that the question of sequence is not particularly important, provided forgiveness and repentance are intertwined with one another. In practice, as far as a human experience is concerned, some people will experience forgiveness first while others will repent first. Provided the two things are linked, it is not clear why it should matter over-much which comes first, despite the fierce debate there has been about it (Biggar 2001). The important point is that, ultimately, there cannot be any forgiveness without repentance, and there cannot be repentance without forgiveness.

It is also very important here to avoid distortions of the concepts of both forgiveness and repentance. It would be a gross over-simplification to see repentance as entirely negative, and forgiveness as entirely positive. They are actually much more closely intertwined than is often realized. In English translations they both probably have significantly more negative connotations than was intended by the New Testament writers. The New Testament was first translated into English in a guilt culture, and that seems to have distorted the way in which it was translated. Modern translations have become more intelligible, but have not always corrected these initial conceptual distortions that came from the guilt culture of the Reformation period.

The English word repentance is related to the Greek *poine*, which means punishment; it was the name for the Goddess of Vengeance. The main Greek word that is translated as repentance, *metanioa*, means a change or renewal of the whole psyche, indeed, the whole person. Though repentance involves an element of the person putting past mistakes behind them, it also includes an element of renewal.

Forgiveness is another English word that has more negative connotations than were probably intended by the corresponding word in the Greek New Testament, *aphesis*. It is not necessarily a religious word, and is used when something is left behind, abandoned, let go or released. 'Forgiveness' in English has come to mean something like exoneration. *Aphesis* means something closer to liberation.

The problem, and it is one to which we will return, is thus that the word 'forgiveness' has come to mean something much narrower than the concept of forgiveness in the New Testament. Psychology has often implicitly adopted this narrow contemporary meaning. However, there would be merit in its working with a broader concept of forgiveness closer to that found in the New Testament. The extent of the contrast between the scriptural concept of forgiveness and the everyday one is often not fully recognized, though Werner and Lotte Pelz (1963) put it with characteristic force when they emphasize that the biblical understanding of forgiveness is a 'flat contradiction of our own' (p. 120).

The key difference is that forgiveness is now understood much more moralistically than it is in either the Old or New Testaments. Christianity is much less concerned with morality, as it is conventionally understood, than is normally assumed. Moralism is not necessarily a virtue or a blessing; on the contrary, it can be a problem. As Pelz and Pelz (1963) say, it can be our 'subtlest camouflage, for it keeps us preoccupied with a few symptoms while the rot spreads' (p. 116). As the New Testament sees it, moral failings are simply not the main issue, whereas forgiveness addresses our real needs and deepest problems.

Aphesis is about liberation at the deepest personal level; it is not about exoneration from moral shortcomings.

Divine and Human Forgiveness

For religious thinkers, and perhaps especially for Christians, human forgiveness needs to be placed in the context of divine forgiveness. However, there are at least two distinct issues here that need to be clearly separated. One is the closeness of the analogy between divine and human forgiveness, and how far it is feasible or appropriate for human forgiveness to be modelled on divine forgiveness. The other issue is about facilitation, the extent to which human forgiveness is made possible by taking place in the context of divine forgiveness.

It is not uncommon to find theologians saying that divine forgiveness should be the model for human forgiveness, but I suggest that considerable caution should be exercised about that. We humans are not God, and not everything that is characteristic of God is possible or appropriate for human beings. There is a parallel issue about the currently fashionable theological claim to the effect that the pattern of relationality that exists within the persons of the Trinity provides a model for human relationships. That is also a very doubtful proposition, in part because each human being is separate from every other human being in a way that the persons of the Trinity are not separate from one another. The two kinds of relationality are simply not parallel: the mode of relationality that is possible for humans is different from the Trinitarian one.

In a similar way, I suggest that caution needs to be exercised over the idea that human forgiveness should be modelled on God's forgiveness. We do not have, and cannot hope to have, the resources of grace that God brings to forgiveness. Also, there is a degree of asymmetry in the relationship of God to each human being that is not paralleled in the relationships between human beings.

However, the question of the dependence of human forgiveness on the context of divine forgiveness is entirely another matter. Though human forgiveness can be never be exactly like God's forgiveness, all theologians would see God's forgiveness as providing the indispensable context within which human forgiveness arises. It is because we are forgiven that we are able to forgive. R.C. Moberly puts it rather well in *Atonement and Personality* (Moberly 1901), one of the first approaches to forgiveness to integrate both theology and psychology, when he says, 'Human forgiveness is to find its inspiration in man's experience of the forgiveness of God. God's forgiveness must find an expression of itself in man's forgiveness of man.' (p. 63).

There are two aspects to this divine context of forgiveness, the objective and the subjective. There is a sense in which God's unconditional forgiveness is part of the objective context in which all human life exists, and within which it flourishes. That remains true regardless of whether people recognize that unconditional forgiveness, or seek it. However, there is also the important subjective matter of how far people have a sense of having been forgiven by God. The more people have a lively sense of that, the more their lives will be enhanced by it and, in particular, the better they will be able to forgive others. The key point is what Jones (1995) calls 'the priority of forgiveness to our forgivingness' (p. 174). Having been forgiven by God facilitates human forgiveness, and the stronger the sense people have that they have been forgiven, the more they are able in turn to forgive. This is, incidentally, an empirical claim, and one that could be tested empirically in the psychology of religion.

It makes a very important difference, psychologically, whether people have a sense that the forgiveness they experience and practise is part of a broader grace of forgiveness that comes from God. The sense of participation in something broader and more powerful may make forgiveness possible in situations where it would otherwise seem hopeless. Just as the practice of intercessory prayer depends on belief in a God who is capable of answering prayer, so the continuing practice of forgiveness in difficult circumstances may depend on belief in a God who is capable of potentiating limited human acts of forgiveness.

Conditional and Unconditional Forgiveness

The way the analogy is drawn between human and divine forgiveness has a bearing on another theological controversy about forgiveness, whether it should be conditional or unconditional. It is rather close to the controversy that we considered above about whether or not forgiveness requires prior repentance.

Those who emphasize prior repentance are inevitably led to see forgiveness as conditional. Moberly (1901) sets out the case for conditional forgiveness, though he has been much criticized for it. He thinks that true forgiveness has to be right and proper forgiveness, in the sense that for someone to be forgiven they have to be forgivable. That makes forgiveness conditional.

As a representative voice on the other side of the debate we find, for example, Richard Holloway (2002) who sees true forgiveness as being based on an 'abandonment of code and conditionality' (p. 82). He hazards the view that, in Jesus' story of the Prodigal Son, the son's repentance may not have been the necessary condition for the father's forgiveness but that 'the forgiveness that was unconditionally given actually caused the repentance that followed it' (p. 82).

Though Holloway extols unconditional forgiveness, he is forced to admit that it is 'beyond most of us' (p. 86). Nevertheless, his approach to human forgiveness starts from his understanding of the nature of divine forgiveness as being unconditional. Moberly appears to proceed in the opposite direction. For him, true forgiveness 'is strictly and absolutely correlative to what may be called the "forgiveableness" of the person' (p. 56). This is partly based on his concern to safeguard divine forgiveness from being capricious or arbitrary. However, it is hard to avoid the suspicion that, having been persuaded of the inescapable conditionality of human forgiveness, he has simply extrapolated from there to assert the conditionality of divine forgiveness as well.

One solution to this problem may be to weaken the analogy between divine and human forgiveness. There are many reasons for seeing God's forgiveness as absolute and unconditional, as a gift to humanity, made despite our being unworthy of it. However, to imagine that human beings can display the same kind of an unconditional forgiveness is perhaps a kind of hubris; we cannot become like God in that sense. For us, forgiveness is, as Jones (1995) says, a 'craft' that needs to be patiently learned. Forgiveness does not flow from our very nature in the way that it flows from the nature of God.

Jacques Derrida (2001), in a recent essay on forgiveness, also takes a line that is similar to Holloway's, and is in marked contrast to Moberly's concept of right and proper forgiveness. For Derrida, forgiveness only comes into its own when something unforgivable has happened. 'Must one not maintain that an act of forgiveness worthy of its name, if there ever is such a thing, must forgive the unforgivable and without condition?' It is precisely because forgiveness is impossible that it is 'the only thing that arrives, that surprises, like a revolution, the ordinary course of history, politics, and law' (p. 39).

Gift or Initiative?

This brings us to another important difference between the theological understanding of forgiveness and that found in contemporary secular culture. Theologically, forgiveness is seen as something in which we are caught up, it is primarily something that we experience rather than something that we do. It is not something that we initiate, but something in which we are invited to join. Forgiveness breaks upon us; as Pelz and Pelz (1963) say, it is an 'eschatological' event. 'It faces us with the promise of our beginning and the hope of our end.' (p. 118)

Forgiveness, the unconditional forgiveness of the unforgivable of which Derrida speaks, may seem an impossible dream. However, it still has an eschatological power as a vision, promise, ideal and calling. The human reality of forgiveness may often be very different, regrettably limited and conditional. We are thus caught between the limited forgiveness that we normally experience and practise, and the higher forgiveness to which we are called. It is important in a proper eschatology of forgiveness not to collapse these two, but to keep a sense of both their distinctness and their relatedness.

We trivialize forgiveness if we see it as only something that we have the capacity to dispense to others, and do not realise that it is also something bigger than ourselves in which we can participate. One reason why we cannot hope to dispense adequate forgiveness is that we are ourselves involved in the failures of other people:

> We are implicated in every crime, in every act of faithlessness, hopelessness and apathy. We shall never know whether any particular outrage was not a direct result of our lack of faith, hope and love... There is no 'innocent' party to a divorce, just as there is no innocent party to a war... there is no accused who is not also an accuser, no offender who has not first been 'offended'. (Pelz and Pelz 1963: 119)

The implication is that the forgiveness that we presume to extend to others will usually be shallow, and of limited value to both parties:

> The belief that forgiveness is at our disposal is a misunderstanding and leads to hypocrisy. It is corrupting to behave as if one had forgiven when one has not.... such forgiveness is based on an unbearable and unjustifiable arrogance: Who am I to forgive, to degrade my fellow-man by treating him as one who needs me more than I need him? (Pelz and Pelz 1963: 119–120)

The current psychological literature sees forgiveness primarily as something that we do. In contrast, from a theological point of view, forgiveness is something in which we participate. There is a sense in which it is 'more blessed to give than to receive'. However, for many people it is harder to receive from others than to give; learning an attitude of receptiveness towards our fellow human beings is a crucial pre-condition to having anything to offer them.

This view of forgiveness has important psychological implications. For example, it leads to a different attributional perspective on forgiveness. In conventional thinking, forgiveness is something that we attribute to ourselves. However, from the alternative perspective that we are developing here, it should rather be seen as something that we attribute externally, whether to God or to our fellow human beings.

Also, in much current thinking about forgiveness, there is a simplistic view that sees forgiveness as something we can decide to do or not to do. However, this is an over-individualistic, over-rationalistic perspective that exaggerates the scope of the individual will in ways that are psychologically unrealistic and unhelpful. It distracts us from a proper recognition of our interconnectedness with others. Furthermore, the focus in the current psychological literature on forgiveness has been almost entirely on helping people to extend forgiveness to others. The comparable task of helping people to learn to recognize their need for forgiveness, and receive it from others, has scarcely been begun.

Note that this is not a complaint about the inherent and unavoidable limitations of a psychological approach to forgiveness; it is just a complaint about the limitations of the psychology of forgiveness as it has developed so far. There is no reason why these limitations should not be redressed and remedied within a psychological framework.

Giving and Receiving

The psychological literature on forgiveness has been very largely concerned with the problem of offering forgiveness. However, as has been seen, there is also the problem of how to receive forgiveness. Resentment makes it difficult to extend forgiveness to others, but there are various problems that make it difficult to receive. Psychologically, a key problem is poor self-esteem, and the defensiveness associated with it. For some people, to accept the forgiveness offered by others involves a humiliating acknowledgment that one is in the wrong and morally indebted to others.

In this context, shame may represent more of a problem than guilt (Watts 2001). Guilt, the sense that one is responsible for specific misdeeds, can often be assuaged by receiving forgiveness. However, shame, a more pervasive sense that one is unworthy, is less easily assuaged. Furthermore, it is part of the sense of shame that makes it difficult for people to receive the help that they need.

If the theology of offering forgiveness has not been very fully developed, even less attention has been given to the theology of receiving forgiveness. This is surprising, in the sense that Jesus, like the Old Testament prophets before him, is much concerned with the hypocrisy, self-righteousness and hardness of heart that make it difficult for people to accept the blessings of his kingdom. When he taught his disciples to pray for forgiveness, one suspects that the hardest challenge for them was to make that prayer with the appropriate sincerity.

The forgiveness that Jesus extends thus becomes a kind of judgment, in that it separates out those willing to receive forgiveness from those who are not. People often cut themselves off from the forgiveness that is extended to them because they are unwilling to admit their need. That is perhaps the central challenge that Jesus presents to people. Receiving forgiveness is as much a developmental task in the redemption of humanity as is the offering of forgiveness. To receive forgiveness, both from God and from one another, is a spiritual task, and one that contributes further to the spiritual development of humanity each time it is realized.

This broad understanding of the significance of forgiveness for human personality is entirely consistent with the line taken by Moberly a hundred years ago. As Moberly (1901) says, forgiveness

> is no mere transaction outside the self, a mere arithmetical balance, which leaves the self unchanged. Even the earliest touch, on the conscious moral life, of the most provisional forgiveness, must be a bracing touch, enhancing moral power, or (at the least) adding flame to moral desire. [In so far as it does those things] already the content and character of the I who am forgiven is to that extent changed. (pp. 71–72)

What is true of the one who is forgiven is also true of the one who forgives.

Detachment and Identification

Psychologically, forgiveness is never straightforward. We can easily find ourselves standing on a fixed piece of ground, harbouring pride or resentment, unable to move backwards or forwards. However, in order to give or receive forgiveness, we do need to move on. Basically, two directions of movement are possible.

We can move nearer to the person who we might forgive, identify with them more closely, empathize with them, and 'get into their shoes'. On the other hand, we can stand back, become more detached and dispassionate, give up our own particular point of view, and try to see things more objectively. There is a case for movement in both directions, and it will be helpful, theologically and psychologically, to explore what is at stake here.

The best exponent of the detachment approach is Bishop Butler (1970), in his famous sermon on resentment and forgiveness. Psychologically there is much to be said about forgiveness by detachment from the standpoint of cognitive therapy, and Bishop

Butler can be seen as an interesting antecedent of the contemporary approach to forgiveness in terms of cognitive therapy. This will be explored in more detail in chapter 6, but essentially it involves recognizing distorted judgments, and rebalancing them; also recognizing obsessive preoccupations, and exercising control over them.

Butler's approach to forgiveness is an example of what would now be called attribution therapy. He recommends a reattribution of blame, and in particular that we do not regard the injury that has been done to us as having been done deliberately but rather, as he says, through 'inadvertence and mistake'. Rather than attributing blame entirely to the other person, he recommends that we should recognize failings in ourselves. Thus, we move from casting all the blame on the other person to a more balanced perspective. As he correctly observes, once we have removed the attribution of intention from the other person, the injury that we feel has been done to us is much reduced.

What is particularly interesting from our present point of view is that Butler sees this perspective as depending on the achievement of a 'due distance'. It also involves drawing back from that 'self-love' which he sees as the source of the tendency to blame others rather than ourselves. He seems to be recommending a degree of detachment that is close to what would be endorsed within the Buddhist tradition. From this perspective, obstacles to forgiveness arise from too close a personal involvement.

Forgiveness through detachment, for a Christian thinker, raises questions about judgment and discernment. 'Judgment' is another Christian concept that is often understood in too negative a way; it should be seen not as judgmentalism, but as seeing things in the clear light of truth, which of course means seeing them as God sees them. For a Christian to judge correctly, as God does, involves in some measure surrendering his or her own limited, human vantage point, and seeing things more from a God's-eye point of view.

When people feel themselves to be victims they can easily be drawn into making judgments. Indeed, being a victim can make people feel they are entitled to make judgments. However, Christians will always remember, even when they are victims, that judgment belongs to God, not to themselves. It is one of the helpful things about approaching forgiveness within a Christian framework that there are resources to help people move on from the limited and distorted judgments about the victim that they initially form to the more constructive and balanced judgments that emerge in the context of the felt presence of God. It is central to this process to recognize that judgment belongs to God, not to human beings.

There is a helpful strand of thinking about God's forgiveness of the world through the work of Christ that sees it as a completion of the incarnation. In Christ, God identified himself with the world, and entered deeply into it. Through uniting himself with the world, God overcame the world's estrangement from himself. That overcoming of estrangement is central to what is meant by 'forgiveness' in Christian thinking. The work of God in Christ also led to a fresh outpouring of the Spirit, which was experienced in a new way as springing up within humanity. Through planting the Spirit within us, God again overcame creation's estrangement from him.

There is an interesting analogy to be explored between God's reuniting of himself with the world in Christ, and the human capacity for empathy. Empathy is a psychological capacity that is as yet not very well understood. It seems, though, to be an example of emotional intelligence, and to arise at the intersection of emotion and cognition. Empathy is, in one sense, clearly a cognitive capacity. However, it is one that arises from, and is heightened by, emotional sensitivity. As will be seen in chapter 6, one of the current psychological approaches to understanding forgiveness is couched in terms of empathy. If one person is to forgive another they need a degree of empathic identification with them.

It thus seems that the detachment of cognitive reappraisal, as presented by Bishop Butler, and greater empathic identification, both facilitate forgiveness. This may seem paradoxical; in one sense, they seem to be moving in opposite directions. However, it is a recurrent paradox that opposites can meet in unexpected ways. The common element in both detachment and identification is perhaps that they help people to extricate themselves from a narrowly egocentric point of view. Detachment can help with that, but so can empathic identification with the other person.

There are resources within Christian discipleship to help with both detachment and identification. It is part of the regular spiritual practice of a Christian to reflect on experience in the presence of God. Because a God's-eye perspective is a much broader one than our own, and one that rises above the constraints of all particular vantage points, to reflect on events in God's presence inculcates a helpful detachment. On the other hand, the Christian is called to follow in the path of God's identification with the world in Christ, and to follow Christ's call to his followers to identify themselves with those who have not yet responded to his promise and invitation. Following in the footsteps of the Incarnation can also, in a different way, help people to surrender a narrowly egocentric vantage point.

Discernment and Forgiveness

It is important to be alert to the ways in which acts of forgiveness can vary. There is no single prototype of forgiveness to which all examples correspond. Theology and psychology can make different and over-lapping contributions to understanding the variety of acts of forgiveness, and to discerning the power and authenticity of particular acts of forgiveness. For example, some acts of forgiveness have much broader ramifications than others.

It is an important feature of the tradition of miracle stories in Christianity that apparently limited human actions can have unexpect-edly wide implications. In the Gospels, the sharing of a few loaves and fishes led to a multitude being fed. For a more recent example, and one that is relevant to the current theme, we can turn to the bombing of the cathedral in Coventry during the Second World War. Bombs set the cathedral alight and it burned fiercely through the night; by the following morning only the outside walls were left standing. The Provost and others visited the ruined building next day and dedicated the cathedral to a ministry of reconciliation. Subsequently, the words 'Father forgive' were inscribed on the walls behind where the altar had been. That single act led to a creative and far-reaching ministry of reconciliation that has continued for over fifty years and been a significant force for forgiveness and reconciliation throughout the world.

The act of forgiveness from which it flowed was evidently a profound and spiritual one that was blessed by God. From a theological point of view, one of the crucial questions about acts of forgiveness is how much they are, in that sense, blessed by God. That in turn perhaps depends on the human question of the spirit in which the act of forgiveness was carried out, and how far the person who practises forgiveness was drawing on the resources of God's grace.

There is an interesting contribution to discerning forgiveness in a recent book by Sergei Prokofieff (1992) within the framework of thought stemming from Rudolf Steiner. As would be expected within that tradition, Prokofieff has a strong sense of the spiritual tasks facing humanity at different stages of its development, and argues that forgiveness is 'an essential part of the modern path to Christ' (p. 48). He sees it as part of the spiritual calling and destiny of humanity to rise above the confines of the 'lower ego', and move towards a more spiritual form of existence. Forgiveness represents an important developmental task for humanity, in that each act of true forgiveness (a) depends on overcoming egocentricity, and (b) contributes further to the spiritual development of humanity.

It is within this context that he develops the distinction between true forgiveness and pseudo-forgiveness. As he observes,

> what may at a cursory glance appear to be forgiveness is really only a particular form of conscious or unconscious egoism – a hidden wish to present oneself in as advantageous a light as possible, to don a mask of false virtue. This so-called forgiveness does not really make any great inner demands, even though it can easily be made use of for achieving some kind self-seeking purpose. (p. 72)

Prokofieff goes on to suggest that there are two key features that distinguish true forgiveness from pseudo-forgiveness. One is the 'overcoming' of oneself. He sees true forgiveness as arising from the 'permeation of the lower ego by the forces and substances of the higher ego' (p. 72). True forgiveness, he suggests, involves a degree of a sacrificiality, i.e. a sacrifice by the lower ego so that the higher ego can permeate it. Not all ostensible acts of forgiveness are characterised by this sacrifice of the lower ego. His distinction between lower and higher ego is analogous in some ways to Jung's distinction between ego and Self. Jung might also claim that the ego needs to sacrifice itself in order to receive the resources of the Self.

The other key distinguishing feature of true forgiveness, Prokofieff suggests, is the amount of inner activity associated with it. He emphasizes that forgiveness can never be mere forgetting, but includes 'an inner obligation to make amends for that objective harm which the evil action has wrought not only upon us but also upon the world' (p. 73). Acts of forgiveness thus carry obligations with them; they have behavioural consequences and involve moral commitments. The expression of forgiveness by the Provost of Coventry after the bombing of his cathedral illustrates the quality that Prokofieff calls true forgiveness. It was a sacrificial act of forgiveness, rising above the natural resentment of the lower ego. It was also an act of commitment that led to serious effort for the cause of reconciliation, and issued, for example, in the subsequent rebuilding of a bombed hospital in Dresden by the people of Coventry.

Ethics and Forgiveness

Whether acts of forgiveness represent true forgiveness or not depends crucially on the spirit in which they are undertaken. That brings us to the question of why people forgive. How people forgive will be much influenced by why they do it. This is essentially a moral question of a kind that is familiar within ethical theory. It is always possible to argue a moral case in terms of consequences, and to see a close identification between actions that are morally right and actions that have good consequences. One can press the case for forgiveness entirely on such pragmatic grounds, arguing that the world is a better place if forgiveness is practised than if it is not. The pragmatic case for forgiveness is a strong one. Though there may be contexts in which forgiveness seems impossible for one reason or another, or in which attempts to forgive are counter-productive, forgiveness has a remarkable capacity to heal relationships and to heal the past. Both those who offer forgiveness, and those who forgive, can be liberated by an act of forgiveness. The recent therapeutic forgiveness movement has been impressed by this pragmatic case. It is because the secular world has increasingly seen the good that forgiveness can do that it has found ways of bringing forgiveness out of a narrowly religious context into the broader arena of secular life.

This widening of the practice of forgiveness is undoubtedly to be welcomed, and I have no concerns about forgiveness being practised outside an explicitly religious context. However, the question is whether something important is not lost by approaching forgiveness in such a narrowly pragmatic spirit. We live in a consumerist society, in which everything tends to be approached with a consumers' mind-set. We have become consumerist even about forgiveness, seeing it as a practice that will do us good if we 'buy into it'. However, there is a danger that forgiveness practised in a narrowly pragmatic spirit will degenerate into what Prokofieff calls 'pseudo-forgiveness'. True forgiveness may continue to elude those who see only practical, not moral, value in it.

This is a point made by Richard Holloway (2002), who says that 'pure forgiveness is not an instrumental good, a prudent management technique or a damage-limitation exercise; it is an intrinsic good, an end in itself, a pure gift offered with no motive of return' (p. 78). However, it is not clear how consistently Holloway takes the line that forgiveness is not an instrumental good. Elsewhere, for example, he says that if people cannot forgive, it 'may have the tragic effect of binding them to the past and condemning them to a life sentence of bitterness' (pp. 54–55). That sounds rather like seeing forgiveness as an instrumental good. Holloway is clearly right to emphasize that forgiveness is intrinsically good. However, it would be exaggerating the point to imply that it is not also an instrumental good. It would be better to say that forgiveness is not only an instrumental good, and should not be approached solely as an instrumental good.

We are touching here on a specific example of the long-standing debate about whether ethics should be approached in terms of the desirable consequences of good actions, or simply in terms of moral authority. My own view, both in general and in the specific case of forgiveness, is that it is a mistake to go entirely with one side of the argument at the expense of the other. To put it in terms of the particular example of forgiveness, it makes no sense to state the case for forgiveness simply in terms of moral authority and to ignore its practical consequences. Equally, it represents a limited understanding of forgiveness to argue for it simply in terms of consequences and to fail to see it as an absolute good. The case for forgiveness properly needs to be stated in both/and terms, not in either/or terms.

Forgiveness as Virtue

Yet even a both/and approach does not adequately state the case for forgiveness. Dorothy Emmet (1979) in her book, *The Moral Prism*, endorses the view that we need to approach ethics both in terms of consequences and in terms of moral authority. However, she adds a third strand, which is less easy to define, in terms of virtue or character. The approach taken by Jones, who sees forgiveness as a craft, fits into this third approach. Seeing forgiveness as an absolute good, and seeing it as having useful consequences, needs to be complemented by seeing it as a virtue or craft that can and should be cultivated.

Jones introduces a helpful analogy between learning the craft of forgiveness and learning the clinical practice of medicine. In both cases there are overriding values and commitments that are so deeply learned that they dominate the thoughts and actions of the practitioner. The cultivation of that kind of commitment to the life of forgiveness is rather like the education of conscience, something acquired through patient and sometimes costly self-discipline, in which other conflicting objectives and priorities have to be set aside.

Jones is also right to emphasize the involvement of the whole personality in enacting forgiveness. It is much more than the mere uttering of particular words. It involves sensitivities as well as forms of expression, and the relevant forms of expression involve much more than simply what is said. As Jones says, 'we learn to judge our progress in the craft of forgiveness, not by examining isolated actions, feelings, or thoughts; we must see how they are contextualized in broader patterns of life' (1995: 233). An important aspect of this broader contextualization of forgiveness concerns the transformation of the person who forgives. Forgiveness is not something that can be undertaken adequately without any preparation. On the contrary, forgiveness requires a gradual transformation of personality. In Jones' view, if we are to engage in forgiveness we need to need to learn to 'diagnose and discern the craft of forgiveness in the situations and contexts that we and others face in the world around us'. We also need to learn 'what it is about ourselves that needs to be transformed if we are to become holy people' (p. 227).

Forgiveness has a complex relationship with our personal histories. There is a sense in which we need a lifetime of preparation for each act of forgiveness. However, forgiveness also involves the healing of the past. Jones is again right to point out that there is much more to forgiveness than the absolution of guilt. Forgiveness, he says, 'is focused on the reconciliation and healing of our broken pasts, not simply on the absolution of guilt'. Here Jones disagrees sharply with Haber (1991), who claims that 'our own moral history is not an issue'. In contrast, as Jones says (and I agree with him), from a Christian point of view 'our own moral history is precisely what is at issue' (p. 213). In forgiveness, there can be a transformation of the past history of both parties, both the one who forgives and the one who is forgiven. Memories often hold people captive in broken patterns of relationship, and that is as true of divisions between societies as divisions between particular individuals. As Charles Elliott (1995) has emphasized, the path of salvation includes a transformation of memories. Once again, there are particular resources within the Christian faith to assist with this, and contextualization is again of the essence. For the Christian, the story of the life, death and resurrection of Jesus provides a narrative within which the more particular narratives of personal hurts and offences can be set. It is through such contextualization that forgiveness is rendered possible and the past is transformed.

We normally see forgiveness as addressing something that has gone wrong in the past, whereas the forgiveness of the Bible is at least as much about a promise for the future. 'Forgiveness is of the future. It has nothing to do with forgetting or wiping out the past; for the past is unchangeable, hopeless, dead...' (Pelz and Pelz 1963: 115). Jesus, they say, 'understands forgiveness exclusively as an opportunity grasped, a call answered, responsibility shouldered, as the giving of what one expects' (p. 115).

Yet even that may not exhaust all there is to be said from a Christian point of view. Rowan Williams (1994), in discussing the parallel question of the case that can be made for sexual morality, sees both 'rule-keeping' and 'being nice to people' as inadequate approaches. As he says, what is supposed to be Christian about either of them? There is also the possibility of a sacramental approach to sexuality, in which the key question about sexual relations is how much we are prepared for them to signify, whether we are prepared for them to be an outward and visible sign of a profound giving and receiving, of integrity, love and fidelity.

In a similar way forgiveness, undertaken in conscious obedience to the purposes of God and with the resources of grace that God offers, can be a sign of the presence of God. When we undertake forgiveness in that spirit, we encounter God in the people we forgive and the people who forgive us. We discover him also within ourselves as we engage in the personal struggle to offer and receive forgiveness in the way he has shown. By giving and receiving forgiveness, we extend God's kingdom and make his presence among us a more tangible reality. The practice of forgiveness can, in that sense, be a sacrament of the presence of God.

5
———————

Forgiveness and Liturgy

Roger Grainger

This chapter on liturgical aspects of forgiveness is psychological rather than historical; it will focus on the experience of liturgy rather than the history and construction of liturgical rites. It will not focus primarily on liturgies of forgiveness, but on liturgy more generally, because all liturgy is designed to embody an experience of forgiveness. The need for forgiveness arises when a relationship has become damaged, and forgiveness leads to the restoration of relationship. So, in order to understand how forgiveness is transacted and experienced in liturgy, we will need first to understand how liturgy embodies and transforms relationality. In accordance with this emphasis, the psychology that will be used in this chapter will be mainly the existential and psychodynamic psychology that helps us to understand the human experience of being in relationship.

Forgiveness and Relationality

Public rituals are corporate. It is not just that we relate to one another as if we were the limbs and organs of a social body; rituals are literally *corporate* because we use our bodies in order to 'do this', co-operating in sound and movement, using the physical distance between us, our individual personal presences to signal and confirm the relationships that exist among us; embracing, joining hands, singing in harmony, acting out stories which concern us, both individually, all together and in groups-within-groups. We do not just think about these things, we actually do them.

At first sight there seems to be a great difference between the actions carried out as part of a corporate religious ritual and those carried out in non-religious settings (what we usually call 'ordinary life'). However, from at least one point of view they turn out to be very much the same, in that our daily lives are made up of giving and receiving gestures of information, attitude or intention (Shorter 1996). For human beings, conscious action taken towards someone else is always meaningful, reinforcing and extending what Kelly (1963) called our 'personal construct system', the way in which we have learned to make our own personal sense of life. Even those actions we make unintentionally, or to mask our real intentions, are, in this sense, gestures of the soul. By virtue of being human, our gestures reach out toward the Other; they make contact with that otherness which is the source and principle of what we call 'relationship'.

Relationship is central to religion. The corporate awareness of the congregation is rooted in, and founded upon, the actions and dispositions of individual members in a very particular and special relationship, their attempt to keep faith with God. Sin is defined precisely as a breakdown in this relationship. Righteousness is keeping this precious relationship intact, and living in obedience to it. In contrast, the common duty towards other men and women is a secondary consideration. We know God in the actual experience of acceptance by him, the infinitely blessed knowledge of our deliverance from ourselves. In other words, we know him in the forgiveness of our sin – sin which is private in origin, however public its effects may be.

In acts of corporate worship, 'private' and 'public' reinforce each other in an experience of interpersonal validation. In this sense, liturgy focuses the personal. In ritual, the action of reaching out is wholly intentional, the expression of a well-made wish. From a 'personal construct' point of view, self-awareness is intensified in ritual because it takes place at the edge of our self-system, which normally exists so that we can at least exert some kind of control over the things that happen to us. Religious ritual, in contrast, takes place on a frontier that defies this kind of control. That is why it is a transforming experience.

Liturgy and Theatre

We can put this in another way, in terms of an analogy between liturgy and theatre. Whereas in the theatre we find ourselves drawn towards one another across the distance which separates *theatron* (auditorium) from *skene* (stage), in religious ritual this aesthetic distance is located elsewhere – in the distance between human beings and God, in what Buber calls 'the stern over-againstness of I and Thou' (1957: 66). 'The difference between religion and drama,' says R.L. Grimes, 'has to do with the degree to which acting in both senses is felt to be in touch with inescapable rhythms (like the Tao), definitive transitions (like the Exodus) or deep processes (like the collective unconscious)' (1982: 59–60).

There is good reason for talking about theatre in a discussion of the relationship between liturgy and forgiveness. Theatre, like any kind of drama, functions by means of separation, and I have argued elsewhere that the same is true of liturgy (Grainger 1974, 1988, 1994). Both liturgy and theatre work dialectically in order to express and promote a relationship between different realities, whether that is humanity and divinity, or the audience's everyday world and the imaginative construct which is theatre. Theatre is a paradigm of ritual, a coming-together of realities which are normally both experienced and understood as being opposites – what Jung refers to as a *co-incidentia oppositorum* (in McGuire and Hull 1978: 328). It is in this coming-together of separateness that relationship itself consists; it is an encounter, not a fusion, because the new relational reality preserves and ratifies the identities of those involved.

In religious rituals we have a sense of meeting God. In the case of initiated people, this is a genuine human experience affecting our lives as human beings; indeed, it is the most important thing about our lives. Ritual 'seen from the inside' has a particular effect on us, as all passionate encounters do. As the anthropologist Van der Leeuw pointed out, 'the virtue of a religion is not in its texts but its effects' (1938). Ritual takes our minds off who we are: we lose our self-consciousness and throw ourselves into the arms of the Beloved. While this is going on we forget about differences, even ultimately significant ones, and enjoy what we experience as a timeless moment of union.

I have chosen to stress theatricality for two reasons. First it allows the ritual symbol to retain its metaphorical force and point beyond itself to what is cognitively and affectively unattainable. In this way, it allows us to enter into relation with a reality which is otherwise perceptually outside our range and cannot be known by mere description, or even illustration, however expressive (Grainger 1974). Indeed, the more expressive it is, the more it encourages us to confuse symbolism with the straightforward transfer of identity. Whatever the Mass is, it surely ought not to be seen as a process in which people are brought psychologically into a frame of mind in which they are able to accept the truth of their union with Christ without surprise, without a sense of the impossibility of that which has taken place by faith.

The second reason for referring to theatre brings us explicitly to the experience of forgiveness. Ritual, like theatre, consists in the exchange of realities that takes place in the encounter between persons. The gospel message about reconciliation with God is expressed in terms of forgiveness as something to be passed on, spiritually present in every personal encounter, embodying the essence of personhood itself. To be in relation with someone else is implicitly to accept them and to be accepted by them. Even when forgiveness is not explicitly called for, such acceptance carries a relational requirement.

In rite, as in theatre, the fundamental gesture is one of exchange, a reaching out toward the Other in an exchange of awareness. For human beings, forgiveness involves not fusion but sharing, the interchange of love. In Holy Communion, Christ establishes God's forgiveness by sharing himself with sinners so that they too may share themselves. Both being accepted by the Other, and the acceptance of the Other, are of God.

A Space for Forgiveness

Next we will explore some of the psychological factors involved in the way in which people set about creating the conditions of time, place and intention which promote the mutual giving and receiving of regard, which is personal relationship.

For both theatre and ritual, it is crucial to set aside a space for encountering the sacred. The sacred place is the place of safety, encouraging adventure, permitting self-disclosure. It is the embodiment of an idea or image of security which we carry with us from the first moments of self-awareness when, for the first time, the self is experienced as existing 'in context'. Describing a child's relationship to the image of the mother, Kelly says that 'armed with such a construct the person can face, not only his world of people, but his world of physical events, with equanimity' (1963: 151). This vision of the self as existing within a 'superordinate' (Kelly's word) relationship affects all our experience. It is never 'just an idea'.

From another angle, H.S. Sullivan defines security as 'freedom from anxiety' (1953). Just as anxiety is necessary for the growth of personhood, so is the experience of deliverance, the place of freedom; life is lived, says Sullivan, 'in the broad dialectic between needs for satisfaction and the need for security' (Greenberg and Mitchell 1983: 100). Similarly, Margaret Mahler describes 'an eternal longing for the actual fantasied "ideal state of self" which characterises the entire human life cycle' (1972: 338).

Such security is not the denial of anxiety but its resolution. Simple avoidance of anxiety does not work. In fact, repressing or denying things which get in the way of security has precisely the opposite effect, resulting in psychopathology. The safe space, as D.W. Winnicott demonstrated, is an opportunity for self-disclosure, the abandonment of the apparent safety which comes from hiding behind a 'false self' system, when the 'defensive function is to hide and protect the True Self, whatever that may be' (1960).

Winnicott also sees a more positive, even creative, function in defensive structures of this kind: 'the False Self has as its main concern a search for conditions which will make it possible for the True Self to come into its own' (1960). The safe space, then, is the awareness of safety and danger at the same time. It is a continued challenge and a liberated security. It encourages us to show ourselves despite our urge to remain hidden, and gives us something to cling onto on our journey into the unknown. As such it might be described as 'the spar to which we cling in order to stay afloat in the ocean of life'. At least, this is how we imagine it – as a state of being in which opposing forces are held in tension, as they are in the cathartic balance which Aristotle characterised as the heart of the theatrical event.

Forgiveness and Catharsis

The kind of theatre to which Aristotle was referring had a close affinity with religious ritual, and the phenomenon of catharsis occurs in both places. Indeed it can be reproduced wherever the degree of emotional threat is balanced against that of psychological safety. The actions of ritual and theatre are 'safe' because they are designed in advance. This means that self-disclosure is pre-arranged, limiting the risk of the self being found unacceptable, or even culpable, and consequently rejected or rendered invalid. Both explicitly in religious ritual, and implicitly in theatre, selves are invited into relationship with the Other by the promise of acceptance and deliverance from fear. In both theatre and ritual, deliverance takes the form of cathartic experience in which anxiety on behalf of the self is redeemed by the self's responsive gesture towards the Other. That corresponds to Aristotle's description of the transformation of our own fears by involvement in someone else's sufferings: the 'purgation' brought about by 'pity and fear' (*Poetics*, vi, 2).

In catharsis a vulnerable or suffering person achieves a degree of distance from their anxiety by taking on the role of somebody else. This is not done in order to deny the reality of their own potential pain, but to gain help in bearing the burden of it. Our ability to bear pain is reinforced by our awareness of someone else's love; and we respond by identifying with that person to the extent of sharing our own painful experience. Thus a mother's reaction to her child's anguish helps to make her child's pain shareable by endorsing its reality and granting permission to weep. In this way, what is shareable becomes bearable. According to Scheff (1979) being allowed to cry helps children adjust to the burdens which 'appear to be an inescapable feature of infancy as a result of intense and incommunicable feelings of separation and loss' (p. 62).

Ritual and theatre allow incommunicable feelings to be acknowledged. In other words, they give us 'permission to weep' about things that are both true and unbearable – unbearably true, in fact. Scheff describes how people who are protected and exposed at the same time can abandon their psychological defences and begin to make contact with aspects of reality they have trained themselves to deny. For effective catharsis to occur, we need to feel secure enough to 'see ourselves feeling'. This involves recognizing ourselves in other people in a way that acknowledges their otherness without seeking to include them within the self.

Within the secure world of a spiritually shared experience we find courage to be ourselves, and perceptiveness to recognize truths we have worked hard to keep at arm's length. Catharsis is not simply deliverance from tension in the sense of a release of pent-up emotion – the usual psychiatric definition of the term – it is also the place of revelation. Indeed, it is primarily this, constituting as it does a global experience of personal meaning that is concerned with ultimate truth, beautiful enough in itself to bring tears to our eyes. It is also more extensive than the experience of cognitive 'closure' which the Gesaltists identified with the mental mechanisms that give rise to understanding and insight (Ellis 1966). In fact it includes all four of the psychic functions described by Jung, 'sensation' and 'intuition' as well as 'cognition' and 'affect'.

Catharsis, with its combination of spontaneous feeling and revelatory insight, is hard to define in precise psychological terms, and is best described in less exact ways, such as the '*éclairage*' which Sartre sees as the defining quality of theatrical truthfulness or Ian Ramsay's 'disclosure experience'. According to Robert Landy, 'the moment of catharsis is a creative moment, rather like the discovery of a pun,' (1995: 115); and he points out that such experiences are no less powerful for not being 'large, tearful moments'. They are, in essence, those moments of recognition, upon which theatre depends. Religious ritual is full of them.

The ritual process, then, is one in which need, structure and safety lead to recognition, encouragement, encounter and reconciliation. Once 'recognition' has taken place, encouragement, encounter and reconciliation are experienced all together within the cathartic moment. It could be said, then, that rituals 'speak the language of reconciliation'. The structure of the rite constitutes a way of approaching a reality – a Presence – which is otherwise felt to be unapproachable, not only because it is too sacred, but also because we are too unworthy. The rite is both a confession of need and a plea for forgiveness. Although the effect of this Presence may be to discourage or dissuade, its intention is to welcome, and to change things by doing so. We come forward 'in penitence and faith'. Once this special kind of meeting has taken place, and contact has been made under the terms of the rite, a spiritual transformation has been brought about. Our world is changed and we are changed with it. We are cathartically liberated from spiritual anxiety.

Being Forgiven so as to Forgive

Another, simpler way to put this is to say that we feel radically forgiven. We have been reassured of forgiveness in a way we find hard to ignore or misunderstand; we have encountered it in circumstances in which we are able to let ourselves accept it. Metaphorically speaking, God has revealed himself to us in a way we have been able to accept, despite our painstakingly elaborated deafness to anything we construe as too painful to tolerate without distortion. This, I would argue, is the psychological purpose of religious ritual – to transmit a message about unworthiness as explicitly as possible, so that ideas about the possibility of communicating with God on our own terms may be ruled out of court from the very beginning (Grainger 1974, 1988).

It is primarily to this general sense of unworthiness that liturgy speaks. Whereas sacramental confession focuses rather narrowly on specific misdeeds for which people feel guilt, the more general liturgical experience of the Eucharist can, at its best, take people from a state of estrangement to one of acceptance. It is arguable (see Watts 2001) that we live in a society that is characterized more by shame (a general sense of a unworthiness) than by guilt (remorse over specific behaviours). If so, sacramental confession may not be speaking as powerfully to the need for forgiveness as it once did. However, the liturgical experience of the Eucharist will still be highly relevant to providing an experience of being forgiven.

Being forgiven oneself leads on to forgiving others; forgiveness involves reaching out to another. To put it at its crudest, we cannot forgive somebody without endorsing their own personal existence. The cognitive psychologist G.A. Kelly points out that the fact of simply living alongside other people, if we want to interact with them in any effective way, necessitates a degree of involvement with them. In order to be human at all requires a willingness to at least try to understand one's neighbour as oneself: 'to the extent that one person construes the construction processes of another he may play a role in a social process involving another person' (1963: 93). Thus, the only people we can have any kind of a relationship with at all are those whose actions and reactions we can anticipate. This kind of 'cognitive empathy' is basic to our survival as social beings. To understand is always to some extent to let oneself become perceptually involved (Mearleau-Ponty 1962) and this is never more so than in our relationships with one another. This being so, if we are to understand those who have harmed us, we have no option but to try to forgive them.

However, forgiveness requires more than willingness to understand; or rather the willingness itself depends on something more basic than an ability to imagine what someone else may be thinking or feeling. It needs a sense of security which is established emotionally, and is not simply a matter of constructs, either cognitive or liturgical. In other words, it needs a history of being forgiven because one is loved.

Christian theology revolves around a proposition which is made very succinctly in the First Epistle of John, that 'we love because he first loved us' (1 John 4.19). Theologically speaking, our loving is a response, made in kind, to God who 'is love' (v. 16). The statement has more than a theological resonance; or rather, its theological meaning strikes home because it refers to a psychological experience with which we are familiar, that of loving in exchange. We love people who love us, the point scarcely needs to be argued; and even if we dislike someone, the revelation that they have loving feelings, a loving attitude, towards us cannot help lessening our dislike – unless, of course, we are determined not to let it. The key issue is the degree to which being loved by someone affects our attitude to other people, not simply to people we associate with the person who loves us, but to people in general. Because we are loved, is it actually easier to love our neighbours to the extent of forgiving them hurts they may inflict on us? Within the ritual event, an event which we have identified as a cathartic experience, claiming for it a specific quality and intensity uniquely associated with a particular kind of socio-aesthetic event, we find a degree of acceptance that transforms our attitude to our neighbours.

Object relations psychology stresses the fact that love begets love. To experience love is to be given the power to bestow it – and on other 'objects' apart from the person first associated with the giving and forgiving. Suttie is in no doubt about the way these things happen: 'the love of others comes into being simultaneously with the recognition of their existence' (1988: 30). It is not an instinct but a relationship. 'Not sexual desire degenitalized by repression, as Freud would have it ... I believe the love bond to the infant mind has the quality of tenderness from the beginning' (1988: 31). This tenderness is mutual: 'the need to give is as vital as the need to get' (p. 53); without it there will be little or no tenderness, little or no real loving which is shared with others later in life: 'because it is in fact this first love that we exchange that teaches us how to love, as we "put the whole social environment" in the place it once occupied' (Suttie 1988: 16; also Bowlby 1971).

This argument depends upon taking account of the safety provided by the structure rather than any inherently spiritual or aesthetic value or significance it may possess. It applies to all corporate rituals, not only those that are explicitly religious, but to every moment of metaphorical encounter between persons, because safety is fundamental to the way such metaphors communicate their meaning. The security provided by the structure permits us to transcend those factors of defensiveness and preoccupation within the self which inhibit spiritual awareness.

Eucharist and Baptism

The Church's central liturgy, the Eucharist, demonstrates the use of ritual as an active symbol of loving, one firmly rooted in the human experience of being loved. The forgiveness represented – embodied – here is not only the theological origin but the actively remembered experience of being forgiven. Earlier in this chapter we looked at the cathartic effect of ritual, its ability to encourage us to reach out towards an encounter with the unknown and un-assimilable. Catharsis reproduces an existential situation in which we feel loved and secure, yet irresistibly impelled to take risks with our own safety. In fact, the balance between safety and danger gives rise to a kind of emotional paradigm shift in which movements 'away from' and 'towards' occur at the same time, as we find ourselves seized by fear for ourselves and pity for someone else. We become involved, simultaneously, in the living and dying of someone who is at once like and unlike ourselves.

In the Eucharist this cathartic effect, lying as it does at the heart of the rite's action, opens us up to feelings associated with the protagonist of the drama. It is his love, his forgiveness, with which we identify – not only to receive, but also to give. These are moments of cathartic insight, in which emotional release is accompanied by spiritual revelation, and the world feels renewed. If, for us, loving is a courageous action, then the cathartic experience has the effect of making us feel loved and able to love, being at the same time both demand and gift.

Writing about the Mass, Ronald Murphy (1988) tells us that 'the union of opposites and the "warping" of time, which in a sense is the union of opposites (i.e. ambiguity of time present and time past), is exemplified repeatedly in the ritual of the Mass' so that 'one is never quite sure whether one is present at a church service in the twentieth century, or at the last supper, at the crucifixion and resurrection, or for that matter before the Heavenly Throne as presented in the Book of Revelation' (p. 319). Father Murphy lays much stress on the 'ambiguity' produced by the 'dyadic oppositions' involved in the ritual. His exposition of the pictorial quality of the Mass brings home its dramatic quality as a presentation of Catholic dogma. The Mass takes us from the entry procession at the beginning of the service to the altar rail at its culmination; the priest approaches the altar first but eventually calls the faithful to approach too. The structure of the Mass prepares people for that crowning experience, and the experience of forgiveness is a key part of that preparation.

Theologically, Christians are, in the most real sense, 'in Christ'; so the message of the rite is one that moves us towards that identification with Christ by eliminating the sense of an unbridgeable gulf between the human and the divine. Rather than being the experience of encounter through awareness of separation, the Mass realizes union with Christ by acting out the transcendence of oppositions. As R.S. Lee emphasizes, the ideal of union with Christ is transformed into actuality within the Eucharist. 'We do not merely imitate his external example, we become Christ. He enters into us and shapes us to himself. He is real in us, made actual in us' (Lee 1955: 109–10). This is the most powerful possible experience of having been forgiven.

Religious ritual is also unavoidably initiatory (Eliade 1965: 114), a symbolic 'movement into higher ground' that requires a being-change on the part of those involved. This is its purpose and its nature. Change of this kind is not easily accomplished, and all such rites involve some kind of symbolic dying, in which the old state of affairs is 'put to death' so that the new one, the condition of future life, might be brought to birth. From this point of view every rite is a 'rite of passage' (Van Gennep 1960) containing within its threefold structure the soul pain which represents the price and the possibility of forgiveness.

This rite of passage from being unforgiven to being forgiven is, of course, symbolised in the rite of baptism. In this sense, as Christopher Jones (2001) remarks, baptism is the 'primary sign of the decisiveness and comprehensiveness of God's act of forgiveness in Jesus Christ and of the new identity and calling which baptism initiates' (p. 45). There is a dual movement in baptism from being outside Christ to being 'in Christ', and also from being outside the Christian community to being welcomed into it and becoming part of it. Though the transformation that takes place in baptism can never be repeated, it stands as a continuing sign, not only of having entered a state of forgiveness, but of the possibility of returning to being at one with Christ and the Christian community whenever estrangement reasserts itself.

Religious ritual can be regarded as a special kind of human language, one whose message concerns the only possible terms on which human beings may be reconciled to God – that is, through overcoming the shortfall between what divinity represents, if we can imagine such a thing, and whatever we ourselves can come up with. Because ritual is the symbolized encounter between the human and the divine it allows those taking part to feel forgiven, to feel accepted. The language encoded within ritual is specially designed for reconciliation. The message of liturgy, if it is to be practical, must be addressed to a need for forgiveness – psychologically and theologically.

Appendix: A 'Ritual and Forgiveness' Workshop

Before carrying out the following workshop, it is advisable to bear in mind that the nature of offences for which individuals are seeking forgiveness could vary enormously. Although it is unlikely that an individual would reveal anything especially shocking after they have been invited to share with their partner, leaders should be aware of this possibility, and the effect it could have on the listener and the group as a whole.

If the symbolism of personal transformation is present then an experience of renewal is likely to emerge, however crude the structure may appear to be. Intention is very much more important than any kind of skill, as the study of ritual makes abundantly clear. The following workshop sets out to demonstrate this. It contains three distinct stages in order to reproduce the symbolic shape of a rite of passage, expressing forgiveness and new life:

- Stage One introduces the motif of the need for change, for 'turning again';
- Stage Two confronts the pain involved in allowing real change to take place;
- Stage Three celebrates the freedom of new possibilities.

Because this is a workshop its general tone is exploration rather than theological or doctrinal statement, but the elements of ritual it contains ally themselves with its overall shape to bring home the idea of forgiveness as a real experience, not simply a pious aspiration. Its obvious aim is to make the Biblical message about God's forgiveness as immediate as possible by encouraging a vivid kind of imaginative involvement. Group work concentrates more on the experience of a shared journey than the definition of a clear-cut doctrine. It is my personal conviction that telling people in advance exactly what it is they are supposed to discover is not the most powerful way of doing justice to biblical material – and the story of the reality of God's generosity is no exception. Workshops like this one are easy to put together, so long as the ritual outline – of a journey into and out of pain – is preserved. The intention is in fact to reproduce a very simple form of corporate art; perhaps the oldest form of all...

Stage I

- Stand together in a circle. Take turns to say who you are. Now go round the circle again, this time saying what is the main thing on your mind at present.
- Listen to one of the group reading from the Bible. They are going to read the parable of the Prodigal Son (Luke 15.11–32).
- Give yourselves a moment to think about the story, then take hands and move around, circling first to the left, then to the right.
- Now divide into two groups, Group 'A' and Group 'B'. Each member of Group A finds a partner from Group B; partners spend about five minutes talking to each other about the story and what it means to them.

(Musical interlude)

Stage II

- With your partner, move to one end of the room, standing next to one another, facing down the room.
- Move slowly down the room in pairs, taking your own time and concentrating on your partner, talking quietly to each other. As ask Bs the question: 'Would you think less highly of me if I told you....?', sharing with them something about which they feel personally ashamed or guilty. Bs acknowledge the question and say one or two words in response to it.
- When you reach the other side of the room, As pick up a token – a small lighted candle, or a flower, or a simple glass bead, for example. They give this to their partner.
- Now retrace your steps silently (you may hold hands if you wish).
- Repeat your journey down the room and back again. This time B asks the question and gives A the token. As before, partners accompany each other back to the starting line.

- Hug your partner (or shake hands if you prefer!), then go and find somewhere to sit and listen to the music. Be sure to take your token with you.

(Musical interlude)

Stage III

- Place the tokens you were given in the middle of the room, and then form a circle around them, holding hands.
- Now send a message round the circle by squeezing the hand of the person next to you (i.e. when you feel your left hand being squeezed, pass the message on by squeezing the hand of the person on your right). Keep reversing the direction!
- Use all the tokens to create a pattern, or perhaps a picture, in the centre of the room. Try to let everybody join in doing this. Take some time to admire what you have created together.
- Say a prayer of thanksgiving together; then pause, to give individual people a chance to pray.
- Say goodbye to everyone, taking particular care to speak to your partner, and to thank him or her for your token.
- Take your token with you when you go . . .

Workshops like this one need to be experienced in order to be properly understood. They do not usually involve 'large tearful moments', but their impact is considerable all the same. Reading about them is not enough to bring home their ability to realise the truth they are designed to communicate – a quality which is intrinsic to the corporate action we call ritual.

6

Intrapersonal Forgiveness

Liz Gulliford

This and the following chapter are primarily psychological rather than theological in tone. It is hoped that this will provide an adequate background from which to evaluate the recent psychological approaches to forgiveness that have been advocated within both individual and interpersonal therapy. The theological 'ideal' of forgiveness can benefit from psychological insights about what we might call 'the human side of forgiveness'. As Watts has indicated (chapter 4), the role that psychology should play in forgiveness has been the subject of vigorous debate. For Jones (1995) 'therapeutic forgiveness' is a distortion of the 'true' forgiveness of the Gospel. Antagonism has also, until recently, cut the other way with psychologists reluctant to turn their attention to a concept which they perceive as 'religious' in tone.

Consequently, until lately, forgiveness received little attention from psychologists, and interventions to promote it were not developed within therapy. This was an unfortunate state of affairs, for other forms of therapy may fail to provide an appropriate 'release' for clients. Forgiveness is a powerful way of allowing this essential 'release' to occur, freeing people from the burden of the past, and allowing a new future to be envisaged on social, interpersonal and individual levels.

Recent years have seen a surge of interest in forgiveness, particularly as a therapeutic goal, as attested by Smedes (1984), Hebl and Enright (1993), Al-Mabuk, Enright and Cardis (1995), McCullough and Worthington (1995), Freedman and Enright (1996), Coyle and Enright (1997), McCullough, Worthington and Rachal (1997), Enright and North (1998), Worthington (1998a, 1998b), Di Blasio (1998), McCullough, Pargament and Thoresen (2000), Enright and Fitzgibbons (2000), Enright (2001), Worthington and Ripley (2002) and Gordon and Baucom (2003) to name a few. It should be pointed out, however, that all of these interventions only aim to facilitate forgiveness *where that is the expressed desire of the client*. People are not *constrained* to forgive, as that places a further burden on those who have already suffered much.

The injunction to forgive in the Lord's Prayer may be problematic for individuals who have suffered particularly damaging injustices. It is not uncommon for people to envisage themselves as unworthy and unloved because they cannot forgive grievous wrongs. Some individuals in this position imagine that they will put themselves out of the orbit of God's love if they cannot forgive an abuser. It is clear that in such cases care needs to be taken to protect the person involved from further shouldering this dreadful burden. It may, perhaps, help people to be reminded that a compassionate God *suffers with* those he loves, and helps bear our burdens. God's forgiveness is also beyond the scope of ours: it may alleviate some strain on the part of the person seeking to forgive to know that, although *they* cannot forgive the wrong, forgiveness is possible for God.

Therapeutic interventions tend to begin by defining forgiveness by contrasting it with condoning, excusing, forgetting and pardoning. However, when it comes down to *positively* defining forgiveness, differences of opinion emerge. Whether forgiveness is conceptualized primarily as a change of emotional tone or behavioural changes towards an individual has a bearing on models of forgiveness, on the putative psychological mechanisms underlying these interventions, and on measures of success and failure in realizing forgiveness.

The eighteenth-century Anglican Bishop, Joseph Butler, defined forgiveness as 'the foreswearing of resentment – where resentment is a negative feeling (anger, hatred) directed toward another who has done one moral injury' (Butler 1970). Richards (1988) qualifies this with the suggestion that abandoning resentment does not constitute forgiveness – a person could stop resenting and still have a hostile attitude of another kind. He proposes that forgiveness should instead be conceptualized as the abandonment of *negative feelings*. But is forgiveness simply a matter of abandoning *negative* feelings?

McCullough and Witvliet (2001) note how there is a heavy bias towards defining forgiveness in terms of the cessation of unforgiveness. While that appears to make some intuitive sense, a recent study suggests that forgiveness and unforgiveness may not represent polar opposites (Wade and Worthington 2003). Wade and Worthington found that forgiveness was predicted by dispositional variables, trait forgiveness, contrition, empathy and effort (in trying to forgive). Lowered unforgiveness was also predicted by empathy and perceived contrition of the offender, but *not* by any of the other variables. While people who had forgiven tended to report less unforgiveness, there was a wide range of unforgiveness in the lowest scorers on forgiveness, suggesting the two are not opposite ends of the same spectrum. In addition, Worthington, Berry and Parrott (2001) found that in a sample of 320 students, 18 per cent were high in forgiveness and unforgiveness, 38 per cent were high in unforgiveness and low in forgiveness, 34 per cent were low in unforgiveness and high in forgiveness, whilst 10 per cent were low in both.

It seems then that the *reduction* of negative feelings and emotions and the *increase* in positive ones are *both* important for a full understanding of forgiveness. North (1987) offered a definition which recognizes this: 'Forgiveness is the overcoming of negative affect and judgment toward the offender, not by denying ourselves the right to such affect and judgment but by endeavouring to view the offender with compassion, benevolence, and love while recognizing that he has abandoned his right to them' (North 1987: 502).

Enright, Freedman and Rique (1998: 46–47) offer a comprehensive definition of forgiveness as 'a willingness to abandon one's right to resentment, negative judgment, and indifferent behavior toward one who unjustly injured us, while fostering the undeserved qualities of compassion, generosity and even love toward him or her'. Their definition includes cognitive, affective and behavioural components. It also emphasizes that forgiveness is a free choice on the part of the person seeking to forgive (i.e. its conative aspect). It also suggests, through its insistence on promoting compassion, generosity and love, that forgiveness cannot be practised out of self-interest alone – an issue which has been prominent in some critiques of 'therapeutic forgiveness.'

The view that forgiveness is primarily a prosocial phenomenon can be contrasted with a view which concerns itself with the effects of forgiveness in the forgiving person. This difference can be expressed psychologically as 'interpersonal forgiveness' (forgiveness between individuals) as opposed to 'intrapersonal forgiveness' (the feelings, thoughts and behaviour associated with forgiveness within the individual seeking to forgive). In recent years the focus on the forgiver has been especially pertinent in therapeutic circles, and forgiveness has been advocated as a powerful means of personal therapy.

Forgiveness does not always lead to the reconciliation of all parties: death may prevent the behavioural acting out of a forgiveness that had been reached intrapersonally, for example. Reluctance to accept forgiveness could prevent the full healing of relationships, or there may be no sign of repentance on the part of the offender. Though reconciliation may not be possible, that need not mean there is no healing whatsoever for the person seeking to forgive. Many people report a profound sense of personal release as they move towards forgiving those who hurt them. That this might not be 'returned' by the offender does not, of necessity, undermine growing positive feelings in the forgiving person. To make forgiveness contingent on repentance or acceptance by the other party places the victim in a stranglehold. It is not inconceivable that wrongdoers may deliberately refuse to accept they are forgiven (because this is tantamount to an admission of wrongdoing) or believe they are in any way accountable for their actions, in an attempt to 'foil' interpersonal forgiveness.

In view of this, some argue that it is simply better *not* to forgive until the other person repents, making forgiveness dependent on repentance. Unfortunately this 'straitjackets' the person seeking to forgive: they cannot begin to eliminate negative feelings and judgments about their offender *until* that person has come to himself or herself and is prepared to repent. This could be a long time coming, if at all. There is also evidence that maintaining bitterness and resentment endangers one's health. There is, then, an argument in favour of forgiveness that rests on its putative salutary benefits.

Anger and Forgiveness

In part, the health benefits of forgiveness have been elucidated against the backdrop of anger, which is widely believed to have damaging effects on health. Enright and Fitzgibbons (2000) hold the view that anger is a significant factor in a range of clinical disorders and promote forgiveness as a means of dealing with out-of-control anger that could play a part in depression, anxiety and a range of other problems. While we cannot be sure that unresolved anger lies at the root of all these clinical manifestations, the link between anger and a number of physiological outcomes is better documented, and provides some insights into why waiting for repentance *before* embarking on forgiveness could prove costly to health.

Anger gives rise to an increase in adrenaline. At length, heart rate returns to normal and the accompanying feeling of rage subsides. In some cases, however, adrenaline production is sustained, resulting in chronic hyperarousal of the sympathetic nervous system which eventually takes its toll on the body (see Thoresen, Harris and Luskin 2000: 258–60). Witvliet, Ludwig and van der Laan (2001) asked 35 women and 36 men to recall a person who had hurt them and react in unforgiving and forgiving ways. Unforgiving thoughts triggered stress responses from higher blood pressure to faster heart rates. Forgiving thoughts resulted in lower physiological stress responses.

In addition to physiological effects, sustained anger increases the likelihood of substance abuse and may exacerbate problems in psychosocial functioning. Angry people are more likely to isolate themselves from others. They often become intolerant and, consumed with their own anger, are less able to demonstrate empathy. Resentment and bitterness disfigure the healthy relationships they *do* have, leaving them even more embittered and lonely than before. Worthington, Mazzeo and Kliewer (2002) suggest that unforgiveness may be a co-morbid condition with addictive and eating disorders. Given that Post-Traumatic Stress Disorder is one of the strongest predictors of substance abuse in both males and females (Kilpatrick, Acierno, Saunders, Resnick, Best and Schnurr 2000), and that cases where forgiveness is sought may often be traumatic, the potential for unforgiveness to lie at the root of addictive disorders could well be elevated. Consequently, forgiveness, it has been suggested, might offer a means of dealing with anger so it does not become channelled in self-destructive avenues.

To wait for repentance *before* proceeding with the task of forgiveness might seem 'just', but it is perhaps not fair to oneself, and perpetuates the pain of the offence rather than working to eliminate it. However, while repentance need not precede forgiveness in all cases, it is nonetheless an appropriate response to having been forgiven. It shows the wrongdoer appreciates that he or she must mend their ways. Failure to change in light of forgiveness devalues the magnanimity bestowed in the act. This point is made theologically by Bonhoeffer (1971), who speaks of repentance as the only fitting response to the gift of grace of God in Christ: we 'cheapen' that gift, he says, if we fail to mend our ways. We may have felt an analogous sense of our forgiveness being devalued by insouciance if it fails to elicit any change on the part of the person we forgave.

Forgiveness and repentance are closely intertwined, but one does not have to assert the temporal priority of repentance. In the New Testament there are repeated exhortations to repent in the light of the coming kingdom. On the other hand, however, Jesus consorted with tax collectors and sinners *without* hearing them first repent, and called on God to forgive his torturers with the prayer, 'Father, forgive them; they do not know what they are doing' (Luke 23.34). There is a dichotomy, it seems, between whether it is better to allow victims freedom to choose their own course of action in the wake of an offence, or whether it is better to deny this personal freedom to uphold a moral code in the interests of the collective. 'Indiscriminate' forgiveness could be cited as antagonistic to societal goals, potentially opening up the way for abuse. It is precisely this concern that lies at the root of the exposition of repentance and forgiveness in chapter 2.

In the next part of the chapter we will consider approaches to forgiveness that have been advocated in therapeutic interventions. The focus is on the individual's journey towards forgiveness. These approaches are based on the assumption that the individual's right to choose to forgive, in the absence of prior repentance, is a legitimate course of action.

Approaches to Forgiveness within Therapy

Lewis Smedes' *Forgive and Forget: Healing the Hurts We Don't Deserve* (1984) was the first therapeutically oriented book about forgiveness to gain a wide and popular audience. The author offered an approach to forgiveness that centred on the well-being of the person seeking to forgive. It described how not forgiving can further victimize the sufferer of wrongdoing, as we have discussed above, and it offered an approach to how forgiveness might be realized which centred on seeing the offence with 'magic eyes'. In other words, by careful re-examination of the matter and 'by putting oneself at a due distance from the offence' (as Bishop Butler said), one may find forgiveness easier, and can be liberated from the binding effect of resentment. Smedes' view was that people who retain a vindictive mind-set in the wake of wrongdoing give the offender another victim. So long as a person is tortured by fantasies of revenge, bitterness and resentment, they remain trapped in the clutches of those who have wronged them. He advocated a means of restoring one's own dignity and health by choosing to forgive an offender, thereby redefining oneself not as a victim of abuse, but as a person who retains the strength to forgive one who has wronged them.

Many people felt this focus on the 'forgiving self' was narcissistic – even irreligious. Critics such as Jones (1995) felt forgiveness had 'sold out' to a self-help culture. While it is true that Smedes focuses on letting go of one's own anger and negativity, it seems he was somewhat misunderstood. Focusing on the person seeking to forgive does not mean we cease to care about the person who wronged us, or the relationship which has been broken, it simply addresses the person whose will we can change – *our own* – in the hope that our forgiveness may lead to the renewal of mutual love and respect. It is, in any case, appropriate for someone to experience some personal gain and release through forgiveness without this being construed as 'narcissistic'. 'Narcissism' is not a word that is appropriate in the context of restoring the worth and dignity of people who have been seriously wronged, many of whom will have very little self-esteem and are likely to have a distorted self-concept that runs counter to that of inflation, as chapter 9 elucidates.

Attention must always be paid to context in any situation. In cases where the balance of power between forgiver and forgiven is more or less equal we should be on our guard against the kind of grandiosity which might lead us to pursue forgiveness in an empty and heartless way, without care for others. However, as we have noted, in cases where this balance has long run against the victim's well-being, forgiveness for one's own sake is surely appropriate.

People should only begin the journey of forgiving if it is something they earnestly desire to do. It should *never* be forced on anyone until and unless they are ready. Some people seem to have a tremendous capacity for forgiveness that is almost Christ-like, yet for many of us the gulf between our capacity to forgive and God's in Christ is much, much wider. An acceptance and awareness of this disparity is important in orienting oneself towards the goal of forgiveness with humility.

Forgiveness in Therapeutic Interventions

In recent years a number of approaches to the question of how forgiveness might be effected have centred on the idea of 'reframing', 'reappraising', 'reattributing' or seeing the offence with 'magic eyes' (see Smedes 1984, Hebl and Enright 1993, Al-Mabuk, Enright and Cardis 1995, Coyle and Enright 1997, Enright, Freedman and Rique 1998 and Coleman 1998, for examples). Reappraisal (or reattribution therapy) has proved effective in treating a variety of clinical disorders, such as depression and loneliness (Abramson, Seligman and Teasdale 1978, Peplau, Russell and Heim 1979), and a number of researchers believe that a reattribution approach is fruitful within forgiveness therapy.

Essentially, reframing techniques aim to widen the perspective of the victim so the actions of the wrongdoer are placed within a framework which expands the narrative of blame to include what might have led the offender to behave in a hurtful way. The process of reframing may, for example, take account of aspects of the offender's upbringing, which could lead the injured party to see the actions of the perpetrator in a different light. In essence, a reframing approach was advocated by Butler (1970), who suggests that those seeking to forgive should 'place themselves at a due distance' from the offence, attributing wrongdoing to inadvertence or mistake, rather than malice and scorn. He spoke of the importance of bracketing out one's own interpretation of events, biased by 'the peculiarities of self-love'.

Butler's advice prefigures psychological approaches to forgiveness that incorporate reattribution. Of key significance in attribution theory is the question of whether events are attributed to personal (internal) or environmental (external) factors. Since Heider's (1958) work on attribution, investigators have found that people attribute the behaviour

Liz Gulliford

of others to both internal dispositions and external (situational) factors. The extent to which internal or external attributions dominate our interpretation of a person's behaviour depends on a number of factors, such as how well we know the individual concerned, and whether they have made us feel unhappy. It is almost inevitable, in the wake of an offence, that an attribution of blame that fails to take account of external factors is likely to be made. Depending on the extent of the hurt we feel, we are less likely to consider that the person could have been distressed about something unrelated to us, preferring instead to see them as rude and inconsiderate.

The theory behind reframing is that if we 'rework' our attributions, mindful of biases that might have affected our judgment, and put the offender in a new frame, taking account of proximal and distal causes for their behaviour, we might find forgiveness easier. Often reframing techniques challenge individuals seeking to forgive to consider their own failures in order to reframe their offender as *someone like them*. Forgiveness is often easier when we accept our own weaknesses, and can see that we are not entirely innocent ourselves.

Reframing in Therapeutic Interventions

Enright and colleagues at the University of Wisconsin, Madison, have been developing a model of forgiveness since 1985. The model, whose four key stages are described in chapter 3, further divides into 20 units, though early versions of the model had 17. The sequence was postulated after informal discussion and philosophical reflection on the subject of forgiveness. They now believe, having used the model systematically in therapeutic interventions, that although there are individual differences in the length of time clients spend in each of the units, and the precise sequence of their progression through the stages varies, the model, nonetheless, can be followed therapeutically to generate forgiveness. The model is described in detail in *Helping Clients Forgive* (2000) and developed as a self-help book in *Forgiveness is a Choice* (2001), in which an individual is led through the 20 units with journaling exercises and other opportunities for reflection.

The first phase of the model is the 'Uncovering Phase' in which there are eight units (see Enright and Fitzgibbons 2000 for a more detailed exposition). The overall goal of this phase is for the client to gain insight into whether and how the injustice and subsequent injury have compromised his or her life. Summarizing the eight units, the client must first (Unit 1) examine psychological defences, such as denial or displacement, that might be preventing the client from obtaining a clear picture of the offence and its effect. In Unit 2 the client confronts their anger: 'An important part of forgiveness therapy is to acknowledge this anger, allow for its expression (within reasonable limits), and set a goal for the diminution of this emotion towards the offender' (Enright and Fitzgibbons 2000: 71). At 3 the client is encouraged to explore the sense of shame they may feel as a result of the indignity they suffered. In the next unit, the person seeking to forgive is asked to become aware of the emotionally draining effects of being preoccupied with thoughts about the person who caused them pain. This helps throw into relief the amount of time a person may spend 'in the continual thrall' of the wrongdoer. Similarly in Unit 5 the client focuses attention on obsessive thinking about the offender – a journal may be kept to document these thoughts as they occur. At 6 the client is asked to reflect on the differences between themselves and the perpetrator in the wake of the incident. This leads, in some cases, to 7, where the possibility that one might have to face permanent change as a result of the offence is addressed – this is especially prominent in particularly traumatic cases. The final unit of the 'Uncovering Phase' addresses the idea that one's view of the world might now have to be revised in the light of one's experiences. The 'just world-view', described by Flanigan (1992) could, in the wake of offence, give way to a more pessimistic outlook on life. This is, of course, especially so where deep trauma has been suffered.

Having 'uncovered' the offence, addressed defence mechanisms and become aware of its implications, the client enters into the second phase of the model: the 'Decision Phase'. Here he or she examines their forgiveness construct, so that distortions may be addressed and the possibility of committing to forgiving (on the basis of an accurate understanding of its meaning) may be proposed. In Unit 9 the client reflects on 'alternatives' to forgiveness (such as revenge), asking how these coping strategies are helping them deal with hurt. At Unit 10 clients explore the construct of forgiveness, differentiating it from related concepts such as condoning or excusing. This enables clients to correct misinterpretations they might have about forgiveness, which have, perhaps, prevented them from considering forgiveness as a viable option.

The point should be made here that this does, to some extent, entail that the client 'buys into' a particular therapeutic notion of forgiveness, and that the success of realizing that goal to some significant degree depends on whether the prescribed view of forgiveness is accepted by the client. The same point about what constitutes psychological 'health' could be made about any form of therapy, and the trajectory that the therapeutic course takes towards that end. The point perhaps ought also to be made that differentiating between pardon and forgiveness is possible in English, but not in French. There is, then, a component of forgiveness that is inescapably bound by language, and this would have to be acknowledged whenever forgiveness is discussed outside the English-speaking world.

In 11, on the basis of reflection on the meaning of forgiveness, clients decide whether to commit to forgiving the offender. Enright follows Fitzgibbons (1986) in believing that a decision (a cognitive act) precedes the affective aspects of forgiveness, unlike Worthington (below) who suggests that empathy for the offender may facilitate the subsequent decision to forgive. Enright and Fitzgibbons (2000) believe that the control one feels in deciding to forgive is, in itself, helpful in the goal of realizing forgiveness, and suggest that this decision does not entail a 'complete' forgiveness, rather the intent to refrain from seeking or entertaining thoughts of revenge. We could say, then, that the 'Butlerian' 'forswearing of resentment' understanding of forgiveness is the focus of this unit.

In the third phase ('Work Phase') there are four units whose collective goal is to gain a new understanding of the perpetrator, resulting in positive affective change towards the offender, the self and the relationship. This phase begins with 'reframing'. The client is posed questions about the offender to help put him or her into a wider 'frame'. According to Enright and Fitzgibbons 'cognitive insight usually comes before positive affective responses towards an offender' (2000: 79). Reframing represents the turning point from a mere forswearing of resentment to the aspects of forgiveness which concern the generation of positive feelings towards the wrongdoer. At Unit 13, having reframed the offender, the client may feel more compassionate towards them. At 14 the notion of 'bearing the pain' is introduced. As Bonhoeffer noted (1971), bearing the pain makes it possible for pain to cease: evil runs aground, absorbed by love. The suggestion that, by bearing the pain, one is a survivor rather than a victim, may be made. The final unit of the 'Work Phase' is giving some gift to the offender to demonstrate goodwill and open the way for reconciliation.

The work of forgiveness does not end here. In the final five units of the 'Deepening Phase', clients are encouraged to find meaning in their suffering and to deepen positive affect towards the wrongdoer. At Unit 16 people reflect on whether their suffering might, in some way, benefit others – perhaps survivors may have grown in their capacity for empathy, which could equip them to help others better. In the next unit forgiveness might be deepened by reflecting on having needed forgiveness oneself in the past. Other researchers, such as Worthington (below), envisage this step as coming earlier in the scheme of forgiveness, perhaps even facilitating empathy *before* a decision to forgive. Unit 18 calls for the client to reflect that they are not alone in their task of deepening forgiveness – a confidant or sense of God's presence might help someone to engage in ever-deepening forgiveness, especially during inevitable periods of relapse. As a result of working through the four phases, a person might, at Unit 19, envisage a new purpose in life – perhaps a desire to counsel others. Finally, in 20, the client is encouraged to become aware of how they have been transformed by their experience. They might feel a sense of personal growth or less anxious and depressed than before.

Enright and colleagues have always maintained a degree of flexibility concerning progression through the stages. They did not want to create a prescriptive and inflexible dogma about how forgiveness is to be realized. However, they believe they have provided support for the model in a number of clinical interventions using treatment manuals based on either the earlier 17-unit model or the 20-unit model summarized here. There is a comprehensive review of these papers in Enright and Fitzgibbons (2000) which includes full details of the instruments used and experimental procedures. Here the essence of each study is presented, with comments about their implications and conclusions. For unpublished research see Worthington, Sandage and Berry (2000) who offer a meta-analytic review of *all* known interventions to that date.

Hebl and Enright (1993) used the 17-unit process model in an intervention with 24 elderly women who completed a self-esteem inventory (Coopersmith 1981), a depression scale (Beck, Ward, Mendelson, Mock and Erbaugh 1961), a test of anxiety (Spielberger, Gorsuch, Lushene, Vagg and Jacobs 1983) and two forgiveness scales: the Psychological Profile of Forgiveness Scale, developed by Enright, whose scores are in the range of 30–120, and the Willingness to Forgive Scale (also Enright) in which participants select a response to a hypothesized scenario. The first three scales were administered pre- and post-test, while the two forgiveness scales were used only at post-test.

After random assignment into either the experimental (forgiveness) group or control (support therapy) group, participants met with the same therapist once a week for eight weeks. The therapist followed a manual which suggested treatment outcomes for each session commensurate with the process model. The control group addressed other issues but did not touch on forgiveness.

The researchers found that there were significant differences before and after the intervention in terms of trait anxiety and depression in *both* the experimental and the control groups, suggesting that the forgiveness intervention had made no appreciable difference to these clinical outcomes.

It is interesting to note that the forgiveness scales were only administered post-test. The researchers found that participants in the forgiveness group showed a significant difference in relation to the control group on four of the Psychological Profile of Forgiveness subscales: absence of negative affect, absence of negative cognition, presence of positive affect and presence of positive behaviour. They also found that Willingness to Forgive scores were higher in the experimental group, suggesting that forgiveness was more readily considered in this group than the controls.

Enright and Fitzgibbons (2000) claim that this study was the first to show that it is possible to effect change in forgiveness through deliberate intervention. However, the study has its limitations. For example, the fact that there were no *significant* differences between the groups in terms of alleviating depression and anxiety and in improving self-esteem suggests that the forgiveness intervention did not make a real, clinical difference. Although the experiment is basically a repeated measures design, the fact that forgiveness scores were not calculated before and after the intervention means that we do not know what the 'base-rate' level of forgiveness in the two groups was. Hebl and Enright's rationale for giving the forgiveness scales at post-test *only* was to ensure controls would remain unaware of the purpose of the study. However, the experimental group would have *become aware* what the purpose of the study was when they received the forgiveness scales and it is possible that 'demand characteristics' influenced their responses.

More encouraging evidence for the process model comes from a number of later studies by Enright and colleagues. Al-Mabuk, Enright and Cardis (1995) conducted two studies, the first of which took college students deprived of parental affection through units 1–11 (Commitment to Forgive) of the process model. In Study 2 a different group were coached through all stages of the model. The two studies aimed, therefore, to throw light on the question of whether forgiveness is primarily a decision, or whether it involves stages *beyond* the commitment to forgive.

In the first study 48 students who perceived that at least one of their parents had been emotionally distant for a number of years while they were growing up were recruited. Twenty-four students were placed in each group. There were 19 women and 5 men in the forgiveness group and 18 women and 6 men in the control group.

Participants completed the same scales as in Hebl and Enright (1993) plus a 30-item hope scale made for the purposes of the experiment, and an attitude towards mother/father scale (also created for the study). Four scales were given both before and after the intervention: the Willingness to Forgive Scale (WFS), attitude towards mother/father scale, hope scale and anxiety scale. The Psychological Profile of Forgiveness Scale (PPFS), depression scale and self-esteem inventory were only administered at post-test – once again meaning that a base-rate score on these scales was not calculated. A treatment manual was used by the therapist which led participants in the experimental group through units of the process model up to and including Stage 12 (Reframing). The control group received a programme dealing with interpersonal skills.

Results showed that those in the forgiveness group were more hopeful and willing to forgive at post-test than the controls. Despite this, however, this forgiveness could be regarded as 'pseudo-forgiveness' since the scores on the attitude toward mother/father scale did not decrease appreciably in the experimental group after the intervention. The PPFS scores (which were measured only at post-test) were *not* significantly different between the two groups. No significant differences were found between the groups in depression or self-esteem.

Al-Mabuk and colleagues surmised from Study 1 that only an 'empty' kind of forgiveness obtained when forgiveness ended with a commitment to forgive, devoid of the Work and Deepening Phases of the model. This 'empty' commitment seemed to have no effect on clinical variables. To investigate this further a second study (with 24 in the experimental group and 21 controls) was carried out using the same measures as in Study 1, although this time only the self-esteem and depression scales were given at post-test only. The same therapist conducted the sessions following a manual which covered six sessions, taking participants through *all* phases of the process model.

Results showed that all of the measures administered both before and after the intervention (except that of state anxiety) showed significant differences in favour of the forgiveness group. Scores on the PPFS went from a mean of 81 to 101.5 (max. = 120) in the experimental group, compared with a modest increase from 82.2 to 86.6 in the controls. Self-esteem was significantly higher in the experimental group than the controls but there was no difference in depression (both groups were not depressed). Twenty-three out of the 24 subjects in the experimental group completed a Commitment to Forgive contract, while only 10 of the 21 controls did.

This more carefully controlled study showed improvements in forgiveness and in other clinical measures as a result of a forgiveness intervention that incorporated the Work and Deepening Phases of the process model. The researchers concluded that forgiveness is more than a *commitment* to forgive. Since they measured forgiveness with the PPSF and WFS before and after the study they could conclude that the intervention had, in fact, brought about improvements in forgiveness.

They also adduced evidence that alongside the improvements in forgiveness were other clinical gains in terms of anxiety and self-esteem. The question remained, however, just how enduring the effects of such an intervention might be.

The question of the longevity of forgiveness increments was addressed by Freedman and Enright (1996) and Coyle and Enright (1997). The participants in the first study were 12 female incest survivors, six of whom formed a wait-list control group. Subjects in the second study were 10 men hurt by a partner's decision to terminate pregnancy. While both of these studies included the necessary 'follow-up' component, it is noteworthy that they recruited relatively few participants. None of the subjects in Freedman and Enright's (1996) study had been abused in the previous two years and all presented with clinical symptoms. A hope scale, the PPFS, and the same anxiety, depression, and self-esteem scales were administered at pre-test, post-test and follow-up. A self-report scale was incorporated to assess when forgiveness was judged to be complete so that therapy could be terminated. Three sets of scores on the scales were obtained at two-week intervals and were averaged to give a pre-test score. The same procedure was followed for obtaining the post-test score, while follow-up scores for the original experimental group were based on one completed form per scale.

Sessions took place on a one-to-one basis with a female therapist, once a week for one hour, until the clients had reached the point of forgiving (this took on average around 14 months). In this study, participants were given a manual of the forgiveness process. Each unit of the 17-unit process model was dedicated a separate section which participants took at their own pace.

Results showed that there were statistically significant differences between the experimental and control groups on all measures except for self-esteem. With regard to the PPFS there were increases in positive affect and positive cognition and decreases in the subscales of negative thoughts and behaviour towards the wrongdoer. The only subscale which did not show improvement was increase in positive behaviour towards the offender. Taken as a whole, the PPFS score in the experimental group saw an increase of around 20 points, from 60.5 to 85.6 (max. = 120). Anxiety and depression scores in the experimental group reduced dramatically. The same trends were found in the wait-list control group on their participation in the intervention. Here all dependent measures (including self-esteem) saw statistically significant improvements. The follow-up for the original experimental group (14 months later) indicated that the improvements on all of the measures were enduring.

Coyle and Enright's (1997) subjects were 10 men whose then-partner had at some time previously had an abortion and who still felt psychological difficulty over their partner's decision. They completed an anxiety scale, an anger scale (the State Anger Inventory – Spielberger, Jacobs, Russell and Crane 1983), the Perinatal Grief Scale (Potvin, Lasker and Toedter 1989) and the Enright Forgiveness Inventory – EFI (an updated version of the PPSF with 60 items on a six-point Likert scale, max. score = 360). As in the previous study, three rounds of scores at pre-test, post-test and, in this case, follow-up, were averaged to yield scores on each of the scales.

The intervention consisted of a 12-week course in which participants met individually with a female therapist once a week. The five controls (who later participated in the study) received no therapy during this time. A written manual based on the process model guided the therapist.

The results showed that the experimental group grew in forgiveness: scores on the EFI increased significantly from a mean of 196 to 251, although again there was no significant difference between the groups in terms of the positive behaviour subscale of the EFI. A reduction in anxiety was found in the experimental group. Anger and grief were also significantly lower in the experimental group than the controls.

The control group, having participated in the intervention, showed significant improvement on all measures except anger. Comparing the second follow-up scores of the first group with the first follow-up scores of the second did not reveal significant differences, suggesting again that improvements in the first group were lasting – or at least endured for 12 weeks.

Enright and colleagues believe these studies have shown a good deal of support for the validity of the process model and its applicability to a variety of populations (Enright and Fitzgibbons 2000). However, while not wishing to undermine the work that has been accomplished, it would seem that there are perhaps a few limitations with these studies. For example, although all of the studies adopted a repeated measures design, not *all* measures were taken at pre- and post-test, meaning that the base-rates on some of these scales were not known. This is particularly problematic in the studies where forgiveness scores were not calculated both before and after the intervention, where the efficacy of the forgiveness programme was the main focus of interest.

Reframing: An Evaluation

There may be cases where trying to put things into a larger 'reframed' perspective will only serve to reinforce how evil was the wrongdoing – we call to mind serious violations such as rape, child abuse, massacre and brutality of any kind. In these cases, forgiveness, even initiated by reframing, may be impossible (how can one understand, even partially, what led someone to behave in such a way?) or even inadvisable. In these cases perhaps a way out of the impasse might be found by reframing the question of ultimate forgiveness beyond the human realm. What might seem humanly impossible may not be divinely so, and people may experience some release knowing that the final judgment on forgiveness does not, in the last analysis, rest with them.

Reframing has its limitations and may not always represent even a 'first step' towards forgiving particularly heinous violations. It may constitute an overly 'intellectual' approach to forgiveness which assumes that, once faulty cognitions concerning blame have been reappraised, affective and behavioural change will necessarily occur. Another problem with reframing is that it may engender repeated rumination of the events which led to the offence. In reframing, distortions in our thinking are still in evidence – we can never arrive at a totally 'objective' interpretation.

Moreover, reframing certain offences may, in practice, reduce forgiveness to condoning behaviour on account of mitigating factors. Condoning, excusing, exonerating and understanding do not wholly recognise the 'wrongness' of an offence, but instead represent an attempt to explain why something occurred and how, within a certain situation, it was 'understandable'. On the other hand, there is something 'inexplicable' about forgiveness – the wrong cannot be neutralised by the application of some 'explanatory balm'. The process may be further complicated by the fact that, even when the process is felt by the forgiver to be more than condoning, it may not be perceived as such by onlookers or by the person who has caused offence. This could have serious implications for the future of the relationship.

Neblett (1974) argues that although, in theory, condoning can be distinguished from forgiveness, in practice 'where forgiveness ends and condoning behaviour begins cannot always be discerned.' (p. 272). Ultimately we cannot be certain whether a person has 'forgiven' someone or whether resentment towards that person was lessened by condoning. By the same token, we cannot know whether the wrongdoer regards himself or herself as excused or forgiven. In the former case, the sense of responsibility for the wrong would decrease, while in the latter condition a person who felt forgiven would still have the same sense of responsibility for their actions, with the knowledge that, in spite of this, the wronged party continued to respect and even love them.

The success of reframing perhaps depends on the nature of the offence, the personality of the reframer and the quality of the reframing exercise. It would not seem an appropriate forgiveness strategy to employ *in isolation* for persons prone to excessive rumination. It may, however, be useful, especially in the initial stages of forgiveness, since it does afford another perspective on the offender and has been shown to facilitate forgiveness in the studies that have been outlined.

Empathetic Routes to Forgiveness in Therapy

In addition to approaches to forgiveness that envisage cognitive reframing as the step which leads to empathy and forgiveness, another model, developed by Worthington and colleagues (the Pyramid Model of Forgiveness), regards fostering empathy as the crucial factor in realizing forgiveness. While Enright and Fitzgibbons (2000) regard anger as the factor which preserves unforgiveness, Worthington (1998a) suggests that, at bottom, 'Forgiveness is a motivation to reduce avoidance of and withdrawal from a person who has hurt us, as well as the anger, desire for revenge and urge to retaliate against that person. Forgiveness also increases the pursuit of conciliation toward that person if moral norms can be established that are as good as, or even better than, they were before the hurt.' (p. 108). He proposes that the state of unforgiveness is maintained by 'fear-conditioning', and provides a neurobiological account of the forgiveness process on the basis of this assumption (see Worthington 1998a: 108f.).

Worthington describes the offended party as having experienced the hurt (unconditioned stimulus) from an offending person who then becomes the conditioned stimulus. On seeing or thinking about the offender, the person experiences stress and the desire either to avoid or withdraw from the wrongdoer, or to react towards him or her in angry, retaliatory ways. The person has, in Worthington's words, been 'fear-conditioned', and this reaction is difficult to shake. In the first stage of the model, the client is asked to recall hurts in a supportive environment, exposing them imaginatively to the conditioned stimulus (the offender) which over time will lessen the impact of thoughts about the perpetrator.

At the relatively early second stage of the Pyramid Model, the client is encouraged to empathize with the offender. The rationale behind this is that because fear-conditioning is an emotional response, it needs to be addressed by a procedure which addresses the emotions – fighting fire with fire, if you will. In this stage, clients try to put themselves in their offender's shoes: what was the other person thinking during the event? Participants might be encouraged to write a letter of explanation *as if they were* the offender, or to recall vividly and imaginatively good times with the person who hurt them. It is interesting to note the similarity of these empathy-generating procedures to cognitive reframing.

At the third stage, Worthington believes humility is crucial in moving clients on from empathy to forgiveness (the model used to be called the 'Empathy, Humility, Commitment Model of Forgiveness'). The third stage (giving the 'Altruistic Gift' of forgiveness) is tackled by asking the client to reflect on their own guilt in times past, the gratitude they experienced when forgiven and, finally, the giving of the gift, having reflected on these. As a result, 'the person identifies with the experience of the offender (through empathy) and sees the other as needy (through humility)' (p. 125) and is asked by the therapist whether they would like to offer forgiveness to the offender.

In Worthington's model, the commitment to forgive (which preceded the Work phase in Enright and colleagues' model) comes *after* the really hard work of forgiveness has been achieved. Worthington believes this commitment should be public, or else lingering traces of 'fear-conditioning' might see the client distrusting their own forgiveness because of a 'conflicting' message – say, when the person reacts to seeing the offender. He suggests people talk about forgiveness with others, perhaps sign and date a certificate of their commitment to forgive to concretize their experience of forgiveness.

The final, fifth, stage of the model (Holding onto Forgiveness) recognizes that the complete silencing of 'fear-conditioned' responses is impossible and suggests ways that people can strengthen themselves when they feel forgiveness might be slipping away; for example, by being aware that recalling past hurts is inevitable and not, in itself, an indicator that forgiveness has not been realized, and by learning emotion management techniques such as imagining or remembering good times with the offender when bad memories threaten to destabilize the sense of forgiveness.

The empathy model has also received some empirical support. McCullough and Worthington (1995) compared two forgiveness interventions with wait-list controls. Eighty-six psychology students participated (76 per cent female, mean age 22 years). Those who had suffered an extreme violation were excluded. Random assignment to either a wait-list control group, a 'self-enhancement' forgiveness intervention or a forgiveness group which stressed the benefits of forgiveness for harmonious relationships (the 'interpersonal group') took place.

The interventions took a group format (with group size ranging from 7 to 14 persons) and were led by two males. Each intervention was structured and of brief duration (one hour). The sessions comprised teaching, exercises to promote empathy and discussion. The only difference between the two forgiveness groups, therefore, was the rationale they received for engaging in forgiveness. Those in the 'Interpersonal' group were told it would benefit their relationship towards the offender and others, while those in the 'Self-enhancement' group were advised that forgiveness might improve their own state of mind. The researchers were thus aiming to address the thorny question of whether forgiveness entered into for one's own benefit had a qualitatively different effect from the rationale to forgive based on more 'altruistic' motives.

The 83-item Wade Forgiveness Scale (1989) was completed by all participants before and after intervention and at a six-week follow-up. Broadly speaking, those who had participated in *either* of the forgiveness groups reported more positive feelings for the offender, less desire for revenge and were more keen to work towards reconciliation than controls. Breaking it down further, however, the rationale of 'self-enhancement' seemed to give rise – at least in this short intervention – to better outcomes: those in this group scored more highly at post-test and follow-up on the subscales which measured conciliation and affirmation – and less on revenge. This suggests that, at least initially, people are perhaps more motivated to forgive for their own sense of release than for the sake of a relationship.

McCullough and Worthington concluded that the study had shown that it is possible to intervene to change some aspects of forgiveness in a brief therapy session. The effects were maintained at follow-up six weeks after the initial intervention. Although there were more participants in this study than in those of Enright, they were perhaps less naïve, being psychology students, than the populations studied by Enright and colleagues, and this may have made the study more susceptible to demand characteristics.

McCullough, Worthington and Rachal (1997) report two studies which they believe provide support for the empathy model of forgiveness. The first study was correlational, while the second was experimental and, they believe, further corroborated the conclusions they had drawn from Study 1. Essentially, Study 1 examined whether the established link between apology and forgiveness (see Darby and Schlenker 1982, Weiner 1993) was mediated by empathy rather than by attributional changes. As previously noted, the researchers believed that an apology signalled to the offended party that the wrongdoer now experienced remorse for his or her actions, thus opening the way for the injured party to feel for them in their evidently distressed state.

In Study 1, 239 undergraduates completed seven scales assessing the degree to which participants felt hurt and wronged by an interpersonal offence, the level of apology they believed they had received from the perpetrator, an empathy scale (Fultz, Batson, Fortenbach, McCarthy and Varney 1986), a five-item forgiving measure, 20 of the 83 items of the Wade Forgiveness Scale (1989), a three-item scale measuring avoidance and a two-item measure of conciliation.

Structural equation models indicated that the relationship between receiving an apology from one's offender and forgiving them is a function of increased empathy for the offender. They also found that 'forgiveness appeared to be more proximally related to interpersonal behavior towards the offending partner than did empathy' (p. 328). In other words, forgiveness was correlated more highly with avoidance and conciliation than was empathy, suggesting that empathy precedes, and mediates, forgiveness.

The relationship between empathy and forgiveness of self and others was also the subject of a recent study by Macaskill, Maltby and Day (2002). Their findings indicated that there was a significant positive correlation between forgiveness of others (measured by Mauger, Perry, Freeman, Grove, McBride and McKinney 1992) and empathy (Mehrabian and Epstein 1972). Interestingly, though, there was no correlation between forgiveness of self and empathy, suggesting that individuals appear to make harsher judgments of themselves than of others.

The results obtained from the correlational study of McCullough, Worthington and Rachal (1997) were further investigated in an experimental study where empathy was manipulated to see what effect this had on the outcome of forgiveness. There were three groups in the study: an empathy seminar of 13 participants (where empathy was promoted as a process which would lead to forgiveness), a comparison seminar of 17 people (where forgiveness was encouraged but not explicitly through empathy) and a wait-list control group of 40 people. The study extended the previous investigation by incorporating two types of empathy (affective and cognitive-perspective taking) which were hypothesized to increase in the empathy seminar and lead to higher scores on forgiveness than in the other two groups.

Participants were randomly selected to a group in a repeated measures design. Scores on six scales – degree of pain, communication with offender, overall quality of relationship, affective empathy (Coke, Batson, and McDavis 1978), cognitive empathy (Self-Dyadic Perspective-Taking Scale, Long 1990, adapted slightly for the experiment) and the five-item forgiveness measure of Study 1 – were taken before, immediately after and six weeks after the intervention. The intervention took place over a weekend in eight one-hour sessions led by four trainers who had received four hours training in using a manual created for the intervention, detailing what would be addressed in each session.

Results showed that pre-seminar, empathy was correlated with forgiving. After the intervention, the empathy seminar had significantly greater affective empathy than the comparison group, whereas the comparison group had no more empathy than the wait-list controls. Interestingly, those in the empathy seminar did not evidence greater cognitive empathy than the comparison seminar, although the comparison seminar was significantly more successful in generating cognitive empathy than the control group. Although the comparison group had received no specific training in cognitive empathy the results suggest that somehow they had attained a different perspective on their offender – this could have been a function of group support and discussion rather than focused training in this domain. In terms of forgiveness, scores were highest in the empathy group post-test. There was no more forgiveness reported in the comparison group than in the controls and, in general, forgiveness increased over time across all three groups.

At the follow-up stage there was not a significant difference between the empathy and comparison seminars in forgiveness score. The comparison seminar had made substantial improvements in forgiveness and a small gain in cognitive empathy in the 'dormant' period between post-test and follow-up. Might this suggest that the effects of cognitive approaches to forgiveness take longer to appear than approaches based on empathy, but with more enduring value? It is especially interesting that the increase in cognitive empathy occurred at all in the comparison seminar in the absence of any special training.

What can be concluded from this study is that forgiveness can be fostered by intervention and that affective empathy promotes higher scores in forgiveness more quickly than other methods. It might be the case that, while affective approaches to forgiveness are effective, they may not show the continual increments in forgiveness that might be associated with cognitive approaches. In the light of this, it might be considered appropriate to incorporate both affective and cognitive elements in an intervention, so that relatively more-immediate effects can be coupled with the, perhaps, more-enduring ones of the cognitive approach.

It ought also to be noted that this experiment is open, as the researchers themselves attest, to the criticism that demand characteristics within the empathy seminar could have led to the expected outcome. A close reading of the aims of each session bears witness to the fact that subjects in the empathy seminar were exposed to the empathy model and its assumption that empathy leads to forgiveness. Second, and as is always the case, were there perhaps methodological limitations in the scales selected? A five-item measure of forgiveness was used which has since been repudiated, and the thorny problem of the adequacy of self-report methods remains.

Approaches to forgiveness based on empathy have weaknesses: if one assumes the priority of empathy, there may be *huge* obstacles in the way of identification with the offender, especially if that person has behaved in an 'inhuman' or 'unfeeling' way. As with reframing, however, we know that it *can* happen, that some people have demonstrated remarkable empathic ability and have been able to forgive the very grievous harm they suffered.

In reviewing the interventions that have been carried out with both the empathy and cognitive reframing models, some closing remarks about the efficacy of the two approaches seems called for. It seems essential to note that in adjudicating between the models one must be aware that one is also taking into consideration factors quite apart from the basic 'treatment' which may play a part in the outcome. For example, the research of Enright and colleagues has taken place in spaced sessions, while those conducted with the empathy model have tended to be massed together over a weekend. In addition, the populations that Enright recruited were specific: those deprived of parental love as children, elderly women, men upset by a partner's decision to terminate a pregnancy and women survivors of incest, whereas the participants in the empathy-based interventions have not been controlled to the same extent and may, as psychology students, have been less naïve about the subject matter than in the other interventions.

The question of how methodological quality in forgiveness research can be improved is extremely important. McCullough (2001) suggests future research needs to be experimental, enabling cause and effect relationships to be established. Surveying the literature of the last ten years, the need for longitudinal designs (despite the expense) is paramount. McCullough and Witvliet (2001) propose that peer and partner reports would help to balance the reliance at present on self-report scales, as would physiological measures, such as those utilized by Witvliet, Ludwig and van der Laan (2001).

Conclusion

In this chapter we have considered some strategies aimed at promoting forgiveness within the individual. In cases where reconciliation is impossible, there can be *release* for people who have been wronged that is independent of repentance or acceptance of forgiveness on the part of the offender. We can hope that our inner transformation brings about an eventual renewal in the relationship. Forgiveness sought for liberation and restoration of personal dignity is not, in itself, wrong. While we must guard against distorting the concept of forgiveness so that we are seeking it purely for ourselves, or as a kind of 'revenge' against the wrongdoer, release from the past is beneficial for those who have suffered, whether or not they can ultimately be at one with those who have wronged them. God seeks to free the subjugated. He comes to proclaim release to the captives, and to set at liberty those who are oppressed (Isaiah 61.1; Luke 4.18).

7

The Healing of Relationships

Liz Gulliford

Forgiveness and Reconciliation

Some authors, as we have seen, regard forgiveness and reconciliation as interchangeable concepts. David Augsberger, for example, described the burgeoning interest in intrapersonal, 'therapeutic' forgiveness, the focus of the last chapter, as a 'product of the age of individualism'. In the Preface to the third edition of *The New Freedom of Forgiveness* (2000) he calls for renewed attention towards the focus of 'true' forgiveness: 'the regaining of a sister or brother. In Jesus' words, that is the goal of faithful forgiving – not the personal release of letting go and healing yourself or finding healing for yourself, but the reconstruction and transformation of relationships.' (p. 9).

In Augsberger's view, theologians and counsellors have 'got it wrong' when they forget that the heart of forgiveness is about regaining a brother. Instead, he says, 'they get caught up in pursuing cultural values of individualism, self-actualization, self-emancipation, and self-healing' (p. 25), claiming that it distorts and reduces the Christian understanding of forgiveness, and that its primary motivation is to make one 'feel better about oneself' (p. 45). Augsberger's relational focus leads him to define forgiving as 'risking a return to conversation and a resumption of relationship' (p. 29).

Similarly, Hargrave and Sells (1997) emphasize the behavioural aspects of forgiveness. Forgiveness is 1) allowing one's victimizer to rebuild trust in the relationship through acting in a trustworthy fashion and 2) promoting an open discussion of the relational violation, so that the offended partner and the offender can agree to work toward an improved relationship.

Although resuming a relationship with one who hurt you may be in some cases desirable, it may not always be possible – or advisable. A 'return to conversation' might be imprudent – at least in the immediate wake of offence. A person might seek to forgive the wrong they had suffered but may be aware that, until the other person had *addressed* the offending behaviour, a resumption of relationship would perhaps not be wise. Thus it would seem that there are two separate movements involved here: forgiving the person the wrong they did, and being reconciled with the person, perhaps after they have addressed a 'chronic' wrong. Augsberger's definition of forgiveness is about the interpersonal process of coming-together rather than the intrapersonal course of forgiveness (the feelings, thoughts and behaviour associated with the individual seeking to forgive).

Baumeister, Exline and Sommer (1998) list four possible combinations of forgiveness, based on the interpersonal and intrapersonal dimensions. 'Hollow forgiveness' occurs where the interpersonal act of forgiveness is not matched by the intrapsychic state of forgiveness. 'Silent forgiveness' arises when forgiveness is reached intrapersonally without a corresponding behavioural overture signifying forgiveness. Clearly where there is no internal forgiveness or outward expression, the result is 'No forgiveness' of any sort. The opposite, 'Total forgiveness', occurs when there is both intrapsychic forgiveness *and* an interpersonal transaction which indicates that forgiveness has taken place – this interpersonal act is reconciliation.

The latter combination is obviously the ideal state but, against Augsberger and Hargrave and Sells, it need not be the *only* valid kind of forgiveness. Of the four possibilities outlined by Baumeister and colleagues, silent forgiveness is also appropriate. Clearly, in some contexts it represents the *only* possibility in the direction of forgiveness. While forgiveness is a necessary pre-condition for true reconciliation (that is, a 'non-hollow' forgiveness), there can be forgiveness without reconciliation.

Victim and Perpetrator Accounts of Interpersonal Conflict

A key psychological issue which must be borne in mind when considering factors which may inhibit reconciliation is the difference in perspective between victim and perpetrator accounts of conflict. In the previous chapter, the focus was on the victim of wrongdoing, and how that person might rework, perhaps through cognitive reframing, their account of wrongdoing to lead them towards a more forgiving stance. When reconciliation is envisaged, the accounts of both parties (or more) need to be considered and reworked.

Baumeister, Stillwell and Wotman (1990) found that there were systematic attributional biases associated with the roles of victim and perpetrator which need to be taken into consideration when negotiating reconciliation. Victims are likely to see the actions of perpetrators as arbitrary, gratuitous and incomprehensible, whereas perpetrators are disposed towards seeing their behaviour as meaningful and comprehensible. A victim tends to see the event as 'open' and ongoing, whereas the perpetrator is more likely to have 'closure' on the same incident. This lack of closure on the victim's part may be regarded by the perpetrator as excessively vindictive, further escalating the conflict. Baumeister, Stillwell and Wotman suggest that 'if people were more able to realise the interpretative discrepancies, they might be less prone to become angry' (p. 1,000). Failure to recognize these biases may hinder attempts at reconciliation. The researchers suggest that apologies facilitate the reconciliation process because they serve two functions: on the one hand, an apology signals to the victim that the perpetrator knows his or her behaviour was wrong, thus 'reaffirming the rule book' and allowing a new attribution about the offender to be made; and on the other, it enables the victim finally to reach closure on the incident.

Relationship Breakdown

Carpenter (1998) describes how forgiveness has barely been discussed in the literature on family therapy, believing that this is because of its unfashionable religious connotations. However, there are estranged sons, daughters, fathers and mothers the world over, and how these parties may be reconciled is often the major theme in family therapy. A large number of people from relatively stable, non-pathological families feel a certain dis-ease with their parents. They may be somewhat resentful about aspects of their upbringing, or blame their parents for certain personality traits or their inability to sustain a long-term relationship.

'Solutions' such as 'letting go of anger' and even avoiding the person who has caused the hurt have been advocated. While this may, in some measure, deal with the immediate problem of dealing with one's family, it hardly needs to be spelled out that merely 'letting go' of anger, without encountering family member/s, does not build bridges between estranged parties, and avoidance indicates that the relationship is perceived to be 'irredeemable'. Even more sadly, people sometimes seek revenge for their past experiences. While this might seem in some sense 'warranted', turning a perpetrator into a victim and a victim into a perpetrator can never 'heal' a rift. Each party will perceive the wrong done to them as worse than that which they administered and the spiral of violence will continue. 'Changing places' with the other perpetuates an alternating imbalance of power within the relationship and fails to offer the option of setting the relationship in a new key.

An Accepting and Forgiving Environment

Mary Anne Coate (chapter 8) describes the importance of the 'depressive position' in enabling an infant to come to the awareness that human life is ambiguous and that the primary object is a composite of good and bad. Failure to negotiate this leads to the phenomenon of 'splitting': there is no one, integrated mother but instead an all 'good' mother, who is responsible for all the good things that come baby's way, and an all 'bad' mother, who is the root of all frustration and unhappiness.

In an article drawing from both psychology and theology, Atkinson (1982) summarizes Klein, who theorized that from five to six months onward an infant regards his or her mother as a 'whole' object, capable of being both good and bad: the depressive position. Prior to this stage, the infant has lived in a bifurcated world where the parent has been perceived as two persons: one good, one bad. However, as the infant grows out of this 'paranoid schizoid' position, he or she feels 'guilt', 'depression' and 'sadness' over his or her hostile feelings which have hurt the good object. These feelings of concern are, according to the object relations school, the beginnings of the human capacity for empathy and the desire to make reparation for one's wrongdoings.

However, as Atkinson indicates, forgiveness by the parent has to come first in order for the infant to grasp the concept of reparation: '... before the child can come to understand this peculiar life-drive which we call reparation to be reparation and not another thing, forgiveness has to come from the mother as a gift towards the "wrong" which helps interpret the child's own drives to himself' (p. 20). The capacity to feel for others is, then, developed in an external environment which is forgiving and accepting.

Clearly if the external environment is *not* forgiving and accepting – if there is no parental modelling of forgiveness – this capacity is, at best, underdeveloped. However, this need not mean that an individual finding himself or herself in this situation will never be able to experience the forgiveness that will enable him or her to bestow forgiveness on others. This acceptance could come from another source.

Pattison (1965) and Hope (1987) both suggest that the therapist's role is to model this missing acceptance in the therapeutic process: 'The skilful therapist intuitively practises an accepting attitude towards clients and models accepting behaviour in the course of the therapy' (Hope 1987: 241). Thus therapists can furnish clients with a model for forgiveness. In a similar vein, the sense that one has been accepted by God, despite one's faults, may offer another means by which individuals, whose primary relationships failed to provide the space in which the experience of forgiveness could develop, can now find this freedom.

The healing of parent–child relationships through forgiveness may thus occur 'privately' – in other words, without the actual parent being present. There is, instead, a symbolic parent in the form of the therapist. However, it is doubted how far this makes the individual at one with his or her parent/s in the *real* relationship, as opposed to their internalized representations. Veenstra (1992) suggests that the psychoanalytic approach could, in fact, offer more of a rationale for *excusing* one's parents than forgiving them. Although the therapeutic *process* may offer a transformative, accepting space for 'reparenting', as we have discussed, the *content* of the therapy could resolve conflict towards one's parents by excusing them, in the light of 'explanations' for their behaviour, rather than the deeper freedom and release that might ensue through forgiveness. Clients 'go forward on their own rather than go back to work things out with their parents who are excused instead of forgiven' (Veenstra, 1992: 167).

An excuse may represent a healthy resolution of conflict in some cases, but understanding the aetiology of behaviour may not always lessen the impact that the behaviour has had, especially if the excuses are strained to account for conduct which took place over many years. As Veenstra (1992) notes, abusive parents who attempt to justify their behaviour by asking children to excuse them are, in effect, asking children to collude with them in the defence mechanisms of denial or minimization – reactions which play no part in forgiveness, and which could further intensify antagonism within the relationship.

The best therapy, then, would be the kind which engages *both* victim and perpetrator in honest dialogue. Although forgiveness in dyadic and group settings has lagged behind forgiveness in intrapersonal settings, a number of marital and family therapists have recently begun incorporating it into therapeutic practice. On the positive side, this enables conflict to be worked through with the original 'actors', incorporating different accounts of the problem so that the final resolution is fully-informed and arguably less biased than could be achieved by the victim on their own. It is also possible to work through issues that might recur in the relationship, offering the victim/s reassurances about the future. On the other hand, these same things can make forgiveness in group settings more fraught than in individual therapy: arriving at a shared conception of what went wrong could take many hours, or might even be impossible. Dysfunctional patterns of communication may have to be addressed before any attempts at reconstruction can even begin.

Forgiveness in Dyadic and Group Settings

Despite these caveats, Paul Coleman (1998) found that the concept of forgiveness gave new direction to his work as a marital and family therapist. A casual remark about forgiveness represented the therapeutic turning point for one couple. Coleman incorporated forgiveness into his practice, noting that it, in some way 'appeared to be the glue that held the new behaviours in place for long enough for other factors to be of influence' (p. 78).

As noted previously, part of the problem with forgiveness being accepted within secular therapy has been the overtones of guilt which it carries. The fear is that apportioning guilt and blame will lead to the creation of family scapegoats, perpetuating tension within the family unit. The problem about erecting this 'cordon sanitaire' around guilt is, however, that real issues of hurt are, effectively, repressed – except, perhaps, in cases of serious abuse.

While it is true that family dynamics collude in destructive interactions, it is also true that some individuals can be 'more' or 'less' guilty than others in any given instance. As Coleman notes (1998), those who wield more power within the family must accept more responsibility than those who hold relatively less. By bringing issues of guilt (and its resolution in forgiveness) back into therapy, the relationship can be allowed to be set in another key, without denying what was done (forgiveness faces this squarely), and offering the assurance that there is a future to the relationship beyond the present hurt.

Coleman (1998) in contrast to Di Blasio (1998) places the focus on the person seeking to forgive, rather than on the one asking for forgiveness. However, he points out that because his emphasis is on the wronged party, forgiveness should not be discussed too soon in the therapy: 'A premature discussion of forgiveness insidiously places the entire burden for the resolution of the conflict on the person who sees himself or herself as the primary victim' (p. 83). Although Coleman suggests that the 'victim' may need several months before he or she is willing to move beyond anger (depending on the nature of the offence), he stresses that the decision to forgive is not contingent on actually *feeling* forgiving.

Forgiveness is framed as a choice that can be empowering for the victim. In this sense, Coleman (1998) is in tune with Di Blasio, who also emphasizes the conative aspect of forgiveness.

In a process that is now familiar, the offended person is essentially asked to question their own behaviour – how this might in some way have contributed to the wrongdoing. Particularly salient here is the question of whether the victim perhaps overreacted because the infraction resonated with some experience from childhood. Often failures in primary relationships get 'carried over' into a person's marriage, so that a full reconciliation may involve examining conflicts which began in the individual's family of origin. More proximal causes, such as stress, may also play a part in this *reframing* process. The 'guilty' person, for their part, is to reflect on their culpability – no one made them do the hurtful thing they did – in order for them to feel remorse for their actions which, in turn, facilitates a rapprochement.

Akin to individual therapy, Coleman has identified phases of the process of forgiveness with couples: Identifying the Hurt, Confronting, the Dialogue to Understanding, Forgiving, and Letting Go. In 'identifying the hurt', the person seeking to forgive asks themselves what losses they have sustained through the violation: is it a loss of love/lovability, self-esteem or/and control (p. 88)? This focuses attention on what within the relationship specifically cries out to be restored. The 'confronting' stage, rather than being an opportunity to vent one's negativity, is an important and constructive step. In confronting, one values the relationship enough not to overlook or deny pain. In the third stage the couple attempts to 'understand' why the hurt occurred. This will be part of the process where threads from childhood or previous romantic experiences may contribute towards finding meaning, or perhaps more recent stresses and strains may come into the picture. Coleman suggests that a plan of action addressing these contributory factors may be drawn up, since the knowledge that one has strategies in place to prevent further hurt makes the task of forgiveness easier. Having done this work, the victim is free to offer 'forgiveness' in Phase 4. This is not the end of the process since the residual pain of guilt and resentment will exist after the decision to forgive, and needs 'letting go', on which both parties must work. This can, in turn, lead to a deepening of forgiveness.

Being able to forgive one's spouse as a means of dealing with marital disharmony has also been advocated by Gordon, Baucom and Snyder (2000) in the theoretical model described below, recently followed up by Gordon and Baucom (2003). Gordon, Baucom and Snyder (2000) suggest that as marital adjustment has been shown to be particularly sensitive to the ways couples deal with negative events, having some means in place of dealing with and transforming these negative events is crucial. They noted that existing approaches to marital therapy have inherent weaknesses, which could be lessened were they to incorporate forgiveness. For example, cognitive-behavioural approaches to marital therapy offer a means through which couples can re-examine the ways in which they may be interpreting one another's behaviour dysfunctionally. It has been shown that distressed couples selectively attend to negative events from their partners (Robinson and Price 1980), are more likely to offer negative attributions for marital events (Bradbury and Fincham 1990) and are more likely to make negative predictions about their marriage (Notarius and Vanzetti 1983). Couples are taught to examine their attributions, assumptions and expectations about marriage in order to see where conflicts may have arisen from these distortions.

This is essentially a 'problem-solving' approach which may seem somehow 'glib' and rather superficial where significant hurt has been experienced by one partner in the marriage. A problem-solving approach directed at changing maladaptive interactions to improve future patterns may seem to 'whitewash the past', trivializing the hurt caused by an offending partner's behaviour. What can be done to address and overcome the damage to the relationship caused by such a serious offence?

In reviewing insight-oriented approaches to marriage, Gordon, Baucom and Snyder (2000) note they too have weaknesses, which perhaps result in resolution of marital conflict being incomplete. Insight-oriented approaches to maladaptive relationship patterns from childhood or previous romantic attachments are explored. Previous injuries are identified and unmet needs are brought to light. The therapy enables couples to see how their partner's behaviour is enmeshed in a much wider sphere and affords opportunities for empathy and acceptance. During the course of therapy each spouse is able to express disappointment and anger over unmet needs in a secure environment and learns to make the important separation between previous relationships and the present one, experiencing hope for the future as patterns of relating are resolved.

The focus here is on finding meaning for the present in the past, which *could* overcrowd the present and the future. In contrast to cognitive-behavioural approaches, insight-oriented marital therapy offers fewer opportunities for learning new ways of thinking about the relationship and new behavioural repertoires. They suggest that the former may be more fruitful in dealing with specific concerns while the second is probably more suited to resolving enduring emotional problems.

Neither approach to marital therapy incorporates a mechanism with which to deal with the explicit experience of betrayal. They therefore advocate forgiveness as a specific means of dealing with betrayal, in a model which incorporates insights from both schools of marital therapy. The researchers identify the three stages of forgiveness as: absorption of the impact of interpersonal trauma, the meaning of trauma (the proximal and distal factors which contributed to it and its implications) and recovery. Unlike Di Blasio (1998), the goal of forgiveness is only mentioned at the last stage and is not a manifest component of the therapy from the beginning.

In the first stage (impact), the couple must uncover and face up to what happened, but later, as emotions become less strong, it will be possible for them to search for the 'meaning' of what happened (Stage 2). Thus all approaches to forgiveness, whether they be individual or corporate, begin with some statement of hurt and an exploration of how it may have arisen. In the case of individual therapy this explorative reframing is necessarily one-sided, although the victim is encouraged to project themselves in imagination into the role of the perpetrator. In the marital setting the narrative is constructed by both parties.

Gordon, Baucom and Snyder (2000) regard this first stage as primarily 'cognitive behavioural' in tone: the partners learn how to manage their emotions as they discuss the affair and examine their reactions to its impact. The second stage, however, is marked by a more insight-oriented approach: developmental factors which influenced the partner's behaviour will come into play in throwing light on the event. It seems, then, that the empathic and cognitive aspects of forgiveness we discussed in the last chapter are both integrated in this approach. In 'recovery' (Stage 3), the couple adopts the more present- and future-oriented cognitive behavioural therapy in making necessary changes to prevent recurrence. At this stage the idea of forgiving the offence as a means of progressing in the relationship is discussed and finessed. Thus, in this model, the notion of forgiveness adds another dimension to marital therapies that are currently in use. These therapies, each with their own strengths and weaknesses, can be joined together in a framework enriched by the *telos* of forgiveness which offers a real means of setting the examined relationship in a new and redeemed key.

In a very recent article, Gordon and Baucom (2003) have found preliminary support for an inventory based on the three 'stages' model of forgiveness (impact, meaning and recovery) that they advocated in earlier articles (Gordon and Baucom 1999a, 1999b). As a result of this cross-sectional study, the researchers believe they have identified a means of locating the couple's progress (Stage 1, 2 or 3) so that therapy can be carried out which best matches the needs of the couple.

One hundred and seven couples completed the Dyadic Adjustment Scale (Spanier 1976), a one-item global self-report of forgiveness scored from 1–5, the Relationship Dimension Profile (RDP, Daiuto and Baucom 1994), a marital assumption scale, and an inventory representing cognitive, emotional and behavioural aspects of each of the three stages in the forgiveness process. Some of these couples constituted a control group who had never had to forgive a serious offence. It was hypothesized that the overall level of marital adjustment would increase according to which stage an individual was in.

Participants described an incident of major betrayal in either their current or previous relationship and rated the extent to which they were affected by the incident on a five-point scale. They then completed the forgiveness inventory, bearing the offence in mind and rating the degree to which they experienced each of the items on a five-point scale. By way of an example, a cognitive item from Stage 1 – Impact is, 'Our relationship feels out of balance as a result of what happened' (item 8). In Stage 2 – Meaning, the cognitive item 4 is, 'I want to find out why my partner did this'. Overall there was one cognitive item and there were three emotional items and four behavioural items in Stage 1. Stage 2 was marked by four cognitive items, one emotional item and three behavioural items, and Stage 3 (Recovery) had three cognitive items, three emotional items and one behavioural item. On the basis of responses to the above, participants were categorized as in Stage 1, 2 or 3. It was found, as expected, that spouses in Stage 1 (Impact) exhibited the lowest scores on forgiveness, while those in Stage 3 (Recovery) showed the highest. It should, of course, be borne in mind that, as this is a cross-sectional study, it cannot be guaranteed that differences in forgiving are *entirely* attributable to stage and not dispositional factors. It was also found that individuals in Stage 1 reported the least positive marital assumptions about themselves and their partner, the least closeness, investment and overall marital adjustment. They also felt that their partner wielded most of the power in their relationship. People in Stage 3, broadly speaking, gave the opposite view, with those in Stage 2 falling between these two extremes.

Comparing the stages with the control 'forgiveness-not-applicable' group indicated that, although there were significant differences between scores in Stages 1 and 2 and the controls, there were no significant differences between controls and those who were in Stage 3, except that they exhibited lower levels of psychological closeness than those who had never had to forgive. This might give some support to the notion that forgiveness can 'renovate' a relationship, restoring it to an earlier level of functioning, although as this was a correlational study it does not establish a cause and effect relationship between forgiveness and improvements in marital functioning. Clearly, longitudinal and experimental studies are desperately needed to establish this relationship.

Worthington and Ripley (2002) compared two group interventions to promote marital enhancement with a wait-list control group: a hope-focused marital enrichment (Worthington *et al.* 1997) and an empathy-centred forgiveness-based marital enrichment (Worthington 1998b). The focal point in the hope-focused group was on communication skills and conflict resolution, whereas in the latter on promoting forgiveness as a skill for marital relationship repair. It is of note that previous interventions involving the empathy-based forgiveness paradigm had taken place *without* the offender present. Worthington and Ripley (2002) were keen to see how the intervention would function with both parties present.

It was expected that both types of intervention would improve scores on the Dyadic Adjustment Scale (Spanier 1976) compared with the controls. More specifically, it was hypothesized that the hope-focused intervention would yield higher scores on communication than either the forgiveness or wait-list group, and that the forgiveness group would show more forgiveness of a pre-identified hurt than the other two groups.

Forty-three couples participated in the study, completing two measures of marital satisfaction: the Dyadic Adjustment Scale (Spanier 1976) and the Couples Assessment of Relationship Events (Worthington *et al.* 1997). Communication was assessed in three ways: by an observational coding system and two self-report measures – the Global Rapid Couples Interaction Scoring System (Krokoff, Gottman and Hass 1989) and the Relationships Dynamics Scale (Stanley and Markman 1997). Forgiveness was assessed with the Transgression Related Interpersonal Motivations Inventory (TRIM) (McCullough, Rachal, Sandage, Worthington, Brown and Hight 1998) which measures avoidance and revenge.

Couples were randomly assigned to groups. The interventions took place over a weekend (two-and-a-half hours on the Friday evening and three-and-a-half hours on Saturday morning). Each group consisted of two to five couples with one leader per group. A pre-assessment was carried out a week before the treatment weekend, a post-assessment took place immediately after the intervention (except for the controls) and a follow-up three weeks later. Those in the hope-focused group were taught a technique to resolve difficulties which focused on communication and conflict resolution, while the forgiveness group learned the 'Pyramid Model of Forgiveness' described in the previous chapter. This was slightly adapted to apply to couples, who role-played scenarios involving a hypothetical couple.

The results showed that the hope-focused intervention was particularly effective in that it resulted in more changed categories than the other conditions. However, the self-report measures for marital quality, communication and forgiveness were no different in the experimental groups than the controls. It is especially noteworthy that the forgiveness intervention did not result in higher forgiveness scores. This might have been because the person whom the individual bore in mind whilst completing the TRIM was *not* their partner and so the intervention did nothing to foster forgiveness towards this unrelated individual. Worthington and Ripley (2002) suggest that the use of the Pyramid model in a dyadic context may also have been problematic. To discuss the model and role-play situations with someone against whom one might have a grievance could compromise the effectiveness of a strategy that has proved useful in treating individuals. Worthington and Ripley (2002) suggest that an emphasis on *asking for* forgiveness as well as granting it might be more effective in the dyad. This focus is apparent in Di Blasio's (1998) model below.

Forgiveness in the Wider Family Context

The Journal of Family Therapy 20:1 (1998) published a special issue dedicated to forgiveness which aimed to close the gap between the practice of forgiveness in individual therapy and in the context of family therapy. It was noted that, since the restoration of relationships is the major reason why families engage with therapeutic services (Shontz and Rosenak 1988), it was puzzling that the concept of forgiveness had yet to gain a firm foothold in this domain. As we have noted, part of the reason for this is the fear of isolating individual guilt from collective, family dynamics, since this can lay the way open towards creating scapegoats. It would seem, however, that it is important to look at *both* family dynamics (the family as a 'unit') without losing a focus on the individuals and their relative responsibilities and investments in the relationships which make up that family.

It is true that different factors come into play when considering forgiveness along interpersonal dimensions (whether that be at the dyadic or group level), since the reactions and behaviour of other parties feed back into the ongoing experience of forgiveness of the injured party. In addition to this, there may be implications for the rest of the family when a person seeks to forgive another family member: the actions of that individual then reverberate across the whole family. A well-known example of this is the parable in Luke 15, where the forgiveness of the father towards his younger wayward son creates resentment in his oldest son: 'These many years have I served you, and I never disobeyed your command; yet you never gave me a kid, that I might make merry with my friends. But when this son of yours came, who has devoured your living with harlots, you killed for him the fatted calf!' (Luke 15.29–30).

Worthington (1998b) believes that interactions, even within the family, are always fundamentally dyadic. If, say, we consider the parable above, we would look at the relationship between the younger son and his father as one dyad, that between the father and the older son as another and (although it is only implicit in the parable) that between the two brothers as the third dyad. Worthington holds that it is confession on the part of the wrongdoer and forgiveness for the offender which prevent the hurts characteristic of everyday family life from becoming sufficiently entrenched as to threaten the stability and security of the family.

Worthington believes that if an interpersonal wound is not addressed by forgiveness, the quality of love in the relationship begins to degenerate. The first stage of this degeneration sees *passion* being cooled by unforgiveness. If, however, forgiveness is not realised over a longer period of time, or if there is a build-up of wrongdoing, relationship *intimacy* suffers, as defensiveness escalates and resentment against the wrongdoer begins to solidify. At the final stage, *commitment* to the relationship can be called into question – lack of forgiveness and forbearance having set the stage for the complete breakdown of the relationship. Thus in order for relationships to survive hurts, healthy families must adopt a means of dealing with problems before they progress through the stages described. Worthington, in line with the marital and family therapists we have encountered, suggests forgiveness offers the means to stop the escalation of resentment and the disfiguring effect it can have on familial relationships, going further than techniques such as cognitive behavioural therapy.

The previous chapter highlighted the importance, for Worthington, of empathy in realizing the goal of forgiveness. This is followed by humility on the part of the one hurt: they too must see themselves as capable of inflicting hurt and pain on others. Finally, a commitment towards forgiveness must be made – some overt and public act which is as useful for the forgiver as it is for the one being forgiven, since it signifies the making of a permanent change of attitude. The three 'moments' of this forgiveness model parallel the stages advocated by Worthington in individual therapy. However, while the process may be similar to that of individual therapy, the techniques used in family therapy must be different. For example, in a dyadic interaction, establishing the cause of upset is likely to be more challenging, since both members present will be constructing events from their own perspectives. There will be dialogue and dissent from family members as the narrative of hurt is pieced together. Dysfunctional communication and attributional patterns which might only be discussed in individual therapy will actually be played out 'live' in dyadic or group settings. This might mean that it takes longer to establish the more impartial perspective required for therapeutic insight. It also increases the likelihood of relapse, since one party could react in such a way as to upset another, dismantling progress which had already been made. This highlights the fact that, when more than one person is involved in the therapy, the different rates at which progress is made by the individuals could further compound the problem. In a group interaction, the dyad of injured party and perpetrator may be observed by significant others within the family, and the awareness of this 'audience' could affect the therapeutic process.

The family therapist, therefore, has to bear these more specific concerns in mind when conducting the sessions. It is more important than in individual therapy that negative emotions are not allowed to run riot – or the session could degenerate into an argument where no constructive work could be carried out. Since the 'presenting problem' is likely to be embedded within a network of other dysfunctional behaviours, the therapist must take care not to take on too much and focus on the matter in hand.

The sharing (of narratives and emotions) which is a core part of group therapy can, however, offer opportunities for a fuller extension of forgiveness, despite the pitfalls mentioned. Although it may be difficult to hear someone else's side of the story rather than imagining it, it clearly reduces the risk of distortion or denial. Since all parties to the wrong are present, opportunities for empathy with the wrongdoer may also be more apparent. For example, the therapist could encourage the perpetrator to discuss their fears, experiences and vulnerabilities, potentially fostering empathy in the one 'sinned against'. In addition, the perpetrator may show signs of remorse in the therapy sessions as he or she is challenged by the therapist and the wronged party. This, too, could help the person seeking to forgive to take the first steps in that direction. It could, however, cut both ways if the wrongdoer instead tries to heap up justifications or excuses for his or her behaviour.

While I would agree that many interactions do play themselves out at the dyadic level, I do not feel that is the whole story: interactions could involve more than two people at a time. This could be the case where children and step-children interact differently with their natural and step-parents.

Coleman's focus earlier was on the person *seeking to forgive*, while Worthington speaks of the importance of both *confession* on the part of the wrongdoer and *forgiveness* from the wronged individual. Di Blasio (1998) puts the emphasis on *seeking forgiveness*, rather than granting it, believing that a recognition of one's shortcomings is more likely to generate a collective sense of empathy leading to forgiveness.

According to Di Blasio (1998), the fundamental advantage that forgiveness can confer within the intergenerational family is that it allows old issues to be resolved to prevent 'the sins of the fathers being visited upon the children'. As Byng-Hall (1995) has demonstrated, relational patterns that began in childhood are often recreated in intimate relationships in the future. Essentially, forgiveness inaugurates a 'new order', wherein dysfunctional patterns of relating can be absorbed and prevented from being carried over into the next generation. In other words, rather than maintaining the 'ledger' which keeps account of past and present obligations among family members (Boszormenyi-Nagy and Spark 1973), forgiveness regains homeostasis without direct or indirect retribution within the family system: 'Forgiveness can be one avenue that releases the parent from the replicative script in favour of a corrective attachment script' (Di Blasio 1998: 81).

Unlike Coleman, who does not overtly mention forgiveness until the end of therapy, Di Blasio believes that the goal of forgiveness should be explicit from the start. In his view, this 'frame' will generate goodwill, enabling hurts, communication problems and resentments to be addressed within the larger sense that all family members will be seeking forgiveness for the part they have played in familial disharmony.

The therapeutic session (Di Blasio envisages one session in two parts, lasting four to six hours in total) begins with family members taking it in turns to share their perceptions of family life: what was it like parenting/ being a child growing up in this family? Next, the idea of forgiveness is discussed against its religious background which might be important for some of the family members. The benefits and limitations of forgiveness are evaluated and individual family members are encouraged to seek forgiveness for their own offences while being secure in the knowledge that they are free to forgive others as they choose.

Each family member must make a statement of the offence for which they are seeking forgiveness which should be as specific as possible. Following this, family members, but more particularly the 'victim/s', ask questions of the offender – the purpose of this is to try to reconstruct and explain what went wrong. When this has been done, the victims are given a forum in which to disclose the pain they experienced as a result of the (now 'reframed') offence. Although it is helpful to put the offenders through some measure of suffering, as this widens the potential for empathy, the therapist is to ensure that the expression of pain is not calculated to cause further upset – a form of revenge. When the victim has told his or her side of the story, the offender, in an act of validating the pain they have caused, must offer a summary of the victim's account.

In the penultimate stage, the therapist encourages family members to draw up a plan of action to prevent the recurrence of the offensive behaviour. Clearly this helps both the victim/s and the offender, who can be heartened that he or she has a strategy in place to prevent relapse. The plan should incorporate specific ways in which the offender can mend their behaviour. Before each family member confesses their need for forgiveness, a caution that forgiving the offender will mean that the offence can no longer be held against them is made. This need not mean that the event is forgotten, but it should not now be remembered in the same 'key'. The offender then makes their confession. Di Blasio suggests that they perhaps kneel before the victim in a gesture of repentance. If the victim accepts their overtures then the date and time of forgiveness might be recorded to make the experience more concrete. Finally, Di Blasio suggests that some ceremonial *rite de passage* be performed to show that a transition from one relationship reality to another has been achieved. For example, family members could burn or bury written expressions of resentment and anger.

It would seem that the main problem with this approach is that it is really only as successful as its least involved member. Clearly, if all members are willing to express remorse for their actions it works well. However, should anyone decide to 'opt out of' confessing their need for forgiveness, perhaps on the grounds that they are an innocent party caught in the crossfire of pathological family dynamics, there could be problems. Although Di Blasio believes that all family members should confess *something*, it should not be the case that confessions are somehow 'constructed' and have a contrived ring about them. As discussed earlier, family members can be relatively more or less guilty for interpersonal hurts. The good thing about asking everyone to confess, however, is that it can create a more accepting climate: all have fallen short – though perhaps the various degrees by which different members have missed the mark should not be minimized.

Conclusion

At the moment much of the work on forgiveness in the context of the family is theoretical, and the methods put forward are largely those of individual therapy adapted for the dyadic or group context. The question remains as to how these methods can be appropriately accommodated to the familial setting, especially with the complications that arise from disclosing the hurt in the presence of the perpetrator and perhaps others. As we have noted, being able to work together to reconstruct an account of relationship difficulty can be extremely positive and rewarding but it also carries risks. It would seem that those involved in interventions of this sort might benefit from some training in communication skills as a pre-cursor to the target intervention in order to maximize its efficiency.

Sells and Hargrave (1998) have indicated that there is a huge need for the claim that forgiveness prevents dysfunctional patterns in the intergenerational family from being replicated to be empirically validated. Once again the need for longitudinal, perhaps even intergenerational, study would be necessary to throw light on this question.

In this chapter we have seen how therapists are beginning to use forgiveness in group settings in the effort to reconstruct and transform family relationships. This interpersonal forgiveness represents an attempt to move beyond the individual's experience of release towards the fuller experience of forgiveness and reconciliation in a complete renewal of the relationship. The importance of intrapersonal forgiveness, however, should not be occluded by this ideal resolution of conflict. We inhabit an imperfect world and, ultimately, can change only our own will towards others and not the will of others towards us.

8

The Capacity for Forgiveness

Mary Anne Coate

I began to address the theme of our capacity for forgiveness as part of a broader-based exploration (Coate 1994) of the relationships between sin, guilt and forgiveness. I had the sense then that I was thinking and writing in something of a vacuum – even if that was not in fact as true as I thought it was! Be that as it may, in the ten years since 1993 the psychological dimension of forgiveness has attracted ever-increasing attention. There has been, concurrently, development in therapeutic practice and in the wider world of political reality, such as the Truth and Reconciliation Commission in South Africa and the growth of the 'forgiveness movement' particularly, but not exclusively, in the USA. The theme of forgiveness has acquired, overall, an enhanced context and remit.

This chapter has five sections. My aim is, first, to review and re-evaluate some of my original assumptions in order to identify the most salient issues for this current exploration, particularly those which, in the light of experience and contact with other people – not least my colleagues in this present book – strike me rather differently from the way they did ten years ago.

Second, I want to explore what I have identified as a paradox at the very heart of the task of this chapter. Can the concept of a *human capacity* for forgiveness – and the implication that we may indeed have differing capacities – sit easily or at all with the overarching and universal precept of the Lords' Prayer: 'Forgive us our sins as we forgive those who sin against us'? The universal status of the Lord's Prayer identifies forgiveness as a central and indeed 'required' element in the Christian tradition; the implication is that the charge to give and receive forgiveness is laid upon all of us, that it is philosophically and psychologically appropriate and is within our capacity. Yet actual

Mary Anne Coate

human experience does not seem to support the claim that it is within the capacity of every person or indeed of any of us under all situations and pressures – or so I shall argue. Are we being asked to do something that is impossible for us? If I am right in identifying such a paradox it is also incumbent upon me to probe it in the hope of offering something towards its resolution.

Thus far I will be working in the *area of overlap* between the theological and psychological dimensions, but my third section will focus on exploring the phenomenon of forgiveness from a *psychological* perspective with the aim of identifying the *psychological* 'ingredients' of the process of 'forgiveness'. The emphasis will be phenomenological, seeking to *describe* rather than to *explain*. This seemed to me to be the most constructive way to proceed in view of differences and disagreements – sometimes sharp and fundamental – between psychological thinkers which emerge when once we attempt an explanation of *'how'* human processes develop.

It is only in my fourth section that I will offer a way of looking at how individual differences in the capacity for forgiveness arise, though in doing so I will need to acknowledge the other explanatory frameworks that are available.

Finally, I will reopen the dialogue between psychological and other dimensions, and explore briefly how the capacity for forgiveness can be maintained, increased or even nullified over time.

Forgiveness: Assumptions Revisited

Where does Forgiveness belong?

I am on record as claiming that ' "Forgiveness", unlike "sin", has ordinary human currency – it is a word we all tend to use whether we are of a religious persuasion or not. It seems best, therefore, to begin to explore this theme from within this ordinary stance ...' (1994: 78). To be sure, I went on to explore what I then called the religious and psychological stories of forgiveness, but I saw it earthed in ordinary human experience rather than in either of the narrative dimensions. Walrond-Skinner, writing for family therapists, appears to concur: 'the term forgiveness has a common sense ring about it. Family therapists are probably much more at home with other terms ....but forgiveness is a term that everyone understands something about.' (1998: 9). She goes on to cite, in support, pieces of common folklore such as 'Forgive and forget', 'Kiss and make up'.

But I have come to realize that others do not see it like this. To many people forgiveness is a religious concept and the exploration of it belongs firmly in the religious or theological dimension. Walrond-Skinner goes on to say that 'it feels a religious rather than a psychological construct...it may remain for many therapists too religious a concept in its tone and colour' (1998: 5). Sherrill Durham (2000: 68) talks of the dis-ease of many therapists with the idea and practice of forgiveness because of its religious connotations, and my own trawl of a selection of the classical psychoanalytic literature yielded no references to forgiveness as such – the nearest are to 'reparation' and 'concern'. The one exception I found was in Melanie Klein (1937); somewhat ironically for the author of much rigorous and seminal exploration of the psychoanalytic construct of 'reparation', she uses the humanly-related word 'forgiven' without technical exploration or explanation but almost as a commonplace, as if she assumes that everyone will understand it. She writes, 'If we have forgiven them [parents] for the frustrations we had to bear then we can be at peace with ourselves and are able to love others'. (1975: 343). This quote is also interesting in its affirmation of the importance of the act of forgiveness for the well-being of the 'forgiver'.

The sense that forgiveness is essentially and indeed determinatively a religious concept is validated by one powerful strand in the theological literature well summarized by McFadyen (2001):

> It is Christian faith that is taken to give the full and proper account of what is good. Hence the norms and criteria for discerning the nature of forgiveness and for judging what is realistic, what counts as therapeutic and indeed the nature of the pathology to be healed by forgiveness – all are to be found within the circle of Christian faith.....Natural reason, common sense and the truth claims of secular disciplines or culture may be made use of, but only in an ad hoc fashion, to help extrapolate the account of forgiveness to be found within the distinctive integrity of Christian faith. (p. 3)

Watts (this volume p. 5) both validates and moderates this claim in writing, 'We would make the assumption that all human forgiveness occurs within the life of God', while also maintaining that 'the premise that there is no forgiveness without God does not lead to the conclusion that theology provides the only way of comprehending forgiveness'.

This has led me to reappraise my original assertion that forgiveness is essentially a human activity. I conclude that I cannot follow Watts all the way because I see the assumption that there is no forgiveness without God as a *statement of faith* to which not all may be able to subscribe. I am not sure that I can *start* an exploration from that affirmation, though I cannot predict its end-point and do not believe the endeavour to be invalidated by my hesitation.

Furthermore, though I have previously used the words 'religious' and 'theological' interchangeably I now see this as unhelpful. Theological exploration and formulation of forgiveness can proceed independently of my unresolved question as to whether the concept and experience of forgiveness are essentially religious in nature.

The 'Forgiver' and the 'Forgiven'

In 1994 I focused on one 'side' of the forgiveness process, that of being forgiven. Perhaps it was easier that way; perhaps it seems more respectable and acceptable to admit difficulties in feeling forgiven than difficulties in being forgiving. This present endeavour requires increased emphasis upon the role and activity of the person doing the forgiving. Nevertheless, 'forgiving' and 'being forgiven' are linked in the Lord's Prayer as two aspects of the same reality.

I have become uneasy with some of the therapeutic and philosophical literature which seems to be able to separate out, definitively, the injured party and the perpetrator, the forgiver and the forgiven. I do not think that, psychologically, the demarcation can necessarily be as clear as this – though it may be more or less so in individual instances. The view taken here does, however, have implications for the consideration of the extremely difficult and painful question as to whether some actions or persons *should not* be forgiven.

Psychological Story or Psychological Stories?

Psychological thought, like theological thought, is not one-dimensional. It addresses issues of human functioning on all of the emotional, cognitive and behavioural levels, as well as the relational and societal aspects of human interaction. Furthermore, psychological explanations are diverse, not necessarily interdependent, sometimes conflict and are differentially amenable to substantiation through empirical enquiry.

Watts makes the very valid point, 'though the psychodynamic psychology of Freud is an important strand within the discipline, there are many other psychological approaches within which it has no place at all' (this volume p. 7). In this current chapter I will, nevertheless, be drawing considerably on psychoanalytic thought and psychoanalytically based reflection. In particular, for this exploration of the forgiveness theme I have found common ground with, and so also have become indebted to, the writing of psychoanalytic clinicians Hunter (1978), Galdston (1987) and Sherrill Durham (2000).

Part of my reason for sticking – perhaps obstinately – with the psychodynamic and psychoanalytic stance is that I have come to internalize it over many years and on many levels. It is therefore a natural medium, though I hope that that does not mean that I approach it uncritically. It is not easy to substantiate empirically, and this must be acknowledged; furthermore there are sharp differences within psycho-analytic thinking as well as between it and other constructs. It is also important to recognize the complementary, and sometimes conflicting, perspectives of learning theory, cognitive theory and other develop-mental formulations such as that of Piaget.

Nevertheless, within the psychoanalytic construct there are proposi-tions made which address a broad and deep range of human experience. These include the acknowledgment of the unconscious as well as the conscious levels of our being, the presumption of the operation of defences against psychological pain – so Freud, A. (1937); Hinshelwood (1991: 122–37); Brown and Pedder (1979: 25–33) – and the assertion of the determinative importance of early experience, particularly the various aspects of our experience of parents and significant others (often described rather esoterically in the literature as 'part or whole object relationships'). The *potential explanatory power* of psychoanalytic thinking in relation to psychological processes is therefore considerable and far-reaching.

Given, however, my acknowledgment that the psychoanalytic construct is but one way of interpreting experience, it has seemed important in this chapter to focus strongly on the *phenomenology* of the psychological processes underlying forgiveness. It is hoped that this will be useful even to people for whom the psychoanalytic explanatory framework does not have credence.

The Paradox of Forgiveness: A 'Divine' Activity with Human Limits?

Despite my reservation in relation to the assumption that all human forgiveness occurs, ontologically, within the life of God, it is important to acknowledge that this is, however, exactly the perceived context and location of forgiveness through the ages. Pope (1711) asserted 'to err is human, to forgive divine', while Shakespeare says of mercy that 'it droppeth as the gentle rain from heaven upon the place beneath... and earthly power does then show likest God's when mercy seasons justice' (*Merchant of Venice*, Act IV, Scene 1). William Blake (1789) holds the human within the divine:

> For Mercy, Pity, Peace and Love
> Is God, our Father dear,
> And Mercy, Pity, Peace and Love
> Is man, His child and care.

For Mercy has a human heart,
Pity a human face,
And Love, the human form divine,
And Peace the human dress.

In Susan Howatch's novel *Mystical Paths* (1992), human and divine aspects of forgiveness are shown as intermingled yet separate. The healing of a father and son's relationship through their achieving psychological separateness takes place within the religious setting of sacramental prayer; yet the way in seems to be via a struggle to forgive a dead wife and mother on the human level (pp. 519–44).

There is also, as Sherrill Durham discerns (2000: 68), 'for many individuals an inescapable *right-and-wrong* association with the word forgiveness'. If I go to the religious, Christian dimension I find the parable of the unjust steward, the injunction of Jesus to forgive to seventy times seven – in effect without limit (Matthew 18) – and the 'Father forgive them' of the Passion narrative (Luke 23). See also the speech of Prospero:

Though with their high wrongs I am struck to the quick
Yet with my nobler reason 'gainst my fury
Do I take part. The rarer action is
In virtue than in vengeance:
(*The Tempest*, Act V, Scene 1)

Thus far, forgiveness inhabits the 'higher plains' of virtue and, at highest, divinity. It is extolled and required. But – and herein lies the paradox – the human dimension of forgiveness presents a more tortuous and tortured face in respect of whether forgiveness can, humanly, always be desirable, appropriate or possible. There is even the thought voiced by Hunter (1978: 168), and ruefully acknowledged by perhaps many of us, 'that sometimes the word [forgiveness] can have about it an unctuous or smug quality, as though the forgiver is possessed of astonishing and irritating virtue'. The human face of forgiveness is not always attractive to us.

My brief is to explore the '*possibility*' theme, the human *capacity* for forgiveness, rather than to rehearse the literature and arguments for its desirability. Suffice it to say here that '*desirability*' arguments range over theological, philosophical and psychological disciplines. But I have discerned three aspects of the 'desirability' issue as having important relevance to the 'possibility' dimension.

First, people have – in my opinion rightly – voiced concern about so called 'instant' forgiveness or premature closure to which the excessive use of psychological defences such as repression or denial or of certain forms of religious faith and practice may predispose us. In psychotherapy there is a danger, Sherrill Durham (2000), that forgiveness may inhibit the awareness and expression of negative feelings and so block the therapeutic process. In the religious tradition, over-ritualized confessional experience or stereotypic conversion experience may block the taking of personal responsibility.

Second, there is the question of our *need* to forgive. Some question the appropriateness of the act of forgiving being motivated by need. Yet Shakespeare could say of mercy 'it blesseth him that gives and him that takes' (*Merchant of Venice*, Act IV, Scene 1). Walrond-Skinner (1998) and I (1994) argue that the move towards forgiving often does in fact start from an awareness of a deep personal need to do so, even though I have the caveat that 'forgiveness starts in the acknowledgment of personal need, but if it also ends there it is not really forgiveness and will be doomed to failure' (p. 85). Joel Edwards (2002), writing in *The Times* from a evangelical Christian viewpoint for the anniversary of 9/11, can say of the power of forgiveness over revenge that 'it is more liberating than raw vengeance... unforgiving adults are more susceptible to illness... forgiveness releases both individuals and communities from a legacy of hurt and suffering – it is also the only hope for reconciliation'. The dimension of the mutuality of need in forgiveness is one in which the boundary between victim and perpetrator becomes blurred.

Third, we live increasingly, particularly at times of disaster and tragedy, in a culture of audit and enquiry. These have the essentially laudable and mature purpose of minimizing human negligence and dispensing appropriate compensatory justice, but they can sometimes be motivated by a need to apportion blame and inculcate a sense of shame, and come to serve primitive punitive and retributory impulses. By contrast, forgiveness in these situations would require us to confront the unbearable sense of helplessness that is virtually the hallmark of tragedy; it is often, not surprisingly, a casualty of our inability to do this. Such reflections begin to open up the theme of the human capacity to forgive and be forgiven and it is now appropriate to consider it in more detail.

We can say, and have some sense of what we mean, 'so-and-so is or is not the forgiving type'. We can review instances when we, personally, have wanted to forgive but found it impossible: against our better nature we have continued to fester, sometimes fuelling our state with obsessive vengeful fantasies. We see mismatches in situation and response. Sometimes the enormity of the situation is such that forgiveness seems impossible, yet some such as Edith Cavell, Nelson Mandela and Victor Frankl (1962) manage it; in these instances the charge that forgiveness is a weak option will not stick. Other apparently more 'gettable-through' or forgivable situations are not experienced as such by everyone.

Religious or liturgical pronouncements of forgiveness 'work' for some people, and not for others.

Reflection upon experience forces upon us the realization that the capacity to forgive is not a level playing field. But this conclusion is not palatable; it seems invidious. We have imputed a value 'good' to forgive; to have difficulty in being forgiving can attract the value 'bad'. Forgiveness is required and revered, yet for many it is not easy or perhaps even possible, and there is a danger of those who can forgive being seen – by others or themselves – as constituting an 'elite' band possessing elite skills.

To think in this way is to distort the nature of forgiveness. It has its active behavioural aspect but is not defined solely as a behaviour. We could say that it represents a change in emotional attitude to negative experience, having confronted that experience as completely as possible, but that still – in my opinion – represents less than the whole. For this I believe we have to return to Shakespeare, Blake (1789) and the prophet Hosea. (I am taking 'mercy' in Shakespeare and Blake as synonymous with forgiveness; our current understanding of the word mercy is nearer to pardon.)

Forgiveness is 'enthroned in the *hearts* of kings' (*Merchant of Venice*, Act IV, Scene 1), that is, at the centre of our being. It is not an abstraction for its language is personal; it is the language of Hosea: 'My heart recoils within me, my compassion grows warm and tender. I will not execute my fierce anger' (Hosea 11.8–9). Yet the anger is not denied. Its habitat is with Pity (compassion), Peace and Love (Blake 1789); these four are superordinate to other human virtues and abilities. In them the divine and human most closely reflect each other, but in them also the inevitable human falling short of the divine can be most sharply experienced.

To rest our thought at the level of painful dilemmas posed by differences *between* us in our capacity for forgiveness may defend us against confronting a pain that arises *within* us which affects, deeply, our ability to forgive *ourselves*. This is the pain of the *shame* of falling short, individually, of the image of God within us and its human correlate, our 'ego ideal'.

Human and Psychological Ingredients of the Process of Forgiveness

I make, first, some general points in relation to the nature of the forgiveness process.

Forgiveness is a process; it is not instant

This may appear most obviously true on the interpersonal or societal level where progress towards an outcome is observable. But in achieving the outcome a – usually more hidden – psychological process is worked through *within* individual people.

The 'forgiveness process' appropriately covers both the exercising and the receiving of forgiveness

My thesis is that if a person finds it hard to forgive they are also likely to find it hard to accept forgiveness because the act of accepting forgiveness does, it seems to me, always include our forgiveness of ourselves. I am less sure that the argument always holds the other way round. Some people who seem to have difficulty in feeling forgiven can nevertheless apparently forgive others. But I wonder in this case about the likelihood that the process is being short-circuited – motivated by a fear of the other, a need to placate the other, to avoid being abandoned by the other or to assuage a persecutory kind of guilt.

Forgiveness is not the same as forgetting

I have argued, 'It is not possible, nor may it be wise to forget in the sense of deny or blot out' (1994: 89). On one level the adage 'forgive and forget' does not hold and cannot work, in so far as it depends on an excessive operation of the psychological defences of repression, denial or idealisation. Forgetting may be achieved by these mechanisms but positive and transforming energy also gets locked up, causing psychological impoverishment both to individual people and to relationships. But maxims do not usually pass into folklore if there is no truth in them. If not forgetting comes to mean an obsessive rehearsal of grievances and the harbouring and 'fattening' of revenge fantasies then forgiveness cannot come to its full fruition. There is a sense in which being able to give up vengeance leads to a sort of forgetting, in the sense that vengeance becomes inactive. It is forgotten in the sense that it no longer presses for attention, but not forgotten as if it had never been. Forgetting in this sense is hard to achieve for the thought of revenge is hard to give up. Sherrill Durham puts it thus: 'Revenge we know is sweet, and has even been described as an appetite in itself... vengeance easily becomes gratifying, even addictive' (2000: 40).

A post-forgiveness situation cannot be a reassertion of the prior status quo

Or, if it is, forgiveness has not happened and indeed the stage is set for endless repetition of the cycle. In a forgiven situation there is likely to be both loss and gain: loss of an ideal, aspects of a relationship, or innocence; gain in maturity, responsibility and that form of love that is forged from compassion and the will to reparation.

I would like now to explore the detail of what may be the psychological process of forgiveness. I necessarily use the word 'may' because we are in the realm of considered reflection rather than of empirical proof. Helpful paradigms may emerge, but no single psychological paradigm is likely to illuminate fully so multifaceted a concept.

One of the challenges in thinking about forgiveness lies in the range of situations and experiences that we have necessarily to take into consideration. They range from ups and downs in everyday life and relationships that none of us will escape – that is perhaps why on one level the word and sense of forgiveness is commonplace – to the extreme and intense experiences of severely abused and deprived individuals, groups and, sometimes, whole societies. A potentially distorting factor is that interest in forgiveness from a psychological stance has been generated mainly through consideration of when things have gone badly wrong; it is almost as if a 'new' and specialist therapeutic tool has been discovered. Yet its use over centuries in 'ordinary' religious settings – as a permanent part of both creedal formulations and the liturgy, not just in times of extremity or personal and corporate disaster – shows us just how ordinary and universal a concept and experience it actually is. Forgiveness-needing situations are inescapable, ordinary and 'normal' rather than psychopathological. The 'seventy times seven' dialogue between Jesus and Peter (Matthew 18.21f.) indicates this. Peter's question is not about whether people are going to need to forgive each other – that is a fact of life; it is about whether the process has limits.

The attention to the detail and the depth of human interaction and inferred intrapsychic processes in the psychoanalytic literature is, I believe, unparalleled and potentially of great value to an enquiry of what goes on within and between people. On the other hand, most psychoanalytic reflection is based upon interpretation of material arising from clinical, therapeutic settings; it does not automatically generalize beyond the consulting room. There is therefore danger in over-depending upon it as a tool for understanding the 'ordinary' process of forgiveness. In what follows I shall be drawing upon this literature to illumine the range of psychological processes presumed to contribute to the phenomenon of forgiveness, but it is important to be mindful of the limits of extrapolation.

It is my thesis that a forgiveness-needing-situation has certain identifiable psychological features irrespective of whether one is in the role of the 'forgiver' or 'forgiven'. I have come to prefer these words to 'victim and perpetrator' or 'injured party and wrongdoer', just because it does not always – or perhaps often – seem possible to make an absolute demarcation of these roles. To do so may result in the process of forgiveness becoming boxed into a quasi-legal framework and, while I am not, of course, submitting that factors such as pardon, justice, retribution, punishment, mercy, mitigation are irrelevant in forgiveness situations, I do not think they *define* such situations. But some or all of the following are likely to be definitive.

First, and inevitably, *loss* is involved – of relationship, the status quo or the self-esteem of those involved. But there is often also denial that the loss matters or even sometimes that it has happened, and a difficulty in confronting the situation or the other people involved. We may also have ambivalence towards the outcome of the situation. Either we want it back as it was before and for all the unpleasant feelings and experience to 'go away'. Or we have a desire to negate and blot out all that went before.

Second, there are a number of factors constellating in the sense of '*role*'. There is often a delineation, 'a priori', of the roles of forgiver or person needing to be forgiven. We are 'sure' we know who belongs where...or are we? We experience feelings of guilt, shame or omnipotent self-righteousness consonant with the chosen or allotted role, but interestingly there are often twinges of the feelings – usually hastily suppressed – thought to be more appropriate to the role not taken. Dimensions of experience and feeling tend to be *absolute*: the other person is all bad; there is no ability or will to understand or accept provocation or mitigating circumstances – for to do so would dent the defence of self-righteousness. Alternatively, absoluteness is perceived as relating to the situation – irrevocable breakdown, nothing can ever be the same again. Together with absoluteness comes an *inability to empathize*, for to be able to empathize would blur the roles adopted and pierce the defences of righteousness or provocation. But inability to empathize opens the door to other unpleasant experiences and fears, notably isolation or the fear and sense of being abandoned or helpless. To avoid confronting these requires more psychological defence – more denial, more fixed roles, more absoluteness; a vicious cycle develops.

Some feelings are, however, often felt strongly: those of anger and/or hatred, together with desires for revenge that can reach obsessive proportions. Sometimes the object of our feelings is personal and easily identifiable to us; in other situations, notably those that partake of the nature of corporate disaster or tragedy, we often have a pressing need to personalise them, to find someone or something to blame, partly at least so that we can focus our anger. We perhaps hope that in so doing we may ward off other feelings of mindless rage, helplessness, randomness, or – for people who profess religious faith – profound uncertainties and fears about the activity and nature of a so-called loving and redemptive God. It may even seem to us as it did for Andrew Elphinstone in his *Freedom, Suffering and Love* (1976: 147) that we are actually being asked to forgive God, and that the task is well-nigh beyond us.

In many ways the other 'normal' human situation of which many of these 'ingredients' are characteristic is *bereavement*. A possible paradigm or template for the forgiveness process is, therefore, the *mourning* process. I have argued this before in saying of forgiveness that 'it may properly involve a grief and mourning for what was and now cannot be.... The act and process of forgiveness thus to me always includes an element of quiet grief' (1994: 89–90). If I am right in this association then the following ordered stages of the mourning process stand potentially, therefore, as stages of the forgiveness process.

The process of mourning requires, first, that we come fully to experience and then accept the loss, sometimes after an initial reaction of denial. Such acceptance involves also the experience of feelings of separation, helplessness and isolation. Second, we need to acknowledge, certainly, and express, sometimes, the feelings of anger, even hatred, that emerge. A difficulty in acknowledging these feelings if they are unconscious to us or masked by guilt are possible reasons for a mourning process becoming 'stuck'. Third, we then need to be able to let these feelings go and move, not back but on and into something new, which will be tinged inevitably with a degree of pain and sadness, but in which good memories also can be recovered.

To use mourning as an exact template for forgiveness in this way is, however, over-simple; the processes are complex and there are differences as well as similarities between them. The writing of others on the nature of mourning and its relation to forgiveness is important for the refining of the comparison and the ongoing debate. For instance, Hunter (1978) writes, *pace* my points above concerning loss and grief, 'Forgiveness has to do primarily with the psychodynamics of aggression, not grief. In forgiveness there is no necessary object loss. In forgiveness a resented object becomes an accepted object. In forgiveness the angry affect changes to a rueful or regretful one not a grieving one.' (p. 172).

What, precisely is the loss that needs to be mourned during the process of forgiveness? Forgiveness-needing situations do not necessarily involve an actual death in the external world, though of course they may do. On mourning, Freud (1917) is inclusive; it may be for the loss of an abstraction or ideal as well as of a person. Sherrill Durham (2000: 70 and 106–10), if I have understood her correctly, identifies what is lost and mourned in forgiveness as the internal wish for revenge. I accept that the passing of revenge is certainly a primary element in forgiveness, but I submit that it is not the only loss involved. It seems to me that there is a loss which is partly external and partly internal and this is the loss of the situation – both actual and psychological – which existed before the need for forgiveness arose. This situation may have been perceived as idyllic or as nightmarish; surprisingly it is sometimes as hard for people to give up a nightmarish and suffering situation as it is to relinquish an ideal. Such psychological phenomena as 'the negative therapeutic reaction' or 'kickback' against therapeutic progress attest to this. It is not easy to clarify why people hang on to bad situations, but fear of loss or of the unknown may be contributory factors. As Fromm (1942) identified, we seem to have a deep level ambivalence to freedom – we both want it and fear it – and in so far as forgiveness involves an element of becoming free a similar ambivalence may manifest itself.

Mourning includes a necessary element of anger at loss – and the source of loss – which has to be confronted, experienced and gradually worked through. Loss causes pain and part of the natural reaction to pain is anger. Anger and hatred are not synonymous; anger is normally time-limited, but unrelieved anger can settle into the more stable and difficult-to-dislodge negative disposition we may define as hatred. Only sometimes, usually when there has been previously a deeply conflicted or negative relationship with who or what has been lost, does the dimension of hatred come to dominate the mourning process. But hurt, anger and hatred are centrally implicated in the forgiveness process. Galdston (1987) contends that the capacity to forgive is forged from the ability to hate and to get over hating, and that both pose a psychological challenge. He writes that 'hatred enables the ego to retrieve aggression though a process comparable to mourning' (p. 371). He submits that the achievement of at least some sense of self and of psychological separateness and some degree of object constancy is necessary if hatred is not to turn back, unbearably, upon the self. During a normal developmental process some degree of repression of hatred is temporarily necessary as a defence against destructiveness, but if hate is to play a positive part in the development of forgiveness it needs to become conscious and then to be got over – though this is sometimes avoided through the mechanism of scapegoating. Galdston posits that a difficult obstacle in getting over hating arises when powerful injunctions signalling threats of abandonment – often non-verbal and sometimes unconscious – have been 'swallowed in' during early life and relationships. Such 'introjects' contribute to a weakened sense of self and come to block the recovery of hatred and its redirection towards a new goal that is characteristic of the process of forgiveness.

Yet for me hatred is not the last word in the debate. Although anger, vengefulness and hatred are seminal to the forgiveness process, the pain of grief and separation may be even harder to bear. John Donne (1623) seems to have thought so; in his great prayer 'Wilt thou forgive' his greatest sin is of the fear of abandonment:

> that when I have spunne
> my last thred, I shall perish on the shore;
> Sweare by thy selfe, that at my death thy sonne
> Shall shine as he shines now, and theretofore;

Nearer to our time Searles submits (1956) that vengefulness functions in part as a psychological defence against the **awareness of repressed grief and repressed separation anxiety**. These may seem 'softer' feelings than vengefulness, revenge or hatred, but the implication from Searles is that their psychological effect can be equally savage. He was writing from his experience of working with psychosis when the extremes of defence and their breakdown are most apparent. He cites Lear as an example of someone who chose to go mad rather than allow the emergence of the tears of grief: 'I have full cause of weeping, but this heart shall break into a hundred thousand flaws or ere I'll weep' (*King Lear*, Act II, Scene 4).

Searles seems to show that the pain of grief and separation is as strong as it is because of their association with dependency, helplessness and, ultimately, survival. For myself, the apocryphal story of the two arch-enemies who could not survive without each other – when one died the other quickly followed – or the symbiotic relationship that sometimes seems to develop between victim and persecutor illustrate how hard it can be to let go the negative dimension of relationship and still survive as a separate person. In so far as the work of forgiveness requires the letting go of potentially destructive internal forces which may also be, as it were, keeping us alive, it is likely to be similarly hard and similarly resisted.

In some sense both mourning and forgiveness also involve the giving up of omnipotence. In bereavement we come to find that we cannot make the lost person come back. In forgiveness we cannot magically restore a lost ideal or a lost relationship. In forgiving and being forgiven we become subject to the other, we risk rejection for we cannot compel the other to accept our overture. When Prospero forgave he also forwent his magical powers: 'Now my charms are all o'erthrown, and what strength I have's mine own; which is most faint' (*The Tempest*, Epilogue). He needs, himself, to pray for pardon and freedom.

One of the outcomes of 'successful' normal mourning is that it becomes possible to access and draw upon – as a source of comfort and strength – internal memories of what was good in what has been lost. This supersedes the phase in which memories serve only to intensify, tormentingly, the pain and disillusion of loss. This must also happen in the work of forgiveness if the past is not to be either completely disavowed – thus resulting in the loss of learning that could come from reflection upon it – but allowed to be integrated into the development of something new.

We turn now from description to explanation. How is the capacity for forgiveness determined, developed and maintained?

The Capacity for Forgiveness – Explanatory Frameworks

I make first the relatively simple point that the capacity to forgive or be forgiven varies with the situation and the severity of the hurt or injury. This is observably true and, indeed, peoples' expectations that forgiveness should or should not be possible will take account of this. But other aspects of the total interpersonal situation will contribute, such as the degree of sympathy or outrage in public opinion as shown in the sustained refusal of forgiveness to Myra Hindley. But reflection on our experience shows that there is a greater variability in our ability to forgive than can be explained by only taking into account variations in the *situation*. We are forced back on the question, 'Do some *people* find it easier than others?'

There are two ways of approaching this issue. We can approach it normatively, and explore how people in general become able to forgive, or we can approach it via the exploration of individual differences in the capacity to enter and carry through the forgiveness process.

Considering the issue normatively raises the questions, 'Are there whole categories of people of whom it would be unreasonable to expect the capacity for forgiveness? Does it require that we have reached a certain stage in the developmental process?' Piaget (1932 esp. pp. 314–23) traces – through direct questioning of children – the development of moral judgment, from concern with rules and authority, through revenge and punishment, to co-operation, respect and the idea of justice. From his third stage onwards there is a move from crude ideas of reciprocity – 'give as good as you get' – to 'do as you would be done by' as the basis for articulated compassion and forgiveness. Kohlberg (1968) also posited six stages; he saw the ordering of the stage steps as invariant but acknowledged that actual individuals went through them at different rates and might not reach the last and most mature. Erikson's eight developmental stages (1963 esp. ch. 7) do not specifically touch upon the forgiveness dimension though something of it is implied in his final stage of 'ego integrity'. We have already noted Galdston's hypothesis (1987) that the cognitive achievement of Piaget's stage of object constancy is required for the development of the capacity to hate and so to forgive; furthermore he does attempt to trace the development of hatred through alternating and age-related periods of awareness and repression.

The sharp disagreement, constellating in their 1960 exchange, between Bowlby and prominent analytic colleagues, Bowlby (1960), A. Freud (1960) and Spitz (1960) – all claiming a degree of empirical validity for their conclusions via observing children directly – over the age at which mourning becomes possible is relevant for this discussion. The discrepancies are large; Bowlby, for example, maintained that mourning is possible from six months, Anna Freud that the mental capacities required for mourning make it impossible before the age of two. Some subsequent writers put the age even later: Furman (1964) suggests three-and-a-half to four and Wolfenstein (1966) adolescence. It is of course arguable that different definitive criteria for mourning are being used and there is some need to discriminate between incapacity to mourn, failure to mourn and failed mourning (Furman 1964).

There is not sufficient consensual evidence for a normative threshold – in relation to chronological age – for the development of, specifically, the capacity for forgiveness. Sherrill Durham (2000: 105–12) discusses the issue both theoretically and through case material, but does not I think come to a definitive answer, though she does identify as salient qualitative aspects of development such as a child's understanding of his or her rights, and whether forgiveness has meaning as distinct from being a ritual guilt-averting obligation.

Clinicians exploring the themes of vindictiveness and revenge and, for some, its implication for forgiveness – for example Horney (1951), Joseph (1982), Lane (1995), Sherrill Durham (2000) – have sometimes defined typological categories by 'clustering' people in terms of their assumed psychopathology as inferred by their presentation in the setting of psychotherapy or psychoanalysis. People are differentiated along the active/passive and hidden/overt dimensions of their vindictiveness – whether it is turned outwards towards other people or inwards against the self – and the degree to which it is initially conscious or unconscious. So we read, for example, in Sherrill Durham, of 'exploited repressive' and 'vindictive' types (correlating with Galdston's 'can't hate' and 'can't stop hating' categories); in Horney of 'vindictive expansive' and 'self effacing' types; in Joseph of a 'malignant destructive' cluster.

Such typologies are linked with negative developmental experiences such as temperamental mismatches between mother and infant with concomitant difficulties in bonding and attachment, early deprivation, difficulties in the weaning process, malevolent childrearing that hardens a child against all softer feelings, a clinging need for the person who is at the same time the object of vindictiveness, the requirement to take precocious responsibility beyond one's years, or the need to triumph omnipotently over others. This list could continue. Across the clinical literature virtually every possibility of parental and care-giving failure is cited but this literatures focuses on *when things have gone wrong*. It can, to an extent, help account for the incidence of vindictiveness and concomitant *inability* to forgive, but it does not provide a coherent picture of what makes it possible – *more universally and 'normally'* – for the *positive capacity* for forgiveness to arise.

In my opinion what can contribute to such an explanatory picture is the psychoanalytic hypothesis of the **'depressive position'** in psychological development. It is most definitively formulated in the writing of Melanie Klein (1935, 1940) and indeed the concept is usually linked to her name, but seminal contributions and criticisms are made by Winnicott (esp. 1954, 1963, 1988) and Fairbairn (1952). Both Winnicott and Klein derived their theoretical position from observing and interacting with children, Winnicott in the naturalistic paediatric environment, Klein in the analytic setting. In essence, the 'depressive position' presumes the development – within the first year of life – of a psychological process that is both universal and normal and which brings together 'opposite' aspects of infant experience hitherto split apart. There will have been 'need satisfying' and 'need frustrating' experiences, and the related experience of mother as giving or frustrating, as all good or all bad, as hating or loving but not both at the same time. Furthermore, at the pre-depressive point infants cannot own their own hating or destructive feelings – they provoke unbearable dis-ease or anxiety – and so they are felt to emanate from the outside 'object'. According to Winnicott (1954), at this stage the infant is ruthless, that is, without concern for the result of its instinctual love, but with the depressive position comes the rise of concern – in Winnicott's language, 'there comes the change over from pre-ruth to ruth' (1954: 265) – and the beginnings of toleration of ambivalent feelings and experience.

I quote from Mitchell's summary (1986) of the Kleinian formulation:

as developmentally the ego becomes able to take in the whole person, to see that good and bad can exist together in the same person, it continues to rage against the mother for the frustration she causes, but now instead of fearing retaliation it feels guilt and anxiety for the damage it itself has done in phantasy. This Klein calls the depressive position. In overcoming this position the baby wishes to undo or repair the earlier phantasised destruction of the actual and internalised mother. As it does so it takes in the damaged and restored mother, using these new internalisations as part of the self's inner world. (p. 20)

Despite the linguistic clarity of this summary it poses problems because of assumptions made within it about the nature of infant experience. Winnicott's use of the nonsense words 'ruth' and 'pre-ruth' points up that we cannot accommodate the essentially inaccessible nature of infant experience to our adult vocabulary. Furthermore, there are differences and disagreements in formulation between Klein and Winnicott on the relative contribution of infants' own 'innate' feelings and of the mother–baby environment, and with Winnicott putting the age of onset at five to twelve months rather than the four to six months postulated by Klein. Fairbairn and Klein diverged – see Klein (1946), Sutherland (1989) – mainly in relation to Fairbairn's understanding of aggression as a reaction to frustration rather than an innate drive, the weight that should or should not be given to a child's destructive hate, and Fairbairn's sense (Sutherland, 92) that the child cannot take responsibility or initiative in developing the capacity for loving reparation – that has to come from the experience of being loved.

Debate has continued and the literature has become prolific. But the central plank of the hypothesis remains; in the **depressive position we, so to speak, come – in the service of the task of personal integration – to risk letting the loving and hating aspects of experience meet in rudimentary 'trust' that hate will not destroy love**. Salient for this chapter is that the set of 'ingredients' involved – hurt, hate, ambivalence, reparation and love – are the same as those of the processes of mourning and forgiveness. My thesis is that the 'depressive position' is their prototype. Klein (1940) herself submits that mourning or any pain caused by unhappy experience reactivates the infantile depressive position.

Resolution of the depressive position is – so Winnicott (1988: 70, 155) – achieved over time and the establishment of 'good' internal 'objects' (representations in our inner world) through repeated experience of 'hurting made good'. Resolution is individualized, not uniform; it cannot be perfect; at best it will be – in a favourite phrase of Winnicott – 'good enough', and some people do not get over the threshold. Furthermore, the depressive position is defined *as a position, not a stage* – it is not negotiated once and for all. Situations in present day life can, so to speak, take us back, psychologically, to the old battlefield. The ensuing engagements are made more or less difficult by the extent of the resolution made in early life. In any specific situation we do not begin with a blank screen.

The foregoing paragraphs have been theoretical and have not given a sense of how the depressive position construct 'works out' in practice. It may, therefore, be useful to 'earth' it in concrete examples. Consider first a scenario of two 'best friends' aged, say, about seven or eight. In a rough and tumble game a favourite toy of one rolls into the middle of the floor, gets sat on by the other and broken. In an instant friendship seems to have vanished – 'You've broken my car; I hate you and I don't want to play with you any more'. And that might be that; they don't. Yet for a child who has been able to reach the depressive position in their development this will hopefully not be the last word. They will as it were remember, 'But I really like being friends with you; I don't want not to play .... it wasn't all you – the car rolled; I'm upset and cross and I can't not be but let's go on playing after all.' Here are the beginnings of more mature reality testing and of the taking of personal responsibility. The opposing feelings do not go away, they continue to bump into each other, but one does not destroy the other. Furthermore the process can be aided or hindered by how others – in this case probably the 'big' people such as parents – react. Do they take sides, maybe in this repeating their own past patterns, or can they help the children tolerate and begin to understand the mixture of feelings so that the experience of ambivalence – at first perhaps shaky – can become stronger and more secure?

Let us now move several light years away from this scenario to the well-known Biblical characters, Saul and David. In their stories in 1 and 2 Samuel we surely see the pre-depressive and depressive positions acted out? The two characters, once close, have become enemies. In Saul the dark destructive jealousy and hate of David remains constant and strong. Even after he has spared Saul's life David realizes (1 Samuel 27.1) that Saul will still seek to kill him. Saul struggles to acknowledge David's superior abilities and to take responsibility for his own negative feelings (1 Samuel 26) but he cannot; he cannot reach the depressive position.

David can. In him strong anger and the will to fight and beat Saul are mingled with compassion for his distress and the sparing of his life on more than one occasion. And not only Saul; Absalom conspires against him, yet in his (David's) moment of triumph he can say (2 Samuel 18.5), 'Deal gently for my sake with the young man Absalom.' He is capable of profound grief (2 Samuel 1.19–27) not only at the death of his beloved Jonathan, but also at that of Saul.

Yet to have reached the depressive position does not make David a saint or keep him in that mature place all the time. As with all of us, he is capable of sinking back under certain circumstances. The story of Uriah the Hittite (2 Samuel 11) depicts him sending Uriah to certain death in order to fulfil his own sexual desire. But even then, when confronted by Nathan, he is capable of taking responsibility (2 Samuel 12) and of bearing the pain of the consequent loss of his son. The depressive position still comes through. David is depicted as a flawed human being, but also as someone for whom the whole range of human feelings – love, grief, realistic guilt and compassion as well as anger and hate – is available to experience and use.

It is my submission that the psychological threshold hypothesised in the concept of the depressive position is also the threshold of the capacity for forgiveness. Further, the concept has explanatory power for individual differences in that capacity. Because the psychological processes involved have to be inferred – they cannot be proved – it must remain a hypothesis. What I have written here is inevitably an over-simplification of complex material. I offer it as a starting point.

I first thought and wrote along these lines in 1994, (Coate 1994: 120–25), but did not discover until working on this present chapter that Hunter's paper of 1978, written from a clinical perspective, had already addressed some of the same ground (esp. p. 170). It seems important to acknowledge this; it is an instance of my thinking (and indeed the whole forgiveness theme) not, in 1994, living in the vacuum that I thought they were.

Progress in Forgiveness

I turn finally to some brief consideration of how our capacity for forgiveness can be maintained, increased or, sadly, nullified. Other chapters in this book are concerned specifically with therapeutic approaches and with the place of liturgy. I want to sketch out more general possibilities. First, life itself exercises a strong influence. We have already noted how public opinion can swing towards forgiveness or towards an emphasis on blame and retribution. We can slip back from a corporate depressive position to one where extremes reign and the capacity to perceive and tolerate ambivalence is lost. The capacity for concern for others is also lost. This psychological setting is ripe for a resurgence of so-called talion law – 'an eye for an eye'; if this gains impetus the dangers of a vicious cycle are great.

Individuals are subject to life events which generate forgiveness needing situations of varying intensity. Our ability to handle these will be affected by that intensity, by the support available and by our experience of similar situations. I submit that 'similar situations' include our original experience of confronting the anxieties of the depressive position even though that experience is no longer consciously accessible to us. Some of us will have emerged from infancy with a more benign 'house style' or inner world than others, with internalized good 'objects' (inner representations of relationship) and a truly reparative pattern established at a deep level. Questions to be asked include, 'How set are we in our ways? How determinative is past experience for the present? Can we make up our deficits, and change the hue of our internal world? What can help us to a greater internalization of the sense that hurt, revenge and hate do not have to be the last word, but can be contained by reparation and love?'

As I have already argued, (1994: 135), life itself sometimes helps us. It depends on who we meet and what experiences cross our path. The compassion and forgiveness of others can be mirrored to us in ways that resonate with and increase our own. I am not in this underestimating the psychological tendency to repeat past unhelpful patterns, particularly until we become conscious of them. But I think it is over-deterministic and over-pessimistic to think that we can never take in and benefit from a new and better experience. The greater problem is that life may deal the opposite hand and this is not in our control; the intervention of life can be random.

The religious dimension is also a potential source of help. Whether it actually is or not seems to me to depend largely on the sort of God we have been presented with and come to internalize, both individually and in the communities of faith. There is the God of fear inhabiting a domain of fierce absolutes which cannot come together – good and evil, love and hate, sin and righteousness. This God may still speak the language of forgiveness but there is a danger that it is shame, horror at sin, persecutory guilt and propitiation that are activated in our response. There is the God in whom love and hate are integrated and compassion and forgiveness lived out, who calls forth a response of love, personal responsibility, mature guilt and the disposition to forgive. And there are probably all shades of God in between.

Forgiveness is psychologically complex and demanding. It tests our inner resources to – and sometimes beyond – their limits. In writing this chapter I have come to realise anew that it is not surprising that it fails or sometimes cannot even start, and to marvel – in something approaching awe – that we see as much of it on the human level as we do.

9

Forgiveness in Challenging Circumstances

Stephen Burns

In this chapter I explore some of the complexities which exist within extremely challenging circumstances out of which people may come to forgive others. My primary focus is the legacy of abusive adult–child relationships, and my main concern in tracing some of their dynamics is to outline some contours of an approach to forgiveness that is adequate to the problems that may knot together in such legacies. However, to orientate my discussion of forgiveness in relation to recovery from childhood abuse, I begin by looking for direction through the literature emerging from those remembering another key example of modern challenging circumstances – the Holocaust.

Facing challenging circumstances

The Holocaust

Robert McAlfee Brown suggests that:

> Forgiveness has always been affirmed by Christians as a strong virtue, best exemplified in Jesus' utterance from the cross about the forgiveness of his enemies at precisely the moment his enemies were doing him in. But the Holocaust raises the possibility that forgiveness is a weak virtue that encourages repetition of wrongdoing rather than amendment of life. (1983: 183)

If we begin by attending to testimonies found in examples of Holocaust literature, some possibilities become apparent that are not always acknowledged in many discussions of forgiveness. Perusal of the Holocaust literature shows that Holocaust survivors present no facile homogeneity in their response to their suffering, and least of all a uniform response as promising as forgiveness might be assumed to be. The kind of sentiment that characterises the following extract, found scratched into a wall of Ravensbruck concentration camp, is only one strand of the literature:

> O Lord, remember not only the men and women of good will but also those of ill will. But do not remember the suffering they have inflicted on us; remember the fruits we bought, thanks to this suffering... [and] let all the fruits we have borne be their forgiveness. (Habgood 1993: 27)

Other sentiments are also very evident. For example, one survivor writes: 'For the first time since the occupation, we saw Germans clinging to the walls, crawling on the ground; running for cover, hesitating before making a step in the fear of being hit by a Jewish bullet. The cries of the wounded caused us joy.' (Cohn-Sherbock 1989: 10).

The Holocaust literature witnesses to a wide range of responses to personal abuse between the two poles just indicated. In doing so, the Holocaust literature presents some alternatives to forgiveness that demand serious attention as reactions to inflicted suffering that have been tested by experience. Awful as this test of experience may be, it is in marked contrast to some – perhaps much – theologising of forgiveness conceived apart from contexts in which persons have found themselves diminished and yet able, in some measure, to recover.

A challenging focal-point for the following reflections is, therefore, the chapter 'What Can – and Cannot – be Said' in John Roth and Richard Rubenstein's co-authored volume *Approaches to Auschwitz: The Legacy of the Holocaust* (1987) and the literature that particular chapter surveys. Among the Holocaust authors whose testimonies are considered in Roth and Rubenstein's chapter are Andre Schwarz-Bart, Yehil Dinur, Tadeusz Borowski and Charlotte Delbo. Much of that to which they testify is so thoroughly unpalatable that its import can barely be appropriated, especially in the limits of an essay such as this. Nevertheless, the most basic sense of the perspectives they develop in relation to their experience of the Holocaust presents some massive challenges to any theological construction about forgiveness. In this context we shall focus on the story of Charlotte Delbo.

Delbo's trilogy *Auschwitz and After* was published in English by the Yale University Press in 1995. Its three parts narrate the events of her deportation to Auschwitz in January 1943, her experience of the concentration camp, and her attempt to reintegrate her life with others after the liberation of the camp. Among the most valuable and hard-won lessons of Delbo's experience is the sense, constantly reiterated in the trilogy, that there can be no 'after' Auschwitz, for its marks on her are indelible, drawing everything back to that time. She experiences her confinement in Auschwitz as being so relentlessly pervasive that she feels that it is beyond the kind of transfiguration for which religious traditions might hope for all times and places. For her, 'survival' of Auschwitz is not so much a 'return' to life but at best what she describes as 'death-with-life' – an existence continually marked by her suffering.

As Delbo describes it, the main mark of death-with-life is 'disjunction'. This may be understood in terms of the 'now' and 'then' and 'here' and 'there' which a single person's experience may bridge. Another important aspect of disjunction is evident in the distinction between those who know from their own experience what the 'there' and 'then' of Auschwitz entailed and those 'who only think they know'. An example of this difference is seen in Delbo's reflection upon how, in a post-Holocaust world, when most people say, 'I am thirsty,' they 'just go to a café and order a beer'. She insists that anyone able to exercise this kind of freedom can *only think they know* what survivors of that experience like her *do* know. Yet in a post-Holocaust world, those who do know may experience their memories to be deeply degrading because their memories are in a way 'useless', meaningful communication about them being impossible because of the disjunction between 'then' and 'now' and one's own and others' perspectives. Yet only those who do know can appreciate what it was to be so reduced that 'one can see one's mother dead and not cry'. So Delbo recalls a survivor attending a funeral who was unable to weep because 'one is lucky to have a funeral'. This stark image is one depiction of her sense that for those who do know, 'survival' may seem at best like a 'reprieve'. Moreover, a survivor must wonder if she or he is the same person before and after 'there' and 'then', 'here' and 'now'. Delbo recognizes that she has much to 'unlearn' if she is to re-enter into the 'normal' life of others, and not least because Auschwitz was for her the 'defeat of love'. An important implication of this defeat is that her adaptability to supposedly 'normal' life is, she insists, much more limited than other people's optimism knows.

From this grim experience, we can see, first of all, that if we imagine a continuum, one pole of which is 'flourishing', Delbo's sense of death-with-life disables her from feeling that she might reach anywhere near such a pole. A second significant point that arises in Delbo's testimony is that there may be a huge difference between survivors' and others' understanding of what might have been entailed in the survivors' experience. It is notable that Delbo herself is acid about those who might make assumptions about her situation that she herself is not prepared to justify. Here, then, are two important cautions about considering other people's experience of victimization and approaching any notion of forgiveness in 'challenging circumstances'. Delbo's sense of both death-with-life and the difference between those who know and those who think they know alerts us, in our present context, to be mindful of 'disjunction', survivors' possible sense of separation between past and present, 'before' and 'after', and between themselves and others.

Distilling key points

My selective attention to the merits of Delbo's trilogy suggests a number of convictions that can shape theological appropriation of testimony and that can in turn foster wisdom when thinking about forgiveness. First, it challenges any easy assumptions about the applicability of language (or, indeed, hope) of 'abundance' and suchlike, of fullness of life of which forgiveness might be regarded as part (see Ford and McFadyen 1995 for valuable reflections on the 'scandal' of abundance in other challenging circumstances). Second, it invites affirmation of the priority of survivors' own testimony as a constant test of what is affirmed about forgiveness. An insistence on the priority of speaking from experience in theological discourse is especially important when 'theology' is tied to pastoral practice which is meant to help rather than harm (see Forrester's excellent reflections on the 'bad manners and bad practice' of theologians 'talking behind people's backs', as a recent and powerfully argued reiteration of this point, 2001, p. 14).

In relation to both of these, Isabel Wollaston, in an article that takes its title from the Rubenstein and Roth chapter cited above, states what she regards as the significance of testimony as challenging as that of Holocaust survivors: it amounts to a 'new kind of Bible' that grates against narratives inherited from scriptural canons, so that its 'iconoclastic' potential might indeed smash traditional faith (Wollaston 1992). Clearly, in the case of some Holocaust survivors, faith was destroyed; in other cases, it was radically changed by the reality of the Holocaust. For many, notions of faith proved enduringly problematic. Yet however difficult and grating notions of abundance may be in the light of the Holocaust literature, it is nevertheless the case that there are hints in Delbo's trilogy of her longing for fulfilment, for some reconnection with a sense of abundance – for example, 'I don't know if I can still make anything of me, but if you have the courage to try . . .' So while testimony may test and check theology formed apart from experience, the quest for liberative theological construction is of significance, however sensitively it needs to be presented.

The result of confrontation between traditional narratives and contemporary testimonies and the 'living human documents' who narrate them perhaps need not necessarily be quite so devastating for traditional faith as Wollaston contemplates. They may result, instead of in collapse, in uncomfortable but valuable outcomes such as sparking impetus to recover neglected or marginal elements from within existing traditions and their foundational scriptures, in the kind of process that has been highlighted and practised to good effect within forms of feminist theology, for instance. Confrontation and the processes it entails might lead to an expanded sense of catholicity – of the breadth of resources yielded by the tradition – which is presumably desirable to many religious people. Recovery of elements from within the scriptures of the Christian tradition that are relevant to forgiveness may include – amongst other examples – the gospel pericope about 'sin against the Holy Spirit' (Mark 3.28–29) which is said to be beyond forgiveness, the dominical commission which includes power to 'withhold forgiveness' (John 20.23) and the claim made in the Letter to the Hebrews that excludes restoration of 'backsliders' (Hebrews 6.4–8). These pericopes do not always feature widely in contemporary theological construction about forgiveness, and may indeed after reflection be considered by many as still less than helpful in such construction; they may, however, perhaps come in some way to play a meaningful role in relation to forgiveness considered in the context of acute suffering such as that endured in Holocaust experience, or other extremities. Confrontation with the tradition may, then, yield resources that address complexities of the human condition of which we are just becoming aware, or about which we are just learning to speak.

Personal abuse

In our times, much thought and discussion of personal abuse has focused on the abuse of children in its various forms. However, awareness of other forms of recognized abuse is gradually becoming apparent, notably elder abuse, and – relevant to any discussion of abuse in religious context, or of religious resources which might aid recovery from it, such as forgiveness – the phenomenon of clergy abuse, which covers a range of inappropriate behaviours by religious professionals and which may or may not have specific characteristics of its own.

According to current definitions operative in British law, child abuse appears in four forms: physical, sexual, emotional and neglect. Children may be afflicted by these forms of abuse in various combinations, and even initial attempts at definition of kinds of abuse are frustrated by the opaqueness of the damaging consequences of abuse in relation to those of other – often related – forces. For example, family violence (directed at others than the child) and authoritarian parenting styles may in themselves impoverish a child's interactions and environment, whether or not it is compounded by personal abuse. And 'indicators' of abuse are often highly ambiguous: depression, discontentment, withdrawal, broken sleep, bedwetting and soiling, lack of co-operation and various physical ailments may signal that abuse is taking place in some, but of course by no means all, cases. Likewise, eating disorders in adolescents.

Particularly hard to define are any causal connections between abuse and its outcome later in life. Abuse in any or all of the forms just mentioned may result in a huge variety of legacies in the lives of children so afflicted. At one pole of the continuum, the research literature is even prepared to countenance the possibility that victims may in some cases be traumatized neither immediately nor later in life, presenting little sign of damage. More generally, it is no longer assumed that a child who has suffered abuse will need to undergo therapy, and there is in fact rather a cautious recognition that in some cases therapeutic interventions may undermine creative forms of coping that have enabled a relatively unscathed survival. This fact needs, however, carefully yet firmly to be detached from moral evaluation of what has been done to children, which cannot be excused in terms of this variable response.

What can be established about the after-effects of abuse needs to be discerned in relation to a range of variables and particularities, such as the time of abuse in life, its extent and severity. Even so, it may be that what is most beneficial to survival and recovery depends on appropriation and response to an equally variable range of what have been called 'positive mediators of adjustment', such as supportive relatives and contacts, and creative coping abilities, which each may aid victims' resilience.

Like survivors of Holocaust experience, 'survivors' (as they often themselves choose to be called) of childhood abuse present no homogeneity of response to their experience, and acknowledgment of variables, both positive and negative, in their experience, requires that direct and indirect consequences, and 'potential legacies' of abuse – which individuals may inherit – rather than simple causal connections, are part of genuine understanding. That this is complex can be seen in that direct and indirect consequences may be linked to each other: for example, direct consequences may lead to disorders which persist, becoming established and self-perpetuating, perhaps generating patterns of behaviour which only later become disordered, or perhaps altering attitudes to new situations, affecting selection of environment, or adjusting sensitivities to stress that 'predispose' victims to disorders at a later stage. These possibilities point to the fact that abuse may generate circumstances that in turn generate detrimental legacies.

Yet however opaque some of what is known about abuse may be, one thing that is clear from survivors speaking from, in Delbo's terms, 'what they know', is that the experiential legacy of abuse in children is for many felt in the form of self-loathing. In the research literature exploring the potential affective diminution of abused children, David Wolfe outlines a pattern by which victims may come to experience a pervading sense of worthlessness, as abuse activates or encourages 'stable', 'chronic' and 'global' negative attributions, relating to events whose significance could be reduced if other attributional patterns were possible in more affirming circumstances (Wolfe 1987: 99–100). And John Briere (1992) has paid particular attention to what he calls 'the abuse dichotomy' by means of which cognitive distortions may come about and lead to negative self-perceptions. According to Briere, the abused child may come to make attributions as follows:

> (i) I am being hurt, emotionally or physically, by a parent or other trusted adult. (ii) Based on how I think about the world thus far, injury can only be due to one of two things: either I am bad or the parent or adult is (the abuse dichotomy). (iii) I have been taught by other adults, at home and in school, that parents are always right and always do things for your own good (any other alternative is very frightening). When they occasionally hurt you, it is for your own good, because you have been bad. This is called punishment. (iv) Therefore, it must be my fault that I am being hurt, just as my parent says. This must be punishment. I must deserve this. (v) Therefore, I am as bad as whatever is done to me (the punishment must fit the crime; anything else suggests parental badness, which I have rejected). I am bad because I have been hurt. I have been hurt because I am bad. (vi) I am hurt quite often and/or quite deeply, therefore I must be very bad. (Briere 1992: 27–28)

These attributional patterns, when sedimented, may establish a sense of worthlessness which may in turn build a sense of helplessness, so that the victim expects always to be helpless and incapable of gaining or regaining control over her or his own life.

Sheila Redmond (1989) provides an example of the way in which God-images may bolster the kind of abuse dichotomy outlined by John Briere. The impact of abuse makes the victim look for the answers to the question of why she has been made to suffer: 'Christian children are told that their God is just, merciful and caring. If they are good, then bad things won't happen to them'. When bad things happen, a Christian child is unlikely to question the truth of the statements that God is just ... or that if they are good, bad things won't happen. 'The conclusion to draw is "I am a bad child". The child must, she thinks, have been bad or evil, and she certainly doesn't feel that she deserves to be loved ... she suffers because she has done something bad and is being punished ...' (Redmond 1989: 74). It is not difficult to see how such negative attributions, once inculcated, may affect a child to her detriment.

Such negative perceptions of self do appear to be particularly related to psychological maltreatment but, of course, it is difficult to conceive of forms of sexual or physical abuse that do not inherently entail psychological maltreatment to some measure. So negative self-perceptions may emerge directly or indirectly from exposure to any form of abuse.

Accounts of the potential after-effects of abuse can, of course, become increasingly more complex than the possible scenarios sketched in a basic way here. It is hoped, however, that this incomplete and introductory survey is instructive enough at least to encourage us to think carefully about notions of forgiveness. From this point in this essay, I will attempt to make explicit connections between abuse, its potential aftermath and forgiveness.

Approaching forgiveness with caution

Forgiveness, if it is considered at all by those who have experienced childhood abuse, is considered from within the kind of context sketched above. If this is the context of an individual, it is this context, this past, that must in some sense be addressed by forgiveness (or indeed by any other resources available to pastoral and sacramental ministers). And just as not all Holocaust victims considered forgiveness, neither do all victims of childhood abuse.

Christian Duquoc (1971) narrates a horrific story that illustrates at least one terrible alternative. He presents a story of an adolescent boy living during wartime with a peasant family, who is horsewhipped and spat upon for amusement by the sadistic 'head' of his household. The boy fosters his revenge on his abuser after witnessing one of the man's children die of poisoning, and noting the depth of suffering this causes his abuser. To avenge his own humiliation at the hands of his abuser, he concocts a plan to make the man's other children swallow balls of bread concealing a hook. On the death of the first victim of the hook, the farmer's daughter, the boy reflects:

> I turned away so as not to see her face and forced myself to think only of the lash of her father's whip. As from that moment I could look my persecutors fearlessly in the face, even provoking their blows and ill-treatment. I felt no pain at all. For every stroke I received they were going to pay with a pain a hundred times worse than mine. Now I was no longer their victim; I had become their judge and torturer. (Duquoc 1971: 32)

Frantically, the peasant and others from his village enact magic spells in the hope of turning their fortunes and preserving their children but, as the abused boy continued to exact his revenge, other children in the village continued to die.

Perhaps the key value of this narrative is in the chilling clarity of its depiction of a child demonstrating a capacity to respond to abuse by apparently finding resources for his own esteem in acts of vengeance. However, the value of the story Duquoc tells may rather be that it suggests some of the ambiguities around boundaries of identity between victim and victimized, which is a complexity often little explored in theological reflection on forgiveness (see Wood 1991).

Christian Duquoc's point in relating it is to underscore the destructiveness of vengeance and to insist that, if a cycle of violence that made a victim into a torturer was to have been broken, it would have been necessary, somehow or other, for the boy to forgive. In his discussion of the dilemma faced by the boy, Duquoc insists that, despite the horrors to which he was submitted, as a victim of physical abuse the boy could have chosen to forgive, so stalling the 'hellish circle' of violence, rather than choosing to torture. Yet given ill-treatment such as this, to what extent should a child be considered capable of choosing to forgive? Would forgiveness constitute an appropriate response to circumstances such as this boy's, even if the victim was aware of its potential and however unfortunate this boy's chosen response to abuse in fact was?

An abused child experiences the abuse itself and also its consequences upon his or her development, personality, matrix of beliefs and capacity for relationships. Forgiveness must relate to the abuse itself and its after-effects and not only an isolated event or series of encounters which can be located as having happened 'in the past', 'when one was a child'. Abuse may initiate serious developmental consequences; and the after-effects of abuse 'bridge' the past events and any present consideration of forgiveness.

In the words of one 'survivor' of childhood abuse, 'Why would you want to forgive somebody who has ruined your whole life?' (cited in Imbens and Jonker 1991: 237). Forgiveness does not simply entail a present self considering responses to episodes relating to a past self (and other people). Between abusive episodes and any present considerations about forgiveness are perhaps years' worth of negative after-effects (which may, of course, in some cases have followed years' worth of 'grooming' before the abusive episodes themselves). The point is that as we think about notions of forgiveness, we should consider a potential array of harmful outcomes that may follow the abuse itself: cognitive distortions, affective confusion, an identity grounded in victimhood, the guilt of secrecy, and perhaps in any combination. If a victim is to consider forgiveness, the self who forgives is directly and indirectly related to – constituted by – experience of the abuse. If we are to speak about 'the healing of salvation' in this context, it 'must somehow involve a working through or re-shaping of the identity which has concretely taken shape through life. And that must mean beginning with the damage, not eliminating or ignoring it.' (McFadyen 1996: 99). This is, of course, true of any person considering forgiveness for any offence, but the context of child abuse focuses some of the challenges that all our notions of forgiveness need to face.

Whatever Christians claim forgiveness achieves, it must relate to a legacy of abuse that 'bridges' the past event(s) and any present consideration of forgiveness. This raises a series of questions about the character and potential of forgiveness to address not only an offensive event or relate to a particular abuser, but also to liberate from an array of harmful outcomes. In the context of a mutually critical engagement between forgiveness and contexts like this it is possible that an understanding of forgiveness is severely amended, at least attempting to dispel grandiose understandings of forgiveness detached from the realities of experience that would trivialize the serious and effectively deny real and acutely-felt problems.

Here I have given some sense of the legacy of abuse which forgiveness must face if it is to be of liberating significance to those who inherit elements of this legacy. Apparently, some have found ideas of forgiveness liberating even in circumstances of this kind. But serious attention to insights into the legacy of abuse made available by interdisciplinary study, coupled with appreciation of vast numbers of people who 'remember abuse with concern' (Renvoize 1993: 75) must raise the question of whether it is possible for forgiveness even to begin to address many of those afflicted by the kinds of developmental psychopathology seen above.

Implications of abuse for religious faith

There are few studies of the implications of the legacy of childhood abuse for Christian faith, though what is available suggests that its traumatic effects can extend to the victim's religion and spirituality, including their felt sense of relationship to God. It is important to recognize these, as they belong to the matrix of language and affection to which forgiveness also belongs.

Annie Imbens' and Ineke Jonker's (1991) interviews with survivors concentrated on their perception of the correlation between their experience of incest and their religious upbringing and environment. Images of women, images of men, children, family, 'religious duties' (including forgiveness) and God emerged as difficult areas. All but one of their interviewees stopped attending church as a result, they suggested, of the abuse. Hilary Cashman's (1993) powerful first chapter of *Christianity and Child Sexual Abuse* is simply called 'I lost God'.

Different reasons may account for these reactions and impressions. One of Joanne Feldmeth and Midge Finley's interviewees, Connie, recalls that she 'wanted to be airlifted out of the pain . . . and most of the Christians around me wanted this kind of "rescue" for me too' (Feldmeth and Finley 1990: 90). In Connie's case, the image of God as rescuer appears to have immobilized those Connie needed to support her and stopped them from engaging with her in an obviously helpful way, and consequently the 'airlift' remained unrealised. It would appear that an image of God as saviour, at least in the terms she was hoping for, did not become credible while, arguably, an incarnational emphasis may have encouraged her companions into a deeper sense of solidarity with her.

It is a particular form of incarnational theology that is developed by Janet Pais (1988) in *Suffer the Children*. She promotes a reframing of the image of God in terms of a distinctive incarnational theology, intended to dismantle harmful attitudes to children supported by current theological understandings. She suggests that an attempt to reduce and minimize risks of abuse to children might be made by means of a theology of 'God the child' which involves the clear statement that 'when we abuse a child, we abuse God's creation: we abuse Godself' (Pais 1988: 1). Among the implications of her thesis is the view that 'when a Christian receives a child in the name of Christ, that child is Christ; in fact the child is Godself. Every child received in Christ's name is thus a divine Child . . . '. While Pais' ideas here expand, for example, the christological parable of Matthew 25.31–46, there has traditionally been a reluctance to accept notions of infants as divine representations. Icons, for example, portray an adult face with a child's body, and 'God is not a baby two or three months old' was a classic cry of Antiochene christology (Young 1985: 234). It has not always been accepted that 'the neo-natal baby in Bethlehem is where "the fullness of God is pleased to dwell"' (Maitland 1990: 155).

If appropriate models of God are not available to people as they face abuse – alone or in solidarity with others – reframing views of God may be necessary after such experience. The point at which this reframing becomes necessary if any image of God is to survive might be the point at which the victim cries, 'God, I hate you because you let this happen.' Feldmeth and Finley (1990) relate this cry of their interviewees to the text of Numbers 11.11, which they cite with approval: 'So Moses said to the Lord, "Why have you treated your servant so badly? Why have I not found favour in your sight?"'

Some reflection on abuse has attacked other focuses of Christianity's core doctrine as negligent for sustaining abusive environments, apart from acknowledging that 'child molesters are far more likely to be members of a local church than a devil-worshipping cult' (Feldmeth and Finley 1990: 120). Particularly notable is the feminist collection, *Christianity, Patriarchy and Abuse*, which outlines implications for doctrine about the cross of Jesus which many Christians would regard as devastating. The following serves as an example:

> Christianity has been a primary – in many women's lives the primary – force in shaping our acceptance of abuse. The central image of Christ on the cross as the savior of the world communicates the message that suffering is redemptive...The promise of resurrection persuades us to endure pain, humiliation, and violation of our sacred rights to self determination, wholeness and freedom...Christianity is an abusive theology that glorifies suffering...the predominant image or theology of the culture is of 'divine child abuse'. (Carlson Brown and Parker 1989: 24)

One point that can be drawn from these notions, whether or not we agree with them, is that doctrinal affirmations promise benevolent or harmful outcomes for those who hold them in so far as they create and define expectations about who is around to help and what it is in their power to do when faced with child abuse.

A particularly ambiguous element of Christian traditions which victims may feel a need to reframe are aspects of sexual teaching and ethics. Tracey Hansen writes of awakening to the horrifying possibility that as a child forced into sexual intercourse she is, in Paul's understanding, 'one body with the rapist, forever'. 1 Corinthians 6.15–16 and the ways in which it is traditionally interpreted may confound those who have been abused, especially when allied to the problem that, in Hansen's words, 'when I think of God the father, I think of a man with a penis' (Hansen 1991: 86).

Forgiveness in challenging circumstances

Given the kind of dynamics that this essay has begun to sketch, no simple understanding of forgiveness is possible. However, some points may at this point be made with conviction. If forgiveness is considered to be appropriate to particular challenging circumstances, it must be considered so by, to use Delbo's term, 'those who know', rather than inappropriately proposed by those who do not know what particular experience has been: 'the last word belongs to the victim' (Surin, 1986). Forgiveness must then, if it is to be effective, engage the legacy of abuse rather than narrowly focusing on past events, as if those past events have no after-effects. And in cases where victims' own sense of what is possible by way of creative response following abuse is not as strong as others' 'optimism' might be, resources may yet be available within religious traditions that can foster a measure of recovery. Aspects of New Testament traditions, underdeveloped in theological reflection on forgiveness, have already been mentioned.

These points require a theological and pastoral plurality of approaches to forgiveness, which may be developed contextually in relation to particular circumstances and survivors' own perception of their situation. In developing such a contextual approach, psychologist of religion Paul Pruyser (1991) offers some helpful guidance that he expounds in relation to atonement theories but the wisdom of which is transferable to consideration of forgiveness. He suggests that

> if man's [sic] redemption is to be proclaimed, it is important that not only the positive symbol values, but also the limitations and even the dangers of each of the atonement theories be made clear...My own preference, in the last analysis, is for richness rather than precision of thought with a good deal of tolerance for paradoxes and open systems...(Pruyser 1991: 111)

Bob Lambourne (1991) uses the attractive phrase 'adaptable catholicity' to catch something of the same idea. What Pruyser and Lambourne each in their own way suggest is that contextual consideration is of prime importance in theological thinking, so that 'best fits' between contexts sensitively understood and a wealth of theological resources can be aligned. Pruyser illustrates his own convictions with a sensitive contextual exploration of atonement theories, relating them to psychological health and maturity, mapping some cherished doctrinal perspectives onto mainstream post-Freudian understandings of the human psyche. 'Classical' theories – such as Gregory of Nyssa's image of the cross as a fish-hook and mousetrap, and the twentieth-century revivification of ransom theories in Gustav Aulen's influential *Christus Victor* (1970) – relate, according to Pruyser, to psychological struggles between the ego and the id. For him, the positive symbol value of ransom theories of atonement may be in their insistence on divine deliverance and the gift of adoption by God. This helps to manage anxiety and may indeed invite a movement from anxiety to joy as the believer's sense of estrangement is defeated by a sense of a compassionate God.

Pruyser understands satisfaction theories of atonement to make a different contribution to psychological health. Popular in mediaeval traditions, following Anselm, and a durable feature of the Calvinistic inheritance of faith, these theories manage guilt feelings, mediating between the ego and the superego. Stress on justification and expiation may alleviate guilt related to a sense of transgression. A sense of forgiveness is particularly crucial in this group of theories.

Exemplar theories of atonement function in yet another way. The value of this cluster of approaches to the cross is their stress on the moral influence of their figure of Christ, which functions as a model for adherents' behaviour and may continually open up a sense of the possibilities of new life. In particular, it enables negotiation of feelings of shame. Exemplar theories map a way for shame, in the conflict between the ego and the ego-ideal, to become an impetus to love the image of Christ as enlightened example and to demonstrate one's own intentions by changed behaviour in turn.

Pruyser's models of theology or human psychology are not in themselves novel, but rather the way in which he maps them on to each other is creative: linking ransom theories and anxiety, satisfaction theories and guilt, exemplar theories and shame. Each type of atonement theory relates to a particular psychological conflict, with the corollary that mental health may over time require the mediation facilitated by each of the theories, and that particular challenges at any given time may be 'best fit' to a particular approach to atonement, or to a certain combination of metaphors. Pruyser holds that each one is limited as it stands alone, but may encourage flourishing as part of a wider, eclectic stretch of resources. Of course, Pruyser's pluralist approach to atonement sits happily alongside the sense that the Christian tradition does not offer one definitive understanding of salvation in its core resources of scripture and creeds, but the devotion attracted by particular theories may limit its pastoral applications in some circumstances.

Another helpful book through which to approach contextual consideration of forgiveness is the philosopher of religion Vincent Brümmer's *The Model of Love* (1993) which distinguishes between three kinds of theoretical relationship: 'manipulative relationships', 'agreements of rights' and 'mutual/agapeistic fellowship'. According to Brümmer, manipulative relationships are those in which persons are treated as objects, impersonally and asymmetrically in terms of the power exercised within them. By contrast, personal relationships, which may be defined in terms of either rights or fellowship, involve persons being treated as free agents, each assenting to the establishment and maintenance of the relationship. Personal relationships are, in this view, marked by vulnerability to the other, and by 'give and take' (p. 161). Yet different kinds of personal relationship can be distinguished: a key example is that in agreements persons enter the relationship with a view to serving their own interests or advantage; however, persons enter fellowship with a view to serving the interests of the other, and with each recognising the irreplaceable, intrinsic value of the other (see also Brümmer 1984). Although human relationships are not always as clear-cut as in these distinctions (which Brümmer recognizes), the designations outlined in *The Model of Love* provide some very helpful guidance for considering the kind of relationships in which forgiveness may or may not be appropriate. Conversely, Brümmer's categories imply that the exercise of forgiveness in certain circumstances may invite vulnerability which is not appropriate to particular interactions. For Brümmer, forgiveness is only applicable to relationships of mutual fellowship, where in any case it features alongside penitence as the contribution required by the other when forgiveness is offered. Brümmer holds that outside the bounds of fellowship, relationships are more appropriately restored by means of satisfaction, punishment, and/or condonation. If the context of a particular relationship is not defined, penitence may be confused with punishment and forgiveness with condonation. This is of major importance to reflection on forgiveness in challenging circum-stances, as it suggests that where fellowship has not existed there is no question of employing the tactics of forgiveness. According to Brümmer's definitions, abusive relationships involving manipulation, as almost by definition in the abuse of children by adults, are not the arena of forgiveness.

Other impetuses for exploring contextual approaches to forgiveness come from feminist theologians, who characteristically teach great sensitivity to circumstance. Note, for instance, the wisdom of Rosemary Radford Reuther's statement: 'the essence of servanthood is that it is only possible for liberated persons, not persons in servitude' (Reuther 1978: 54) or relate Ann Loades' logic to questions of forgiveness: 'It is one thing to employ metaphors of sacrifice in the context of love and then be sustained by it in a situation of extremity, but quite another to make the possibility of being in that situation a focus of attention outside the context of love' (Loades 1991: 260).

Conclusion

Each of these perspectives I have just surveyed has much to contribute to developing sensitivity as to where forgiveness might helpfully be encouraged, or not. Circumstances may be so challenging as to require a broader range of perspectives than are mediated by much current pastoral and sacramental engagement with forgiveness. Part of the task of identifying a broader range of resources requires the retrieval, consideration and magnification of elements already within the tradition, but marginal to it. I have hinted, albeit very briefly, at the possible relevance of some New Testament pericopes in this regard. Part of the task is related to expanding options by attending to testimony outside the tradition, even as it may contest the tradition. In this regard, I have included the voices of victims of the Holocaust whose experience witnesses to a breadth of response to suffering in their struggle to survive it. Part of the task may be to vivify pluralistic understandings of doctrinal themes, even when they are commonly regarded as mutually exclusive. Various fragments of the New Testament on forgiveness are again a case in point, and I have explored Paul Pruyser's (1991) 'psychology of atonement' as an example of how doctrines may be expounded in ways which resist a narrow focus. Yet, as Pruyser shows, expansiveness also requires discernment. Inclusion of Vincent Brümmer's (1993) cautious approach to forgiveness is one way in which the importance of discernment has been represented in this essay, and my related references to feminist theologians allude to further resources for critiquing and cautiously employing aspects of the tradition in relation to contextual awareness. In various ways, these elements of expansion and discernment point to the need for the voices of the abused themselves to be recognized as highly significant in approaching forgiveness.

   Within the tension between expansion and discernment, two points can be made by way of conclusion. Views of forgiveness which commit victims to risks of further victimisation and abuse, colluding with oppression or accommodating legacies of wrongdoing, might themselves be regarded as pathological. Adequate theologies of forgiveness will, therefore, steer clear of shallow celebrations of the merits of forgiveness which pay no regard to its complexities and costs, or which bypass the real difficulties encountered in various forms of abuse and their legacies. Each of these is required by forgiveness in challenging circumstances.

10

Forgiveness and Reconciliation in South Africa

Stephen Cherry

In the first part of this essay I will briefly review the way in which questions about forgiveness were being raised at the same time as South Africa was making its transition to democracy, as well as looking at what theologians and activists have more recently had to say about the role of forgiveness in politics. I will then introduce the Truth and Reconciliation Commission (TRC) itself and consider questions of the kinds of meaning and significance that were placed on the concept of forgiveness in its workings. In the second half of the chapter we will consider the significance of some cases of forgiveness and reconciliation which help fill out the picture of what the TRC in the end delivered. Thus in the first half I will discuss some of the rhetoric of forgiveness found in the context of the TRC and in the second I will look at the reality of the role that forgiveness is playing in the emergence of the new South Africa.

Part One

Forgiveness in Public Life

At the same time as South Africa was undergoing its long struggled-for transition to democracy the question of the role that forgiveness can play in public life was highlighted by two theological works, Donald Shriver's *An Ethic for Enemies* and Miroslav Volf's *Exclusion and Embrace* (Shriver 1995 and Volf 1996). Both authors address the question of what it means for people to live together peacefully when they share a history of conflict and hurt. Volf explores the concept of reconciliation from the point of view of fostering 'social agents' and addresses the question,

'What kind of selves do we need to be in order to live in harmony with others?' (Volf 1996: 20). It is in the context of this question that he discusses the dynamics of what he calls 'embrace', which is to welcome others by making space for them non-judgmentally, to accept them as humans. When there are problems with making such an embrace, Volf argues, forgiveness has a central role. More than this, it is only forgiveness that can open up to the future because even restorative justice is doomed as it can never be satisfied. Forgiveness is, he claims, 'an act of the highest sovereignty and inner freedom'. Moreover it overcomes two predicaments, those of 'reversibility' (a point first made by Hannah Arendt, 1958) and that of 'partiality', the problem that the offended against always weighs the offence more heavily than the offender. This is the reason why revenge is always judged to be disproportionate and therefore leads to an escalation of the conflict. It is only by forgiveness that the spiral of revenge can be halted. Against those who are convinced that forgiveness short-circuits justice, Volf argues that it actually 'enthrones' it by 'drawing attention to violation precisely by offering to forego [*sic*] its claims'. Thus: 'It's only if we are able to forgive that we can pursue justice fully' (Volf 1996: 123).

This sense of forgiveness being at the heart of the reconciliation of enemies is explored in the many case studies and narratives of Shriver's *An Ethic for Enemies*. He identifies forgiveness in a political context as a multidimensional human action in which 'moral truth, forbearance (from revenge), empathy and commitment to repair a fractured relation' are the four strands of a thick cable. 'No one element in this cable carries the weight of the action,' he explains; 'each assumes and depends on the others' (Shriver 1995: 9). This stress on the multidimensional nature of forgiveness in politics allows Shriver to 'link realism to hope' and to see the future as being freed from an unthinking repetition of the past. His four-stranded cable is not unlike Jean Paul Lederach's model of reconciliation, which was forged around the same time in the fields of practical intervention in post-conflict Nicaragua and is based on Psalm 85.10: 'Truth and mercy have met together. Justice and peace have kissed.' (Lederach 2001).

For Lederach, who explains his biblically derived ideas very concretely, reconciliation is both a destination and a journey. But the genius of his interpretation of this verse is to take 'Truth', 'Mercy', 'Justice' and 'Peace' not as concepts but as 'energies' and incarnate them as characters in a drama or voices in a conversation. In any conflict or post-conflict situation they have different things to say, different demands to make. And it is in the dialogue of these demands that reconciliation is furthered. Thus, whatever structures are created to facilitate reconciliation it is crucial, he argues, to create a process and a quality of space that gives voice to each energy while at the same time keeping them in connection with each other. For truth without mercy is blinding and raw; mercy without truth is a cover-up and superficial. Justice without peace falls easily into cycles of bitterness and revenge; peace without justice is short lived and benefits only the privileged or the victors. (Lederach 2001: 201)

Both Lederach and Shriver emphasize that memory is crucial to this kind of process, whether forgiveness or reconciliation is understood to be the most appropriate label. (Shriver prefers to use the word 'reconcilia-tion' for the end of the process that 'forgiveness' begins – the destination in Lederach's terms, rather than the journey.) For Shriver, forgiveness begins with remembering and moral judgment, and he comments that it is a sense of being subjected to this that puts people off being forgiven.

What follows from such 'moral assessment' is crucial. Punishment remains an option for Shriver, but not vengeance (Shriver 1995: 8). The forgiver must forbear from revenge and thus open the door to a new future characterized by different dynamics.

It is with the third strand in Shriver's cable that we encounter what he calls 'empathy for the enemy's humanity'. It is not true that the way of understanding inevitably leads to forgiveness, but without a sense of the possibility of the mutual coexistence of former enemies in society nothing approximating forgiveness will occur.

And following logically from this, if not in terms of actual process, is the fourth ingredient, which is a commitment to a new and repaired relationship – a positive rather than a grudging coexistence in which both forgiven and forgiver can let the past be the past and thereby focus on the future while living in the present.

What Lederach, Shriver and Volf have in common is a desire to identify a way forward from a situation of injustice. Each of them forecloses the option of revenge, vengeance or retribution. In this context 'forgiveness' refers less to a process occurring either within a relationship or individual and more to the alternative to revenge that opens up a new relational future. As Shriver has indicated, such forgiveness is a multidimensional process and, as Lederach's model suggests, different moral or transcendent values must be held in balance if progress towards reconciliation is to be made. It is Miroslav Volf, however, who returns us to the forgiving individual, making the point that the believer has somewhere to go with his or her rage and anger, and that bringing this to God can initiate the transformation of emotions and relationships. But Volf also suggests that forgiveness requires both judgment and personal freedom precisely because it does not follow the law of retribution.

It is with these somewhat tentative conclusions in mind that we turn to a consideration of the way in which forgiveness and reconciliation have been negotiated and realised in the context of the South African TRC.

South Africa's Truth and Reconciliation Commission

The South African TRC walked into the limelight of world attention caused by the scandal of apartheid and its dramatic demise. Three aspects helped make the South African model unique among truth commissions. First, it was established by Act of Parliament (Promotion of National Unity and Reconciliation Act No. 34, 1995). Second, it included the possibility of amnesty for perpetrators – provided they gave a comprehensive disclosure and proved that their actions were both proportional and politically motivated. Third, it was conducted in public and attracted enormous media coverage at the time and in retrospect has been subject to unparalleled fascination and scrutiny, adulation and criticism. In addition to this, while the South African TRC was one of many truth commissions (Hayner 2001, documents 21) only two of these have been entitled Truth and Reconciliation Commissions, the other being that in Chile.

The Commission ran for 30 months from 1996 (the original intention was to deal with it in 18 months!) and focused on the gross violations of human rights perpetrated between 21 March 1960 and 10 May 1994 – the dates of the Sharpeville Massacre and the inauguration of President Mandela. During the life of the Commission 21,400 victims came forward, of whom 2,000 testified in public. The amnesty process took longer to get started and of the 7,000 who came forward it would seem that 10–15 per cent are likely to be judged to meet the criteria. (Hamber 2003) The first five volumes of the final report were published in November 1998 despite a legal battle to suppress it (the opposition to publication coming from the ANC) with a sixth volume, referring to the amnesty process which took longer to conclude, being published in 2002. In April 2003 there was a long-awaited response from the Government to the recommendations for reparations to the effect that each of the people given 'victim status' would be awarded 30,000 Rand (approximately £2,500 or $3,750) which contrasts with the Commission's recommendation of R17,000–R21,000 per person, annually, for six years) as well as improvement of community services, symbolic reparation and institutional reparation (Meiring 2000: 193).

As well as recounting these facts it will be helpful to offer an overview of the thinking that was involved in setting up and running the TRC. These factors together constitute nothing more organized than a collage, but this collage is as crucial to the reality of the TRC as the Act of Parliament that established it. Among these I have already mentioned the truth commissions that had already taken place. That some form of truth-recovery was a necessary part of a transition to democracy was a widely held idea and may in the end prove to have been the most successful part of the TRC. Michael Ignatieff, for instance, is among those who refer to it as narrowing 'the range of permissible lies that one can tell in public' (Ignatieff 2001: 20). It is an attempt to bring to light at least some of the accounts of abuse and torture and murder. It includes allowing people to 'tell their story' but also for some positive and practical steps to be taken. For instance, some emergency reparations were paid and, while hastily-buried bodies of the disappeared were exhumed and re-buried, memorial stones were provided for others. In these ways the TRC honoured the need to remember the dead and to bring some closure to the process of grieving.

The attitude of Nelson Mandela as he walked free from prison and into leadership is of great significance, as it was seen to offer a role-model of dignity and forgiveness. Alongside this can be placed a point that was there in the postamble of the Interim Constitution but has also featured in the theology of Desmond Tutu: the idea of *ubuntu*. Most writers emphasize that this word has no precise parallel in Western languages though it is found in different African languages. The closest English word is usually said to be 'humanness' and its use implies the priority of the social over the individual, in the words of John Mbiti's aphorism (Battle 2000: 179), 'I am because we are' or, as it has also been put, 'I am human because I belong'. Alex Boraine points out that this was an important part of the philosophy of the founding president of the ANC Youth League, Anton Lembede, who had a profound influence on Nelson Mandela, Oliver Tambo and Walter Sisulu. What Lembede refers to as the 'philosophy of the African' is a holistic vision in which 'individual parts exist merely as interdependent aspects of one whole realising their fullest life in the corporate life'. It follows that 'His philosophy of life strives towards unity and aggregation, towards greater social responsibility' (Boraine 2000: 362). For this reason *ubuntu* opens the door to a strong empathy in the sense that Shriver uses the term – sense of common humanity and shared destiny. This is what lies behind Tutu's often-made point that the humanity of the perpetrator is bound up with that of the victim and that as one is abused so the other is degraded (Tutu 1999: 34–36). Moreover, a good person is one with *ubuntu* and to have *ubuntu* is to be generous, hospitable, friendly, caring, compassionate and forgiving.

A further cultural and linguistic point is relevant here. While the words 'forgiveness' and 'reconciliation' are sometimes used in overlapping ways they are also distinct. The word used to render 'reconciliation' in the title of the TRC in Xhosa, however, *uxolelwano*, is very close in meaning to 'forgiveness', much closer than it is to the meaning in English of 'reconciliation' (Krog 1998: 160). For Xhosa speakers, therefore, the message that came across was that the Commission was an occasion for them to demonstrate their goodness (*ubuntu*) by forgiving (*uxolelewano*) relevant perpetrators. And this is a different message than that which could come across in Afrikaans or English, where the point is that the TRC was an opportunity to make political progress at a time of negotiated transition by a careful balance of truth-recovery leading to amnesty for perpetrators and reparation for victims.

Of major significance for the TRC, and of enormous importance to those who may consider whether it could model a way forward in other situations, is the way in which the apartheid era came to an end. The Interim Constitution represented a negotiated settlement based on a stalemate. It has been referred to as a 'peace pact', neither side being defeated and neither victorious. There are two ways of looking at this negotiated transition. For those formerly in power it seemed that they were being unfairly put on trial, whereas for the victims, on the other hand, it seemed that the possibility of justice was being lost through the generous amnesty provisions. Thus the TRC can appear very different to participants depending on their location within the contexts created by the very apartheid divisions whose reconciliation it was designed to facilitate or to which it was at least intended to contribute.

Christian Forgiveness

Another factor that gave the TRC a special flavour was its relationship with Christianity. It was chaired by the recently retired Archbishop Tutu who addressed the ecclesiastical part, took the 16 other newly appointed commissioners on retreat, opened sessions with prayer, led the singing of songs and hymns, and used the categories of a psychologically-informed pastoral theology to understand and describe the process. His account of the TRC, *No Future without Forgiveness*, is the polemic of an advocate for a particular understanding of some of the central issues (Tutu 1999). It stands in contrast to the drier and more objective account, by Alex Boraine the vice-Chair who, while a Methodist minister, had been primarily involved in politics since 1974 (Boraine 2000). Tutu's rhetoric and the symbolism of his presence in the chair fuelled the idea that the TRC's process should reflect Christian values. Priscilla Hayner judges that the 'religious overtones' of the TRC were responsible for the prominent focus on reconciliation that contrasted the TRC with the wider family of truth commissions which have, as she puts it, 'generally been regarded as more legal, technical or historical investigations, with very little suggestion of a process rooted in religious convictions' (Hayner 2000: 41).

But more than this, Tutu brought to the TRC his own understanding of forgiveness. This was a form of forgiveness that derives from the fusion of the idea of *ubuntu* mentioned above and some strands in Christian theology. It cannot be said to represent predominant thinking in forgiveness and reconciliation in Christianity today which is based on the belief that repentance is a necessary prerequisite for forgiveness, and that this repentance must include both a sense of remorse and a commitment not to repeat the offence should the opportunity arise. This doctrine is found in both Catholic and protestant circles and was the reason why the Roman Catholic Church in South Africa opposed the TRC in the first instance and why some protestant churches and individuals found it at best unpalatable and at worst unacceptable (Tutu 1999). Alex Boraine, for instance, speaks of 'steps in the reconciliation process' as if they follow a necessary sequence: confession, repentance, restitution and forgiveness (Boraine 2000: 360). But the voices favouring this sort of approach were not only from church representatives. Anthony Holiday put the point very cogently in arguing that the TRC was at fault in failing to recognize the connections between the need for remorse and justice and the essentially internal, personal and uncontractable nature of true forgiveness in Christian doctrine and tradition (Holiday 1998). Priscilla Hayner effectively concurs when she writes that 'Forgiveness, healing and reconciliation are deeply personal processes, and each person's needs and reactions to peacemaking and truth-telling may be radically different' (Hayner 2001: 155).

For others it seems almost axiomatic that the TRC was an exercise in forgiveness. Brian Frost's book *Struggling to Forgive* uses 'forgiveness' as the hermeneutic through which to read every aspect of this complex process and does so in a self-consciously Christian way, positing that 'the commission demonstrates how the reconciliation Christ has brought through his death and resurrection can affect not only individuals but the fabric of society itself' (Frost 1998: xv). But Frost did not originate this way of thinking about the TRC. Kader Asmal writing very early on in the transition process expressed the hope that the TRC would allow victims 'to fulfil a civic sacrament of forgiving' (Asmal, Asmal and Roberts 1996).

The imagery here is potentially muddling. The TRC is envisaged as a confessional, presided over by Bishop Tutu as 'confessor-in-chief', as Holiday puts it (Holiday 1998: 46). But the confessional is precisely *not* public and is not based on the application for an amnesty which can be granted without intimations of remorse or regret. The role of contrition is crucial in the sacrament of penance. Equally, the Bishop's role was not in the Amnesty Committee but with the Human Rights Violations Hearings. Thus those who spoke in his presence were not looking for forgiveness. On the contrary, if this were to be a time of forgiveness then it would be the testifying victim, offering an account of the worst moments of their life in front of the world's media, who would be asked to *do* the forgiving.

Some commentators on the TRC remark that in the course of their hearings, especially the earlier hearings, victims were pressed by Commissioners to express forgiveness (Wilson 2001: 119). The thinking here was that it is a duty on those who have been offended both to give up their initial reactions of rage or anger and certainly not allow them to develop as bitterness nor to seek retribution or revenge or even redress in the courts (Wilson 2001: 120). This is the theology of forgiveness that Tutu brought to the process and is based, as Michael Battle (2000) has argued, on the premise that all are made in the image of God and that therefore no one is a reprobate, all can be redeemed. Significantly, Battle calls this '*ubuntu* theology', the ethics of which imply that to be a good Christian is to be proactive and generous in forgiveness. Alongside this are placed, in Tutu's thinking, two propositions, one of which is psychological and the other political. The first is that to forgive even an unrepentant wrongdoer is good for the mental health of the forgiver because it is a liberation from the damaging burdens of anger, hatred and frustrated wrath (Tutu 1999: 219). The political point is that as they forgive perpetrators, victims are making a significant contribution to the making of a better future for the society as a whole; they are creating the new South Africa. This is summarized in a sentence from Tutu's concluding speech on the first day of the TRC hearings. 'Forgiveness will follow confession and healing will happen, and so contribute to national unity and reconciliation' (Tutu 1999: 91).

Political Forgiveness

Reflecting on the role and nature of forgiveness in the TRC in his recent book, *Reconciliation,* John de Gruchy (de Gruchy 2002) acknowledges that forgiveness talk can be used to manipulate the vulnerable and thereby perpetuate oppression. He makes the point that 'The TRC Commissioners were increasingly aware of the danger of enforcing victims to forgive, recognising that for some it was important to hold back forgiveness and even express feelings of vengeance' (de Gruchy 2002: 171). Many will, of course, wonder how the social utility of forgiveness can be so overstressed that ideas of 'enforcement' could ever be entertained. But critics such as Wilson insist that many people were essentially manipulated into forgiving. 'Many individuals giving testimony that I interviewed were persuaded by former Archbishop Desmond Tutu, or at least so overawed that they dared not resist his views' (Wilson 2001: 240, footnote 11). De Gruchy is at one with Tutu when he expounds an approach to living in the wake of being violated that rules out 'malicious and vindictive vengeance' (de Gruchy 2001: 171) but is not at all clear about what it rules *in* other than unconditional forgiveness. This seems to be one of those junctures where those in favour of forgiveness neglect to notice that between forgiveness and 'malicious and vindictive vengeance' there is a third possibility. That is that there is moral argument for a healthy, and indeed virtuous, form of *resentment*. Jeffrie Murphy (Murphy and Hampton 1988) and Jerome Haber (Haber 1991) have written convincingly about this, arguing that resentment has the function of maintaining the value of the self. To put it most starkly, without the moral emotion of resentment there can be no concept of offence and certainly not of violation. The danger with placing a supreme value on forgiveness is that it 'demoralizes' this essentially moralizing emotion. Miroslav Volf (Volf 1996) argues that forgiveness that is freely given does not lead to a degradation of the self precisely because it is a way of drawing attention to the violation or offence. What is less convincing is that the dignity of the violated can be restored when they tell their story in the context of a process designed to deliver amnesty to those who violated them and when moral pressure is applied to encourage forgiveness of perpetrators by victims, especially when no remorse is forthcoming from the perpetrator. De Gruchy does not salvage the situation by referring back to Shriver and using the category of 'political forgiveness', which he describes as 'a risk taken on the basis of mature insight and political acumen and one that displays moral courage' (de Gruchy 2002: 173). It seems unreasonable to use this sort of language to describe words of forgiveness uttered in or after a TRC hearing, for what was risked and at stake in any *particular* case was not the future of the transitional process but the victim's sense of self, coherence of memories and peace of mind. What is ethically at issue, in short, is whether the Commission leaves victims free to resent while encouraging a process of reconciliation. The political issue is whether the pressure to forgive actually encourages a just reconciliation or a premature closure for a still hurting individual or community.

Shriver's description *would* make perfect sense, however, if applied to an act of political apology or public gestures of atonement by leading politicians. Tutu did appeal to the leaders of the African National Congress, Inkatha Freedom Party and the Pan African Congress as well as to President F.W. de Klerk, asking each to make a symbolic gesture of atonement by visiting the site of an atrocity committed by their force and say to the local people, 'Sorry – forgive us' (Boraine 2000: 372).

None of the leaders accepted the challenge. Looking back at de Gruchy's list of the qualities that lie behind an act of political forgiveness we could speculate as to whether it was 'mature insight', 'political acumen' or 'moral courage' that they lacked. Alex Boraine certainly felt that an opportunity had been missed and that 'the cause of reconciliation suffered as a result'. He is right, and had it been taken we may have had something more like 'political forgiveness' on which to reflect. Equally, had P.W Botha been more generous in his response to the TRC or responded to Tutu's appeal for an apology with something other than anger (Tutu 1999: 201) there may have been an opening for forgiveness that was political. And then again, had the 'handsome' apology offered by F.W. de Klerk in 1996 not been 'spoiled' by being qualified 'virtually out of existence' (Tutu 1999: 202) there would have been something to develop. But in the TRC the only forgiveness that could be offered by victims was personal giving up of resentment in a context which is dominated both by the politics of transition and by an '*ubuntu* theology' of forgiveness; that is to say, in a context that implied that it would be good both for the victim and their country, and which was silent on the possibility that it might, in some cases at least, be good to maintain resentment.

It is intriguing that the psychological study of forgiveness can illuminate what was going on here. The forgiveness that was offered in the context of the TRC was inevitably from victims of gross violations of human rights and seems to be connected with what Enright and others have called 'reframing'. That is to say, the forgiveness flows in partial acknowledgment that the relationship has moved on, for one reason or another, from the way it was at the time of the offence. What was going on in the TRC is, of course, a slightly complex form of this because the TRC itself was part of this process of transition. Nonetheless this must be substantially the case because it is inconceivable that there would have been any forgiveness talk at all outside the context of the end of apartheid. The briefest of glances at the *Kairos* document of 1985 (KAIROS Theologians 1985) will confirm that forgiveness and reconciliation were not seen as appropriate – the ethical and social priority at that stage was for liberation. But after the inauguration of President Mandela the agenda changed. Quite how it changed is yet another contested subject, and the view of Richard Wilson that the TRC was part of a process designed not so much to heal or reconcile the nation as to build a new nation with a new elite, is an example of an independent view based on careful reading of the politics and the social anthropology of justice and reconciliation (Wilson 2001). In the terms of the leadership of the TRC, however, the agenda changed to being one of healing the victims, reconciling the nation and recovering the truth.

And they were, of course, shackled with a responsibility to deliver amnesty as part of the price to be paid for the end of apartheid. But the predominance of the reconciliation agenda, and the particular theology of forgiveness that has been outlined, had the effect not of prioritising the sense of transition or 'reframing' but of *ubuntu*, which in this context is a moral and imperative form of 'empathy'.

Thus, while the psychological *reason* for forgiving, and for forgiveness being part of the process at all, was in terms of the psychology of reframing, which has a legitimate political dimension at a time of transition, the *rhetoric* used to encourage forgiveness was that of empathy. Forgiveness was needed from the victims precisely to demonstrate that a new sense of common humanity was emerging in this tragically and violently divided country. The pressure on victims to forgive was political pressure to testify that the oppressed – of which the victims of gross violation of human rights were taken to be paradigmatic cases – adhered to a world-view or theology which was the complete antithesis of apartheid. Thus the pressure to forgive was at least in part an attempt to invoke the spirit and quality of *ubuntu* as the ethos of the new South Africa. The final report of the TRC contains one perfect example of this when it quotes with approval the words of Cynthia Ngewu, the mother of one of the 'Gugulethu Seven': 'What we are hoping for when we embrace the notion of reconciliation is that we restore the humanity of those who were perpetrators. We do not want to return evil by another evil. We simply want to ensure that the perpetrators are returned to humanity.' (Truth and Reconciliation Commission 1998: Vol. 5, 366). Forgiveness or reconciliation in this context is not so much the exonerating of the perpetrator as the expression of *a* humanness in the project of creating human solidarity. This is the logic of *ubuntu* and lies behind the general pressure to forgive that was seen in the hearings of the TRC.

Part Two

Forgiveness and Restraint

A famous forgiveness story from the TRC can help us develop these thoughts further, namely the case of Brian Mitchell and the Trust Feed Farm massacre (Truth and Reconciliation Commission 1998: Vol. 5, 394–96; Tutu 1999: 137–38). Mitchell was the senior policeman involved in a massacre at Trust Farm township just north of Pietermaritzburg in December 1988. Under Mitchell's orders eleven people were killed and two were wounded; five of the victims were men, the remainder were women and children. Mitchell was given the death sentence for this in April 1992, but this was commuted to life, which allowed him to appeal for amnesty from the TRC, which he was granted in 1997.

As the TRC report puts it, 'The Trust Feed community... was enraged and seemed not to have forgiven Captain Mitchell. The hurt was profound, and the community went through a process of re-experiencing the original pain and anger'. (TRC: Vol. 5, 394). This phenomenon of retraumatization is one that has been discussed in several ways during and since the Commission (see Hayner 2001 and Hamber 2003). Mitchell had however been on a personal journey which involved three elements: he had confessed, but he also, again as the report puts it, 'appeared to repent of his own atrocious deeds and he had made a request for forgiveness. He has also reconciled himself with God and was a member of the Rhema Church' (TRC: Vol. 5, 395). All this was not enough to achieve reconciliation with the Trust Feed community but his intimations that he would like to meet and reconcile with them had the effect of precipitating a community committee that related to the TRC representatives that were seeking to broker the reconciliation. One aspect of this was that it made a space in which some internal community reconciliation between ANC and IFP members could take place. Various mediation consultants were engaged and in July 1997 a reconciliation meeting was held which Mitchell attended. At this it was made clear that full reconciliation would only be possible, as far as the community was concerned, if Mitchell was able actively to participate in – which effectively meant provide funds for – community reconstruction. The report also notes, however, that there was a very positive emotional tone by the end of the meeting with people calling out, 'Bye-bye, go well, Mitchell,' as he left the township.

Whether or not the story of Brian Mitchell is a story of forgiveness depends on your view of forgiveness – in terms of the authors considered at the beginning of this chapter, Lederach (2001) would say that forgiveness was not yet clinched, whereas Shriver (1995) would say that it was mostly in place. He survived his risky return to the village but clearly there is a lack of full reconciliation, and it is probable that a lifelong stalemate will ensue. But the moral suspense created by reluctance to forgive without some serious reparation is, I would argue, very healthy. In particular it opens up a space for the development of a longer-term relationship. The reticence to forgive allows for the possibility of anger modulating to a mature resentment that does not preclude relationship but acknowledges that the relationship is not yet 'right' or fully reconciled.

We turn now to the story of Amy Biehl which is, if anything, more well-known than that of Brian Mitchell and the Trust Farm community. It draws out slightly different aspects of the way in which a reconciliation process might involve elements of forgiveness and non-forgiveness.

On 25 August 1993 the 26-year-old American Fulbright scholar drove three black fellow students to Guguletu township (see Chubb and van Dijk 2001). The car was stoned by demonstrators returning from a rally of the Pan African Congress where the slogan 'One settler one bullet' was used. The stoning soon made it impossible to drive and Amy ran from the car towards a garage where she hoped to find safety. As she ran she was hit by more stones, tripped and then stabbed to death. As a result four youths were tried and imprisoned, but after a year of imprisonment they appeared before the TRC asking for amnesty. In the original trial all had denied being involved in her murder but in their applications for amnesty they gave a full account. That of Monges Christopher Manqina concluded as follows: 'I apologise sincerely to Amy Biehl's parents, family and friends and I ask their forgiveness' (Chubb and van Dijk 2001: 205). In the same hearing her father, Peter, spoke of his daughter's values, quoting a letter that she wrote to the *Cape Times* which said that reconciliation in South Africa might prove to be equally painful as the racist past, but that 'the most important vehicle towards reconciliation is open and honest dialogue'. He said that Amy would have approved of the TRC process. He added that amnesty must be awarded by the state on merit and that the family would not oppose it. 'In the truest sense it is for the community of South Africa to forgive its own and this has its basis in traditions of *ubuntu* and other principles of human dignity.' In a television interview Amy's mother, Linda, spoke of visiting the mother of one of her daughter's killers. She recalled seeing a rainbow poster on the wall and how, when the two women embraced, 'I felt a sense of peace, a peace within myself.'

It was a few years after this, in 1997, that the Amy Biehl Foundation, which was established by donations from Americans who were moved to try to perpetuate Amy's ideals, began its work in South Africa. This led to a project in Guguletu township, 'Weaving Barriers Against Violence'. The work is diverse but the focus is the training of skills that give young people more options and greater hope – skills that create the possibility of an alternative to violence. At least one of those convicted of her murder and subsequently granted amnesty has been employed by the Foundation.

An analysis of this story in terms of forgiveness and reconciliation points to the fact that Amy's father did not presume to forgive in a direct or unequivocal way. Rather he affirmed the congruence between Amy's personal values and the reconciliation process in general and the TRC in particular. This restraint did not limit the scope or the energy of the reconciliation work that was to flow from the sad origin of Amy's murder. Second there is the embrace between the two mothers. This may look like forgiveness but to describe it in that way is to be somewhat imprecise. The embrace was not between a victim and a perpetrator; rather it was of two women who recognized each other's humanness in the context of connected suffering. No doubt it was Amy's death that brought them together, but the encounter was one of *ubuntu* in a broad sense. What is recalled of it is also, significantly, non-verbal.

Resentment and Reconciliation

A non-verbal exchange stands at the centre of another story from the Cape Town area. It is based not on published records but personal conversation with a former member of *Umkhonto we Sizwe* or MK, the armed wing of the ANC. For reasons concerning the future safety of this man a false name, Sipho, will be used in this account of his story, which came to me in conversation at the Direct Action Centre for Peace and Memory in Cape Town. When Sipho was chair of a community court in the Crossroads area the court ordered the 'necklace' killing of four men suspected of being informers. He told me that it was after a TRC hearing that he asked the widow of each man for forgiveness. Three of them said, 'Yes, I forgive you.' But the fourth, as he put it, 'really smacked me'. On the occasion that I met with him he introduced me to this woman. She continued to live in poverty with her small children, like so many in the township, but he occasionally managed to bring her some cash – largely as a result of his work showing visitors like me around some of the main sights of the liberation struggle in Cape Town. I detected no anger or hostility between the two, and he said that he also tried to bring her some bread from time to time. No moment of forgiveness had occurred but there was an ongoing relationship which included continued support for the victim. Revenge and retribution did not seem to be on the agenda at all.

From my conversation with Sipho, who was himself the victim of police torture, it was clear that he was still disturbed by the memory of the 'necklace' killings and the physical suffering of the victims. We do not need to speculate about his own psychological response, however, to make sense of the very firm and clear 'No!' delivered by that smack. It speaks of the pain of resentment but also raises the question of what is at stake in saying 'Yes' to a request for forgiveness. Clearly much depends on the nature of the relationship up to the point of such a request. In this case it was that the two were members of the same community and they spoke the same language but were not connected more profoundly. A quick forgiveness in this context would have two implications, both of which are of great importance. The first and most obvious is that it apparently removes the legacy of resentment. The second is that it removes the need for a longer-term relationship in which a more profound reconciliation might occur.

Things look very different, however, when the relationship is between two people who are committed to each other by a covenanted relationship, for example, a husband and wife or parent and child. In such a case, a request for forgiveness is an acknowledgment that the covenant has been threatened and an offer of forgiveness in this case will, therefore, *perpetuate* the relationship. This in turn would create the opportunity to test whether the repentance or remorse expressed is sincere enough to warrant continuing with the relationship yet further. In other words, if forgiveness is sought, offered and accepted the relationship can continue in a somewhat tentative way until trust is rebuilt. In the context of a covenanted relationship forgiveness is, thus, a step in the direction of reconciliation. But it is not necessarily so in other situations – including the TRC paradigm where the victim and perpetrator were strangers but are taken to be symbolic representatives of their communities, of which Brian Mitchell and the Trust Feed Community is an example.

In the situation that we are examining, however, there is as yet no relationship, certainly no covenant, and yet there *is* the possibility of continued relating. The question is, 'On what terms?' For the answer to that to have any integrity it must reflect the truth with regard to the anger and resentment of the victim. And in the case we are considering the smack speaks for itself. Resentment remains. The onus then returns to the perpetrator. Should that person have a sincere desire to be forgiven they will have to continue to attempt to relate, to converse, with their victim. If not, they can forget the matter. In such a context, then, the refusal of forgiveness is a way of initiating a future that could be reconciling. Had this woman said, 'Yes, I forgive you,' what could have been precipitated was a closure on their relationship, their mutual obligations having been met in apology and response. 'I apologised, you forgave, and that closes the matter.' Whereas restraint from forgiveness created the possibility of a future in which there was a new relationship, more justice, more *ubuntu* and more opportunity for the man to come to terms with both the horror of the victims' deaths and the human consequences of creating secondary victims. By refusing 'instant forgiveness' she created the opportunity for him to atone by relating positively with her. Significantly, the context of the TRC was necessary for this: had he been imprisoned for these murders there would have been very little prospect of any positive outcome and the woman would not have received any ongoing support, however minor.

Conclusions

The South African Truth and Reconciliation Commission provides a fascinating and complex case study for the student of forgiveness. In this chapter I have examined some of this complexity. First, we explored how historically the TRC coincided with an unprecedented interest in the possibility that forgiveness might have a role to play in public affairs. Second, we examined the TRC in the context of other truth commissions but also as very much the product of its own dramatic context. And just as South Africa had become in some ways a microcosm of global injustice so the TRC became a theatrical laboratory of what was possible in terms of the application of certain ideas of forgiveness and reconciliation in the politics of transition. This aspect of the TRC was driven in many ways by the charismatic personality of its Chairman, Archbishop Tutu. As we noted, his theology led to the conclusion that forgiveness was always a possibility because no human being was beyond redemption. But equally his theology of forgiveness was derived from the broader concept of *ubuntu* or humanness. We saw how, especially in cultures where African languages such as Xhosa are spoken, this can lead to a very high moral imperative to forgive.

In the second half of the chapter our attention turned to some stories that tell of reconciliation taking place across some of the apartheid boundaries, but in the context not of overt forgiveness but rather of either silence about forgiveness, or a manifest incompleteness of a forgiveness process, or a straightforward refusal to forgive when asked. Such stories are, I would argue, central to a full understanding of the role of forgiveness in social reconciliation or transitional politics. Some commentators (e.g. Wilson 2001) have been alert to the danger of so encouraging people to forgive that their apparent 'forgiveness' might seem to be yet another acquiescence by an oppressed person to an authority figure. It is reasonable to assume that incidences of this took place – and we have explored the way in which the TRC process may have appeared as demanding differing responses from people from different language communities. But, as the various cases that I have presented make clear, the road to reconciliation is not always paved with instant or overt forgiveness.

Another factor within the TRC was its emphasis on the *personal* within the context of what was essentially a *political* process. There was, for instance, a considerable emphasis in the rhetoric of the TRC on healing victims as well as reconciling the nation. This is a complex study in its own right, but in retrospect there seems to have been considerable naïveté regarding the positive mental health value of telling one's story. Pricilla Hayner explores this issue very carefully (Hayner 2001: 133–53) and is right to make the point that 'those who suggest that "talking leads to healing" are usually making assumptions that do not hold true for truth commissions' (p. 135). And one could make a comparable point about the virtue of forgiveness expressed in the context of the TRC. As Audrey Chapman points out, the circumstances of the TRC did not create the kind of space in which one could reasonably expect to liberate healthy forgiveness. As she puts it:

> Despite the TRC's emphasis on reconciliation and restoring a relationship between victims and perpetrators, there was little actual opportunity for interaction between them. The TRC's Human Rights Committee dealt with victims, the Amnesty Committee with perpetrators. The amnesty process did not allow for dialogue between them. While survivors and victims' families had the right to be present, they did not initially have the right to comment on his testimony. Nor did the TRC seek to arrange such private meetings in advance of or subsequent to the exchanges at open hearings. (Chapman 2001: 270)

It is impossible not to conclude that the therapeutic enthusiasm expressed in some of the rhetoric of leading commissioners was misplaced. And this inevitably leads to the question of whether the therapeutic rhetoric and forgiveness talk as used in the TRC was sometimes manipulative. After all, it was addressed to victims who had otherwise only the vague promise of reparations as a reward for appearing; perpetrators had the much more concrete and instant prospect of amnesty – and indeed often had little more to lose than a jail sentence.

I believe that it is coherent to acknowledge that from time to time the Commission overstepped the mark in encouraging and directing the responses of victims in terms of forgiveness while asserting that the way in which the TRC promoted the values of forgiveness, reconciliation and *ubuntu* was extremely valuable and positive to individuals and to communities and to the nation as a whole. The TRC had an influence far beyond its hearings in terms of participating in and forming the moral and social climate of the new South Africa. This not only contributed to making the TRC unique among truth commissions, it also created a whole new set of criteria against which it was to come to be judged.

As we have seen, the combination of the positive pressure to forgive and reconcile created by the TRC in general and its Christian leadership in particular, coupled with the reticence to forgive of some individuals and communities, helped create the circumstances in which, over time, both resentment and repentance can mature. And it is this mutual maturation that lies behind the possibility of a non-coerced and genuine forgiveness that can not only be healing for individuals but also begin to break down some of the barriers within a society such as South Africa. That forgiveness is part of the process of transition in South Africa is in part due to the Truth and Reconciliation Commission, but it is also due to the fact that many people and communities had more reticence about forgiving than was evident in some of the Commission's rhetoric.

In conclusion, it seems fair to say that the theatrical laboratory of the Truth and Reconciliation Commission has revealed a great deal about the way in which the dynamics of forgiveness, non-forgiveness and resentment may relate together in processes of personal and social reconciliation. There are obvious problems both with the traditional Christian ideal of a forgiveness process of several predictable steps and also with the Tutu approach, which is based on an imperative form of *ubuntu* which leads to pressure being placed on victims who are vulnerable in many ways, not least to retraumatization. The truth about forgiveness is that it plays a somewhat unpredictable part in human affairs and this unpredictability is of its essence, for it is nothing if not freely and generously given. A major conclusion of this reading of the TRC is that the road to reconciliation can be travelled through the valley of non-forgiveness and resentment. However, it is not enough to say this. For this is often a place where individuals and communities can get stuck and there is a role for public figures both in modelling forgiveness and keeping it on the agenda in the most horrific and traumatizing of circumstances. For reconciliation to proceed we need mature understandings of both resentment *and* forgiveness. To the extent that the TRC has drawn world attention to this simple point, it has played a major role not only in our understanding of forgiveness but also of our sense of the way in which forgiveness may influence social, national and global affairs.

11

Concluding Reflections

Fraser Watts

By now it has become apparent that forgiveness proceeds at various different levels. At one end of the spectrum the capacity for forgiveness is an individual matter, dependent on personal development. However, forgiveness is always in some sense also a relational matter, because the occasion for forgiveness always arises within the context of a relationship. Sometimes forgiveness affects no one else except the two people involved. On other occasions it can be a broader, social matter affecting a small network of people, such as a family. We have seen that it is even possible for forgiveness to arise in the context of large social groupings or nations. A clear recent example is the need for forgiveness in South Africa, discussed in the previous chapter.

This raises large general issues about the relationship between the individual and society, which is in itself a vigorous area of debate. The main focus of this final chapter will be to place the psychology of forgiveness in a broader social and cultural context.

Individual and Society

It is often remarked that we live in a highly individualistic society. That can be seen, for example, in our 'entertainment' culture, which leads people to have a clear sense of their individual likes and dislikes, and an expectation that those tastes will be catered for. This affects churchgoing amongst other things; if people go to church at all they want a church that reflects their own preferences. The time is long gone in which it was possible to have an Act of Uniformity, by which only one denomination was permitted, and all churches in that denomination worshipped in the same way. Churchgoing now reflects the pluralistic nature of society, and the choices of the individual.

However, alongside this there has been a strong emphasis within social theory on the primacy of society. Often, this has been expressed in terms of the primacy of language. All members of a society, no matter how individualistic they may seem, speak the same language. So, it is said, their thoughts and patterns of behaviour are deeply and inescapably influenced by that common language. There is also a common culture and historical inheritance. This has led social theorists to emphasise that the individual is profoundly shaped by society, culture and language, however much we may seem to be living in a society of individualism and personal preference.

In religious matters, the view that personal religious experience is primary was reflected in the Gifford lectures given by William James just over a century ago, *The Varieties of Religious Experience* (1902). However, James' view has been strongly challenged. James saw the religious experience of the individual as the foundation of religion, the base upon which doctrinal traditions and religious social structures were built, whereas his critics have always emphasised, in contrast, the extent to which the beliefs and practices of a society shape the religious experience of the individual. The assumptions of recent social theory have led to these criticisms being made increasing trenchantly (e.g. Lash 1988).

My own view is that it is fruitless and inappropriate to debate whether the individual or society is primary, whether society shapes the experiences, beliefs and practices of the individual, or whether society grows out of those individual experiences, beliefs and practices. Surely neither is a foundation on which the other is built; neither is primary, in any strong sense of that term. Certainly, society is shaped by the individuals within it, and individuals are shaped by society. Indeed, it is surprising, in an intellectual climate that has seen the inappropriateness of all kinds of 'foundationalism', that there has been such a strong emphasis on the primacy of society over the individual. Rather, we need to think systemically, in a way that allows for mutual influence between society and the individual.

This general debate is highly relevant to forgiveness. In one sense, the extent to which forgiveness is practised by the individuals in any particular society will depend on the extent to which they have developed the capacity for forgiveness. As we saw in chapter 8, that is a matter of personal development and maturity. However, it is also true that individuals are influenced by society. The extent to which forgiveness is practised by individuals will depend on the extent to which the culture of society is conducive to forgiveness. The title of this book is *Forgiveness in Context*. Society is a crucial part of the context for the practice of forgiveness between individuals. Equally, the practice of interpersonal forgiveness influences the climate of forgiveness in wider society.

It may be tempting to complain that emphasising the psychology of forgiveness encourages an over-individualistic approach to it. Indeed, it is one of the recurrent suspicions about a psychological approach to religious matters that it increases this tendency (Watts, 2002, Ch. 1). However, I believe that this is an unfair criticism. In the first place, psychology is not as exclusively individualistic as is often implied. Within psychology there is 'social psychology' that explicitly takes account of the interaction between the individual and the social group. Also, an emphasis on psychology does not exclude a comparable and balancing emphasis on sociology. On the contrary, I would argue that psychology and sociology need to go hand in hand. It is one of the current limitations of the psychology of forgiveness that it is not yet balanced by an adequate sociology of forgiveness.

In so far as it is reasonable to complain about an over-individualistic approach to forgiveness, the blame for that cannot be laid entirely at the door of psychology. On the contrary, psychology has inherited an individualistic approach to forgiveness that was already predominant in the religious traditions, especially Christianity. Indeed, it is arguable, as Donald Shriver (1995) claims, that Christianity originally took a social approach to forgiveness, and that was apparent both in the teaching of Jesus and in the church of New Testament times. However, even if forgiveness really was a social movement at the inception of Christianity, that emphasis was not maintained. As Shriver says, one has to conclude,

> that . . . forgiveness seldom if ever attained an impressive place in the ethics that the Church sought to commend to its secular host society;
>
> that the medieval institution of penance solidified this tendency, not only in the secrecy and individualization of the confessional but in its ordinary confinement of 'sin' to the sphere of personal conduct;
>
> and that the Protestant Reformation, while making a strong claim to re-socialise the idea of forgiveness and repentance as a function of a Church congregation, continued to stress the power of divine over human forgiveness. (p. 58)

Recent years have seen a growing recognition of the political significance of forgiveness. The Holocaust of World War II and the collapse of apartheid in South Africa have been particularly important in establishing forgiveness as a politically important process. Shriver (1995) himself has written about the political importance of forgiveness for America, both internally and in its relations with Germany and Japan. More recently, Derrida (2001) has written about the forgiveness of crimes against humanity. However, this recognition of the political importance of forgiveness has not been matched by an adequate, theoretically-grounded sociology of forgiveness. Of course, that is not a lack that can be made good in this closing chapter, but it is possible to indicate some of the basic assumptions and principles that will need to be reflected in a sociology of forgiveness.

Towards a Sociology of Forgiveness

Forgiveness, is, of course, a moral activity, and it would be hard to make any sociological sense of forgiveness without assuming that the social order is essentially a moral one. There has been a growing emphasis in recent years on the moral nature of the social order (e.g. Etzioni 1988, Smith 2003, Wuthnow 1987). It is not possible to give an adequate account of society purely in terms of non-moral processes such as social coercion and self-interest. Clearly, the way in which society functions reflects shared values and norms. In this sense, one of the basic prerequisites of a sociology of forgiveness, a sense in social theory of the moral order on which society is built, is already in place.

It is a contingent rather than a necessary feature of social orders that they are essentially moral. It is possible to envisage societies where the moral order no longer obtained, and occasionally examples of such societies are found in practice. Recent theoretical work on the psychology of the evil indicates the conditions under which such societies develop (Baumeister, 1997).

The practice of forgiveness both reflects the moral nature of the social order, and also helps to sustain and shape it. In the first place, it is a reflection of the moral order that certain activities are deemed to have breached moral norms, and in that sense to require forgiveness. It also reflects the moral order of society in a different way, that forgiveness is held by society to be a desirable practice that upholds the moral order. In a healthy society, there are moral norms that support the practice of forgiveness.

A sociology of forgiveness also needs to pay particular attention to what has been called micro-sociology (e.g. Scheff 1990). That is not to neglect the broad assumptions and practices of society as a whole, but simply to recognise that it is within relatively small-scale social structures that forgiveness is most often practised. The social microcosm is influenced both by the broader social order and by the attitudes and capacities of particular individuals. Micro-sociology thus stands at a particularly interesting point of intersection between the individual and the broader society. Micro-sociology shares much with social psychology, which examines the same social microcosm. Sociology helps in understanding the inter-relationship between broader society and the social microcosm. Social psychology helps in understanding the intersection between the individual and the social microcosm.

Sociology is characteristically sensitive to power structures, and the way in which social structures function is often a reflection of power imbalances. This elucidation of power structures has been an important aspect of the related area of the sociology of emotion, and it would also be important in the sociology of forgiveness. To be specific, the nature of forgiveness is radically affected by whether the person practising it is in a strong or weak social position. For a strong person to offer forgiveness can further enhance their social standing. If a weak person extends forgiveness it may be less of a free act, and may further weaken the standing of that person within the social structure. That will often be true of forgiveness by people who have been abused, and chapter 9 made clear how problematic forgiveness can be in that context.

These issues of strength and weakness in acts of forgiveness are ones on which there can be a rich dialogue with theology. The Christian tradition has always understood that there is a close, and sometimes unexpected, relationship between strength and weakness. That stems from Jesus who, though regarded as the Son of God, took a position of human weakness as the crucified one. Thus, paradoxically, strength can be found in weakness, while apparent strength can be much weaker than it appears. In the Christian story, Pilate stands as the paradigmatic example of that. In the passion narrative Pilate, from his position of apparent strength, offers to forgive Jesus, or at least to 'let him off'. However, there is another sense in which Jesus stands in judgment over Pilate, who is in need of forgiveness for his decision to crucify the Son of God. The question of who is in a position to forgive whom is closely intertwined with the question of relative authority, something explicitly discussed between Jesus and Pilate in the passion story in St John's gospel.

A sociology of forgiveness would also place a strong emphasis on processes of interpretation. Social reality is not a given, but something that comes into focus as a result of a process of interpretation. One way of understanding an act of forgiveness is as a social negotiation about how events are to be construed. We saw in chapter 6 that forgiveness is often dependent on reconstruing the events that have caused offence. The particular perspective that sociology would add to this is an awareness of the extent to which that reconstrual needs to be shared between the two or more parties involved in the act of forgiveness, and indeed often needs to be negotiated between them. Recent psychological research in this area has perhaps concentrated too exclusively on how the person doing the forgiving construes the situation.

Forgiveness in the Church

These pointers towards a more explicitly social understanding of forgiveness lead on to questions about the church as a forgiving community. The current spate of interest in forgiveness has so far included surprisingly little on this. 'Therapeutic forgiveness' is being exported to the secular world but, for the most part, it is not yet being enthusiastically practised within the church.

As we saw in chapter 5, forgiveness can be experienced in many ways in the liturgical life of the church. Forgiveness is explicitly offered in two main ways in the church. They both have their value, though neither seems entirely adequate by itself. First, there is the general act of confession and forgiveness practised within the corporate liturgy of the church. However, that is normally so very impersonal that it does little to establish the church as a forgiving community. There is also, in some churches, the confession of the individual penitent in privacy to a fellow Christian, usually a priest. However, even in a church where a substantial proportion of members are practising confession and forgiveness in that way, it is such a private, individual act that it also has negligible effect in promoting the church as a forgiving community.

There are interesting pointers towards what might be possible in Dietrich Bonhoeffer's (1954) *Life Together*, which reflects his experience before World War II as head of a seminary of the German 'Confessing Church' at Finkenwalde. His emphasis is primarily on confession. However, he holds out a powerful vision of how mutual confession and forgiveness can build up a Christian community:

> In confession the break-through to community takes place... Since the confession of sin is made in the presence of a Christian brother, the last stronghold of self-justification is abandoned... He gives his heart to God, and he finds the forgiveness of all his sin in the fellowship of Jesus Christ and his brother. The expressed, acknowledged sin has lost all its power... It can no longer tear the fellowship asunder. Now the fellowship bears the sin of the brother... Now he stands in the fellowship of sinners who live by the grace of God in the cross of Jesus Christ... He can confess his sins and in this very act find fellowship for the first time... Sin concealed separated him from the fellowship, made all his apparent fellowship a sham; sin confessed has helped him to find true fellowship with the brethren in Jesus Christ. (pp. 102–03)

The process Bonhoeffer describes here, based on his experience at Finkenwalde, is clearly a powerful one in which mutual acceptance played a key part. There is perhaps an analogy with the mutual acceptance between husband and wife in a good marriage, where each knows the other so well that failings cannot be hidden, but nevertheless there is such a warmth of mutual acceptance that personal failings cease to be a burden. To be loved by someone who knows the worst about you is always a powerful human experience.

Memories and Forgiveness

An aspect of the psychology of forgiveness that deserves to receive more attention than has been given so far is the transformation of memories. The opportunity for forgiveness arises where there are particularly salient personal memories. Those memories will often be mutual, in the sense that both the giver and receiver of an offence will have a vivid and, in a different sense, painful memory of the episode concerned. However, it is also possible that at least one of them will be oblivious of it. People can certainly give deep offence without realising it, and without any memory of having done so. It is also possible that a person can be mortified by their memory of an occasion when they believe they caused offence, without the other person having taken offence at all.

If interpersonal forgiveness is to be transacted effectively it will involve the transformation of the memories of what happened on the occasion when offence was given and received. That may involve reconstruing what actually happened, or it may involve setting the memory of what happened in a broader context in a way that changes its impact, or yet again it may involve a reassessment of the importance of what happened in a way that diminishes its impact. The transformation of memories seems to be as important in collective as in interpersonal forgiveness (Elliott 1995). For example, forgiveness in South Africa depends on a reworking of the collective painful memory of apartheid.

There are religious resources that can be brought to bear on this process of the transformation and healing of memories. The process of transforming memories to which religious resources can most readily contribute is the casting of those memories in a broader context. For example, the paradigmatic memory that defines the Christian tradition is the collective memory of the crucifixion and resurrection of Jesus. There is a way in which painful personal memories can be associated with that religious memory; such memories can be associated with the crucifixion in a way that points towards a resurrection-like transformation.

There are, of course, dangers in this approach. It is important to retain a sense of the distinctness of episodes of a person's own life from the paradigm of death and resurrection, as well as making connection with it. Also, as James Hillman (1975) has pointed out, it is sometimes important to be prepared to linger over the experience of crucifixion without assuming that it will rapidly and necessarily turn into a resurrection experience. Painful memories can have a 'soul-making' function that is obliterated if they are too quickly healed and transformed by 'forgiveness'.

However, the main point here is that the transformation of personal memories would represent a fruitful focus for psychological theorising about forgiveness, and one to which theology could also make a contribution.

An Age of Forgiveness?

Finally, it is worth asking why the present time is, in a sense, becoming an 'age of forgiveness'. What is it about the human condition, at least in the developed world at the beginning of this third millennium, that makes forgiveness such a timely subject? Charles Taylor (1989) has described how we have moved into an age of interiority and self-expression. It is an age in which the giving and receiving of forgiveness speak powerfully to our human condition. Another relevant approach to the psychological nature of the present age is in terms of its culture of narcissism (Lasch 1978). We live in an age of narcissistic vulnerability in which, among other things, people seem both to have a powerful need of forgiveness, and to be increasingly preoccupied with the personal challenge of extending forgiveness to others. Further, we seem to be living increasingly in a shame culture rather than a guilt culture. That has important implications for how forgiveness is practised and experienced (Watts 2001) though, unfortunately, the liturgical practice of forgiveness speaks to guilt rather than to shame.

It is interesting in this connection that the popular 'therapeutic forgiveness' movement focuses more on giving forgiveness than on receiving it. We seem to live in an age that feels the pain of estranged relationships particularly acutely, and therefore has a strong desire to find the inner resources to extend forgiveness to others in order to achieve reconciliation. It is perhaps also an age of the 'depleted self' (Capps 1993), in which people feel the lack of adequate personal resources to extend the forgiveness they desire to give. People seem to want to forgive, but can't easily find within themselves the magnanimity to do so. Yet another relevant factor is the way in which forgiveness has become intertwined with self-respect. Implicit social norms in favour of forgiveness seem to be quite strong, with the result that it is important for people's self-respect that they should practise forgiveness. Their difficulties in doing so can thus lead to an acute problem of self-respect.

From a theological point of view, it is puzzling that the present age is embracing forgiveness so wholeheartedly, while finding the concept of sin so obscure and unappealing. Theologians have traditionally talked about the 'forgiveness of sins'. However, we are seeing at present a decoupling of forgiveness and sin; the practice of forgiveness is being embraced, but the concept of sin is being rejected. The sense of sin led people in past generations to want to receive forgiveness. In contrast, it seems to be our self-preoccupation that leads us now to want to be able to forgive.

Many will see this attempt to have forgiveness without sin as deplorable from a theological point of view. They may also see it as a regrettable symptom of the recent psychologization of forgiveness. However, things are not always quite as they seem, and these judgments may not be fair.

It has become almost a commonplace of theology to remark that when people reject belief in God they are often rejecting a concept of God that is not the one in whom Christians actually believe. There is a sense in which they are right to reject belief in a God that is a travesty of the Christian one. In a similar way, when people reject the concept of sin as they understand it, they may be rejecting something that is not an authentic part of the Christian tradition. It may be a travesty of the Christian understanding of sin that people reject these days, rather than the authentic concept.

It is probably true that people these days have a less vivid sense of wrongdoing than in the past, but there is more to the acknowledgment of sin than an awareness of wrongdoing. In contrast, people probably still have a strong sense of inadequacy and 'depletion'. In fact, this feeling of depletion may actually be at least close to what Christians have understood by sin as a sense of wrongdoing. The contemporary emphasis on giving rather than receiving forgiveness reflects a lack of any perception of neediness. However, that may not actually be the case. In a way, it may be more difficult and 'blessed' to give than to receive forgiveness. Behind the sense of how challenging it is to forgive someone who has caused offence, there may well be a sense of needing resources beyond oneself in order to meet the challenge.

It is perhaps not so much that the contemporary approach to forgiveness is anti-theological, but rather that it may be necessary for theology to articulate different aspects of a comprehensive under-standing of forgiveness more effectively in order to make contact with the contemporary experience of forgiveness. It would also be inappropriate to say that the approach to forgiveness found in contemporary society is a product of psychology. Psychology is as much a *product* of the current climate, as the *source* of the contemporary approach to forgiveness. To blame psychology for the current approach to forgiveness would be to 'shoot the messenger'.

As was argued in the opening chapter, an approach to forgiveness that is deficient theologically is usually deficient psychologically, and vice versa. Working towards an approach to forgiveness that is more balanced psychologically goes hand in hand with developing an approach that is more satisfactory theologically. We hope that this book has contributed to that twin task.

Bibliography

Abramson, L.Y., M. Seligman and J. Teasdale, 'Learned helplessness in humans: Critique and reformulation', *Journal of Abnormal Psychology* 87 (1978), pp. 49–74.

Adams, M. McCord, 'Forgiveness: a Christian model', *Faith and Philosophy* 8 (3) (1991), pp. 277–304.

Al-Mabuk, R., R.D. Enright and P. Cardis, 'Forgiveness education with parentally love-deprived college students', *Journal of Moral Education* 24 (1995), pp. 427–44.

Arendt, H., *The Human Condition* (Chicago: University of Chicago Press, 1958).

Asmal, K., L. Asmal and R.S. Roberts, *Reconciliation Through Truth* (Cape Town: David Philip, 1996).

Atkinson, D., 'Forgiveness and personality development', *Third Way* 5 (11) (1982), pp. 18–21.

Augsberger, D., *The New Freedom of Forgiveness* (Chicago: Moody, 2000).

Aulen, G., *Christus Victor* (London: SPCK, 1970).

Babylonian Talmud. Tractate Sanhedrin 25a; Tractate Berakhot 10a.

Barrett, C.K., *The Second Epistle to the Corinthians* (London: A & C Black, 1973).

Bash, A., 'A psychodynamic approach to the interpretation of the New Testament', *Journal for the Study of the New Testament* 83 (2001), pp. 51–67.

Battle, M., 'The ubuntu theology of Desmond Tutu', *Interpretation* 54 (2) (2000), pp. 172–82.

Baumeister, R.F., *Evil: Inside Human Cruelty and Violence* (New York: W.H. Freeman, 1997).

Baumeister, R.F., J.J. Exline and K.L. Sommer, 'The victim role, grudge theory, and two dimensions of forgiveness', in E.L. Worthington Jr. (ed.), *Dimensions of Forgiveness: Psychological Research and Theological Perspectives* (Radnor, Pennsylvania: Templeton Foundation Press, 1998): pp. 79–104.

Baumeister, R.F., A.M. Stillwell and S.R. Wotman, 'Victim and perpetrator accounts of interpersonal conflict: Autobiographical narratives about anger', *Journal of Personality and Social Psychology* 59 (1990), pp. 994–1005.

Beck, A.T., C.H. Ward, M. Mendelson, J. Mock and J. Erbaugh, 'An inventory for measuring depression', *Archives of General Psychiatry* 24 (1961), pp. 215–20.

Bible, New Revised Standard Version (NRSV) (New York: Oxford University Press, 1991).

Biggar, N., 'Forgiveness in the twentieth century. A review of the literature, 1901–2001', in A. McFadyen and M. Sarot (eds.), *Forgiveness and Truth* (Edinburgh: T&T Clark, 2001), pp. 181–217.

Blake, W., 'The Divine Image' (1789), in D.H.S. Nicholson and A.H.E. Lee (eds.) *Oxford Book of English Mystical Verse* (Oxford: OUP, 1962), p. 89.

Blumenthal, D.R., 'Repentance and forgiveness', *CrossCurrents*, 48 (1) (1998), pp. 75–81.

Bonhoeffer, D., *Life Together* (trans. John W. Doberstein; London: SCM Press, 1954).

Bonhoeffer, D., *The Cost of Discipleship* (trans. R. Fuller and I. Booth; London: SCM Press, 1971).

Boraine, A., *A Country Unmasked* (Oxford: Oxford University Press, 2000).

Boszormenyi-Nagy, I. and G.M. Spark, *Invisible Loyalties: Reciprocity in Intergenerational Family Therapy* (Oxford: Harper and Row, 1973).

Bowlby, J., *Attachment and Loss, vol. I* (Harmondsworth: Penguin, 1971).

—'Grief and mourning in infancy and early childhood', *The Psychoanalytic Study of the Child*, 15 (1960), pp. 9–52.

Bradbury, T.N. and F.D. Fincham, 'Attributions in marriage: Review and critique', *Psychological Bulletin*, 107 (1990), pp. 3–33.

Briere, J., *Child Abuse Trauma: Theory and Treatment of Lasting Effects* (London: Sage, 1992).

Brown, D. and J. Pedder, *Introduction to Psychotherapy* (London and New York: Tavistock Publications, 1979).

Brümmer, V., *What Are We Doing When We Pray?* (London: SCM, 1984).

—*The Model of Love* (Cambridge: CUP, 1993).

Buber, M., *Pointing the Way* (London: Routledge, 1957).

—*I and Thou* (Edinburgh: T&T Clark, 1966).

—'Guilt and guilt feelings', *Psychiatry* 20 (2) (1957b): pp. 114–29.

Butcher, S.H., *A Commentary on Aristotle's Poetics* (New York: Dover, 1951).

Butler, J., 'Upon forgiveness of injuries' in T.A. Roberts (ed.), *Butler's Fifteen Sermons* (London: SPCK, 1970): pp. 80–89.

Byng-Hall, J., *Rewriting Family Scripts: Improvisation and Systems Change* (New York: Guilford, 1995).

Capps, D., *The Depleted Self: Sin in a Narcissistic Age* (Minneapolis: Fortress Press, 1993).

Carlson Brown, J. and R. Parker, 'For God so loved the world?' in J. Carlson Brown and C. Brown (eds.), *Christianity, Patriarchy and Abuse* (Cleveland: Pilgrim Press, 1989): pp. 1–30.

Carpenter, D., 'Editorial', *Journal of Family Therapy* 20 (1) (1998), pp. 1–2.

Cashman, H., *Christianity and Child Sexual Abuse* (London: SPCK, 1993).

Chapman, A., 'Truth commissions as instruments of forgiveness and reconciliation' in R.G. Helmick and R.L. Petersen (eds.), *Forgiveness and Reconciliation* (Radnor, Pennsylvania: Templeton Press, 2001): pp. 257–77.

Chubb, K. and L. van Dijk, *Between Anger and Hope* (Johannesburg: Witwatersrand University Press, 2001).

Coate, M.A., *Sin, Guilt and Forgiveness*, (London: SPCK, 1994).

Cohn-Sherbock, D., *Holocaust Theology* (London: Lamp, 1989).

Coke, J.S., C.D. Batson and K. McDavis, 'Empathic mediation of helping: A two-stage model', *Journal of Personality and Social Psychology* 36 (1978), pp. 752–66.

Coleman, P., 'The process of forgiveness in marriage and the family', in R.D. Enright and J. North (eds.), *Exploring Forgiveness* (Madison: University of Wisconsin Press 1998): pp. 75–94.

Coopersmith, S., *Self-esteem Inventories* (Palo Alto, California: Consulting Psychologists Press, 1981).

Cordovero, M., *The Palm Tree of Deborah* (translated from the Hebrew with an Introduction and Notes by L. Jacobs; London: Valentine, Mitchell, 1960).

Coyle, C.T. and R.D. Enright, 'Forgiveness intervention with post-abortion men', *Journal of Consulting and Clinical Psychology* 65 (1997), pp. 1042–46.

Daiuto, A. and D.H. Baucom, 'The relationship dimension profile' (unpublished measure, University of North Carolina at Chapel Hill, 1994).

Darby, B.W. and B.R. Schlenker, 'Children's reaction to apologies', *Journal of Personality and Social Psychology* 43 (1982), pp. 742–53.

Davies, W.D. and D.C. Allison, *The Gospel According to Saint Matthew* (3 vols.; Edinburgh: T&T Clark, 1988–1997).

de Gruchy, J.W., *Reconciliation* (London: SCM Press, 2002).

Delbo, C., *Auschwitz and After* (trans. Rosette C. Lamont; New Haven and London: Yale University Press, 1995).

Derrida, J., *On Cosmopolitanism and Forgiveness* (trans. Mark Dooley and Michael Hughes; London and New York: Routledge, 2001).

di Berardino, A. (ed.), *Encyclopedia of the Early Church* (Cambridge: Clarke & Co., 1992).

Di Blasio, F., 'The use of decision-based forgiveness intervention within intergenerational therapy', *Journal of Family Therapy* 20 (1998), pp. 77–94.

Dixon, T., 'The Psychology of the emotions in Britain and America in the nineteenth century: The role of religious and antireligious commitments', *Osiris* 16 (2001), pp. 288–320.

Donne, J., 'A Hymn to God the Father' (1623) in J. Hayward (ed.) *John Donne. A Selection of his Poetry* (London: Penguin, 1950): pp. 176–77.

Dulles, A., *Models of the Church* (Dublin: Gill and Macmillan, 1987).

Dunn, J.D.G., *The Theology of Paul the Apostle* (Edinburgh: T&T Clark, 1998).

Duquoc, C., 'Real reconciliation and sacramental reconciliation', *Concilium* 7 (1971), pp. 26–37.

Edwards, J., 'Forgiveness can be more powerful than Vengeance', London: *The Times* 14th September 2002.

Eliade, M., *Rites and Symbols of Initiation* (New York: Harper, 1965).

Elliott, C., *Memory and Salvation* (London: Darton, Longman and Todd, 1995).

Ellis, W.D. (ed.), *A Source Book of Gestalt Psychology* (New York: Humanities Press, 1966).

Elphinstone, A., *Freedom, Suffering and Love* (London: SCM, 1976).

Emmet, D., *The Moral Prism* (London: Macmillan, 1979).

Enright, R.D., *Forgiveness is a Choice* (Washington: APA LifeTools, 2001).

Enright, R.D. and R.P. Fitzgibbons, *Helping Clients Forgive* (Washington: American Psychological Association, 2000).

Enright, R.D. and J. North (eds.), *Exploring Forgiveness* (Madison: University of Wisconsin Press, 1998).

Enright, R.D. and C.T. Coyle, 'Researching the process model of forgiveness with psychological interventions' in E.L. Worthington (ed.), *Dimensions of Forgiveness: Psychological Research and Theological Perspectives* (London: Templeton Foundation, 1998): pp. 139–61.

Enright, R.D., S. Freedman and J. Rique, 'The psychology of interpersonal forgiveness', in R.D. Enright and J. North (eds.), *Exploring Forgiveness* (Madison: University of Wisconsin Press, 1998): pp. 46–62.

Erikson, E.H., *Childhood and Society* (New York: W.W. Norton and Company, inc., 2nd edn, 1963).

Etzioni, A., *The Moral Dimension* (New York: Free Press, 1988).

Fairbairn, W.R.D., *Psychoanalytic Studies of the Personality* (London: Tavistock, 1952).

Feldmeth, J. and M.W. Finley, *We Weep for Ourselves and our Children* (New York: Harper and Row, 1990).

Fitzgibbons, R.P., 'The cognitive and emotional uses of forgiveness in the treatment of anger', *Psychotherapy* 23 (1986), pp. 629–33.

Fitzmyer, J.A., *Romans: A New Translation with Introduction and Commentary* (London: Geoffrey Chapman, 1993).

Flanigan, B., *Forgiving the Unforgivable* (New York: Macmillan, 1992).

Ford, D.F and A.I. McFadyen, 'Praise', in P. Sedgwick (ed.), *God in the City. Essays and Reflections from the Archbishop of Canterbury's Urban Theology Group* (London: Mowbray, 1995).

Forrester, D.B., *On Human Worth: A Christian Vindication of Equality* (London: SCM, 2001).

Frankl, V.E., *Man's Search for Meaning* (London: Hodder and Stoughton, rev. edn, 1962).

Freedman, S.R. and R.D. Enright, 'Forgiveness as an intervention goal with incest survivors, *Journal of Consulting and Clinical Psychology* 64 (1996), pp. 983–92.

Freud, A., *The Ego and the Mechanisms of Defence* (London: Hogarth Press, 1937).

—'Discussion of Dr. Bowlby's paper', *The Psychoanalytic Study of the Child* 15 (1960), pp. 53–60.

Freud, S., 'Mourning and melancholia', in *The Complete Psychological Works Standard Edition* (London: Hogarth Press, 1917): pp. 243–58.

Fromm, E., *The Fear of Freedom* (London: Routledge and Kegan Paul, 1942).

Frost, B., *Struggling to Forgive* (London: Harper Collins, 1998).

Fultz, J., C.D. Batson, V.A. Fortenbach, P.M. McCarthy and L.L. Varney, 'Social evaluation and the empathy-altruism hypothesis', *Journal of Personality and Social Psychology* 50 (1986), pp. 761–69.

Furman, R., 'Death and the young child', *The Psychoanalytic Study of the Child* 19 (1964), pp. 321–33.

Galdston, R., 'The longest pleasure: a psychoanalytic study of hatred', *International Journal of Psycho-analysis* 68 (1987), pp. 371–78.

Gopin, M., *Between Eden and Armageddon: The Future of World Religions, Violence and Peacemaking* (Oxford: Oxford University Press, 2000).

Gordon, K.C. and D.H. Baucom, 'Understanding betrayals in marriage: A synthesized model of forgiveness', *Family Process* 37 (4) (1999a), pp. 425–50.

—'A multitheoretical intervention for promoting recovery from extramarital affairs', *Clinical Psychology: Science and Practice* 6 (1999b), pp. 382–99.

—'Forgiveness and marriage: Preliminary support for a measure based on a model of recovery from a marital betrayal', *American Journal of Family Therapy* 31 (3) (2003), pp. 179–99.

Gordon, K.C., D.H. Baucom and D.K. Snyder, 'The use of forgiveness in marital therapy', in M.E. McCullough, K.I. Pargament and C.E. Thoresen (eds.), *Forgiveness: Theory, Research and Practice* (New York: The Guilford Press, 2000): pp. 203–27.

Grainger, R., *The Language of the Rite* (London: Darton, Longman and Todd, 1974).

—*The Message of the Rite* (Cambridge: Lutterworth, 1988).

—*The Ritual Symbol* (London: Avon, 1994).

Greenberg, J.R. and M. Mitchell, *Object Relations in Psychoanalytic Theory* (Cambridge, MA.: Harvard University Press, 1983).

Grimes, R.L., *Beginnings in Ritual Studies* (Washington: University Press of America, 1982).

Haber, J.G., *Forgiveness* (Savage, Maryland: Rowman and Littlefield, 1991).

Habgood, J., *Making Sense* (London: SPCK, 1993).

Hamber, B., 'Rights and Reasons: Challenges for Truth Recovery in South Africa and Northern Ireland', *Fordham International Law Journal* 26 (4) (2003), pp. 1074–94.

Hansen, T., *Seven for a Secret that's Never Been Told* (London: Triangle, 1991).

Hargrave, T.D. and J.N. Sells, 'The development of a forgiveness scale', *Journal of Marital and Family Therapy* 23 (1997), pp. 41–63.

Hayner, P., *Unspeakable Truths* (New York: Routledge, 2001).

—'Same species, different animal: How South Africa compares to truth commissions worldwide' in C. Villa-Vicencio and W. Verwoerd, *Looking Back Reaching Forward* (Cape Town: Cape Town University Press, 2000): pp. 32–41.

Hebl, J.H. and R.D. Enright, 'Forgiveness as a psychotherapeutic goal with elderly females', *Psychotherapy* 30 (1993), pp. 658–67.

Heider, F., *The Psychology of Interpersonal Relations* (New York: Wiley, 1958).

Helmick, R.G. and R.L. Petersen, *Forgiveness and Reconciliation* (Radnor, Pennsylvania: Templeton Press, 2001).

Hillman, J., *Re-visioning Psychology* (New York: Harper and Row, 1975).

Hinshelwood, R.D., *A Dictionary of Kleinian Thought* (London: Free Association Books, 2nd edn, 1991).

Holiday, A., 'Forgiving and Forgetting' in S. Nuttall and C. Coetzee (eds.), *Negotiating the Past* (Oxford: Oxford University Press, 1998): pp. 43–56.

Holloway, Richard, *On Forgiveness. How can we Forgive the Unforgivable?* (Edinburgh: Canongate, 2002).

Hooker, M.D., *The Gospel According to Saint Mark* (London: A & C Black, 1991).

Hope, D., 'The healing paradox of forgiveness', *Psychotherapy* 24 (1987), pp. 240–44.

Horney, K., *Neurosis and Human Growth* (London: Routledge and Kegan Paul, 1951).

Howatch, S., *Mystical Paths* (London: HarperCollins, 1992).

Hunsinger, D., *Theology and Pastoral Counselling* (Grand Rapids: Eerdmans, 1995).

Hunter, R., 'Forgiveness, retaliation and paranoid reactions', *Canadian Psychiatric Association Journal* 23 (1978), pp. 167–73.

Ignatieff, M., 'Introduction', in J. Edelstein (ed.), *Truth and Lies* (London: Granta Publications, 2001): pp. 15–21.

Imbens, A. and I. Jonker, *Christianity and Incest* (Tunbridge Wells: Burns and Oates, 1991).

James, W., *The Varieties of Religious Experience* (New York: London: Longmans, Green, 1902).

Jones, C., 'Loosing and binding: The liturgical mediation of forgiveness', in A. McFadyen and M. Sarot (eds.), *Forgiveness and Truth* (Edinburgh: T&T Clark, 2001).

Jones, L.G., *Embodying Forgiveness: A Theological Analysis* (Grand Rapids, Michigan: William B. Eerdmans, 1995).

Joseph, B., 'Addiction to near-death', *International Journal of Psycho-Analysis* 63 (1982), pp. 449–56.

KAIROS Theologians, *The Kairos Document* (London: Catholic Institute for International Relations and British Council of Churches, rev. edn, 1986).

Kee, H.C., Testament of Gad 6:3, 6–7, in J.H. Charlesworth (ed.), *Old Testament Pseudepigrapha, Vol. 1, Apocalyptic Literature and Testaments* (London and New York: Darton, Longman & Todd and Doubleday, 1983), pp. 775–828.

Kelly, G.A., *A Theory of Personality* (New York: Norton, 1963).

Kilpatrick, D.G., R. Acierno, B. Saunders, H. Resnick, C.L. Best and P.P. Schnurr, 'Risk factors for adolescent substance abuse and dependence: Data from a national sample', *Journal of Consulting and Clinical Psychology* 68 (2000), pp. 19–30.

Klein, M. (1975), 'A contribution to the psychogenesis of manic-depressive states' (1935), in *The Writings of Melanie Klein, Vol. 1 Love Guilt and Reparation and other works 1921–1945* (London: Hogarth Press: Institute of Psycho-Analysis, 1975a): pp. 262–89.

—'Love Guilt and Reparation' (1937), in *The Writings of Melanie Klein, Vol. 1* (London: Hogarth Press: Institute of Psycho-Analysis, 1975b): pp. 306–43.

—'Mourning and its relation to manic-depressive states' (1940), in *The Writings of Melanie Klein, Vol. 1* (London: Hogarth Press: Institute of Psycho-Analysis, 1975c): pp. 344–69.

—'Notes on some schizoid mechanisms' (1946), in *The Writings of Melanie Klein, Vol. 3 Envy and Gratitude and other works 1946–1963* (London: Hogarth Press: Institute of Psycho-Analysis, 1975a): pp. 1–24.

Kohlberg, L., 'The child as a moral philosopher' (1968), in J. Sants and H.J. Butcher (eds.), *Developmental Psychology Selected Readings (1975)* (London: Penguin, 1975): pp. 441–52.

Krog, A., *Country of My Skull* (London: Jonathan Cape, 1998).

Krokoff, L.J., J.M. Gottman and S.D. Hass, 'Validation of a global rapid couples interaction system', *Behavioral Assessment* 11 (1989), pp. 65–79.

Kübler-Ross, E., *On Death and Dying* (London: Tavistock Publications, 1970).

Lambourne, B., 'Towards an understanding of medico-theological dialogue', in M. Wilson (ed.), *Explorations in Health and Salvation: A selection of papers by Bob Lambourne* (Birmingham: Birmingham University Press, new edn, 1995): pp. 115–121.

Landy, R., *Drama Therapy Theory: Concepts and Practices* (Springfield, IL.: Thomas, 1995).

Lane, R.C., 'The revenge motive: A developmental perspective on the life cycle and the treatment process', *Psychoanalytic Review* 82, 1 (1995), pp. 41–64.

Lasch, C., *The Culture of Narcissism: American Life in an Age of Diminishing Expectations* (New York: Norton, 1978).

Lash, N., *Easter in Ordinary: Reflections on Human Experience and the Knowledge of God* (London: SCM, 1988).

Lederach, J.P., 'Five qualities in support of reconciliation processes', in R.G. Helmick and R.L. Petersen, *Forgiveness and Reconciliation* (Radnor, Pennsylvania: Templeton Press, 2001): pp. 193–203.

Lee, R.S., *Psychology and Worship* (London: SCM Press, 1955).

Loades, A., 'Eucharistic sacrifice: reflections on a metaphor', in S.W. Sykes (ed.), *Sacrifice and Redemption: Durham Essays in Theology* (Cambridge: CUP, 1991): pp. 247–61.

Long, E.C.G., 'Measuring dyadic perspective-taking: Two scales for assessing perspective-taking in marriage and similar dyads', *Educational and Psychological Measurement* 50 (1990), pp. 91–103.

Macaskill, A., J. Maltby and L. Day, 'Forgiveness of self and others and emotional empathy', *Journal of Social Psychology* 142 (5) (2002), pp. 663–65.

Mahler, M., 'On the first three subphases of the separation-individuation process', *International Journal of Psycho-analysis* 53 (1972), pp. 333–38.

Maimonides, M., *The Code of Maimonides (Mishneh Torah)*, Laws of Repentance, 2.9–11; Laws of Assault, 5.10.

Maitland, S., 'Ways of relating', in A. Loades (ed.), *Feminist Theology: A Reader* (London: SPCK, 1990): pp. 148–57.

Mauger, P.A., J.E. Perry, T. Freeman, D.C. Grove, A.G. McBride and K. McKinney, 'The measurement of forgiveness: Preliminary research', *Journal of Psychology and Christianity* 11 (1992), pp. 170–80.

McAlfee Brown, R., *Elie Wiesel: Messenger to all Humanity* (Notre Dame: University of Notre Dame, 1983).

McCullough, M.E., 'Forgiveness: Who does it and how do they do it?', *Current Directions in Psychological Science* 10 (6) (2001), pp. 194–97.

McCullough, M.E., K.C. Rachal, S.S. Sandage, E.L. Worthington, S.W. Brown and T.L. Hight, 'Interpersonal forgiving in close relationships: II. Theoretical elaboration and measurement', *Journal of Personality and Social Psychology* 75 (1998), pp. 1586–1603.

McCullough, M.E. and C.V. Witvliet, 'The psychology of forgiveness', in C.R. Snyder and S.J. Lopez (eds.), *The Handbook of Positive Psychology* (Oxford: Oxford University Press, 2001): pp. 446–58.

McCullough, M.E. and E.L. Worthington, Jr., 'Promoting forgiveness: A comparison of two brief psychoeducational group interventions with a waiting-list control', *Counseling and Values* 40 (1) (1995), pp. 55–68.

McCullough, M.E., E.L. Worthington, Jr. and K.C. Rachal, 'Interpersonal forgiving in close relationships, *Journal of Personality and Social Psychology* 73 (1997), pp. 321–36.

McCullough, M.E., K.I. Pargament and C.E. Thoresen (eds.), *Forgiveness: Theory, Research and Practice* (New York: The Guilford Press, 2000).

McFadyen, A., 'Healing the damaged' in D. Ford and D. Stamps (eds.), *Essentials of Christian Community* (Edinburgh: T&T Clark, 1996): pp. 91–103.

—'Introduction' in A. McFadyen and M. Sarot (eds.), *Forgiveness and Truth* (Edinburgh: T&T Clark, 2001): pp. 181–217.

McFadyen, A. and M. Sarot (eds.), *Forgiveness and Truth* (Edinburgh: T&T Clark, 2001).

McGuire, W. and R.F.C. Hull, *G.G. Jung Speaking* (London: Thames and Hudson, 1978).

McNeice, M., 'Premature forgiveness', *Self & Society* 24 (1996), pp. 11–13.

Mearleau-Ponty, M.C., *Phenomenology of Perception* (trans. C.Smith; London: Routledge, 1962).

Mehrabian, A. and N. Epstein, 'A measure of emotional empathy', *Journal of Personality* 40 (4) (1972), pp. 525–43.

Meiring, P., 'Truth and reconciliation: The South African experience', in W.E. van Vugt and G. daan Cloete (eds.), *Race and Reconciliation in South Africa* (Oxford: Lexington Books, 2000): pp. 187–199.

Meissner, W.W., *Life and Faith* (Washington: Georgetown University Press, 1987).

'Mid-East Dialog Groups: Building a Grass-Roots Force for Peace (View Points PEACE dialog Forum' *Journal of Peace and Conflict Resolution* 1.3 (online) (May 15, 1998).

Mitchell, J. (ed.), *The Selected Melanie Klein* (London and New York: Penguin, 1986).

Moberly, R.C., *Atonement and Personality* (London: John Murray, 1901).

Muller-Fahrenholz, G., *The Art of Forgiveness: Theological Reflections on Healing and Reconciliation* (Geneva: WCC Publications, 1997).

Murphy, J.G. and J. Hampton, *Forgiveness and Mercy* (Cambridge: Cambridge University Press, 1988).

Neblett, W.R., 'Forgiveness and ideals', *Mind* 83 (1974), pp. 269–75.

North, J., 'The "Ideal" of forgiveness: A philosopher's exploration', in R.D. Enright and J. North (eds.), *Exploring Forgiveness* (Madison, Wisconsin: University of Wisconsin Press, 1998): pp. 15–34.

—'Wrongdoing and forgiving', *Philosophy* 62 (1987), pp. 499–508.

Notarius, C.I. and N.A. Vanzetti, 'The marital agendas protocol', in E.E. Filsinger (ed.), *Marriage and Family Assessment: A Sourcebook for Family Therapy* (Beverly Hills, CA: Sage, 1983): pp. 209–27.

Pais, J., *Suffer the Children* (New York: Paulist Press, 1988).

Pattison, E.M., 'On the failure to forgive or be forgiven', *American Journal of Psychotherapy* 31 (1965), pp. 106–15.

Patton, J., *Is Human Forgiveness Possible? A Pastoral Care Perspective* (Nashville, TN: Abingdon Press, 1985).

—'Forgiveness in pastoral care and counseling', in M.E. McCullough, K.I. Pargament and C.E. Thoresen (eds.), *Forgiveness: Theory, Research and Practice* (New York: The Guilford Press, 2000): pp. 281–95.

Pelz, W. and L. Pelz, *God is No More* (London: Gollancz, 1963).

Peplau, L., Russell and Heim, 'The experience of loneliness', in I.H. Frieze, D. Bar-Tal and J.S. Caroll (eds.), *New Approaches to Social Problems* (San Francisco: Jossey-Bass, 1979): pp. 53–78.

Piaget, J., *The Moral Judgement of the Child* (London: Routledge and Kegan Paul, 1932).

Pope, A. (1711), 'An Essay on Criticism' 1.525, in *Oxford Dictionary of Quotations* (Oxford: Oxford University Press, 5th edn, 1999): p. 584.27.

Potvin, L., J. Lasker and L. Toedter, 'Measuring grief: A short version of the perinatal grief scale', *Journal of Psychopathology and Behavioural Assessment* 11 (1989), pp. 29–45.

Prokofieff, S., *The Occult Significance of Forgiveness* (trans. Simon Blaxlandde Lange; London: Temple Lodge, 1992).

Pruyser, P., 'Anxiety, guilt and shame in the atonement', reprinted in H.N. Malony and B. Spilka (eds.), *Religion in Psychodynamic Perspective: The Contributions of Paul Pruyser* (Oxford: Oxford University Press, 1991).

Ramsay, I.T., *Religious Language* (London: SCM, 1957).

Redmond, S., 'Christian "virtues" and recovery from child sexual abuse', in J. Carlson Brown and C. Brown (eds.), *Christianity, Patriarchy and Abuse* (Cleveland: Pilgrim Press, 1989).

Reimer, D.J., 'The Apocrypha and Biblical Theology: The Case of Interpersonal Forgiveness', in J. Barton and D.J. Reimer (eds.), *After the Exile: Essays in Honor of Rex Mason* (Macon, Georgia: Mercer University Press, 1996): pp. 259–82.

Renvoize, J., *Innocence Destroyed* (London: Routledge, 1993).

Reuther, R.R., *To Change the World* (London: SCM, 1978).

Richards, N., 'Forgiveness', *Ethics* 99 (1988), pp. 79–97.

Robinson, E.A. and M.G. Price, 'Pleasurable behaviour in marital interaction: An observational study', *Journal of Consulting and Clinical Psychology* 48 (1980), pp. 117–18.

Roth, J.K. and R.L. Rubenstein, *Approaches to Auschwitz: The Legacy of the Holocaust* (London: SCM, 1987).

Sartre, J-P., eds. Michel Contat and Michel Rybalka, *Writings of J-P. Sartre* (Boston: North-Eastern University Press, 1974).

Scheff, T.J., *Catharsis in Healing, Ritual and Drama* (Berkeley: University of California Press, 1979).

—*Microsociology. Discourse, Emotion, and Social Structure* (Chicago and London: The University of Chicago Press, 1990).

Schillebeeckx, E., *Marriage: Secular Reality and Saving Mystery* (London: Sheed and Ward, 1965).

Schimmel, S., *Wounds Not Healed By Time: The Power of Repentance and Forgiveness* (New York: Oxford University Press, 2002).

Searles, H.F., 'The psychodynamics of vengefulness' (1956), in *Collected Papers on Schizophrenia and Related Subjects (1965)* (London: Maresfield Library, 1965): pp. 177–91. (First published in *Psychiatry* 19 (1956), pp. 31–39.)

Sells, J.N. and T.D. Hargrave, 'Forgiveness: A review of the theoretical and empirical literature', *Journal of Family Therapy* 20 (1998), pp. 21–36.

Sennott, C.M., 'Faith and Forgiveness', *Boston Globe Magazine* April 4, 1999 (1999), pp. 22–30.

Shakespeare, W., *The Merchant of Venice* (1596–98), Act IV, Scene 1.

—*King Lear* (1605–06), Act II, Scene 4, 1.286.

—*The Tempest* (1611), Act V, Scene 1 and Epilogue.

Sherrill Durham, M., *The Therapist's Encounters with Revenge and Forgiveness* (London and Philadelphia: Jessica Kingsley, 2000).

Shontz F.C. and C. Rosenak, 'Psychological theories and the need for forgiveness: Assessment and critique', *Journal of Psychology and Christianity* 7 (1988), pp. 23–31.

Shorter, B., *Susceptible to the Sacred: The Psychological Experience of Ritual* (London: Routledge, 1996).

Shriver Jr., D., *An Ethic for Enemies: Forgiveness in Politics* (New York and Oxford: Oxford University Press, 1995).

Smedes, L.B., *Forgive and Forget: Healing the Hurts we Don't Deserve* (New York: Harper and Row, 1984).

Smith, C., *Moral, Believing Animals. Human Personhood and Culture* (Oxford: Oxford University Press, 2003).

Spanier, G.B., 'Measuring dyadic adjustment: New scales for assessing the quality of marriage and similar dyads', *Journal of Marriage and the Family* 38 (1976), pp. 15–28.

Spielberger, C.D., R.L. Gorsuch, R. Lushene, P.R. Vagg and G.A. Jacobs, *State-trait anxiety inventory (Form Y): Self evaluation questionnaire* (Palo Alto, California: Consulting Psychologists Press, 1983).

Spielberger, C.D., G. Jacobs, S. Russell, and R. Crane, 'Assessment of anger: The state-trait anger scale', in J.N. Butcher and C.D. Spielberger (eds.), *Advances in Personality Assessment, Vol. 2* (Hillsdale, New Jersey: Erlbaum 1983): pp. 161–89.

Spitz, A., 'Discussion of Dr Bowlby's paper', *The Psychoanalytic Study of the Child* 15 (1960), pp. 85–94.

Stanley, S.M. and H.J. Markman, 'Marriage in the 90s. A nationwide random phone survey' (Denver, CO. PREP, Inc., 1997).

Sullivan, H.S., *The Interpersonal Theory of Psychiatry* (New York: Norton, 1953).

Surin, K., *Theology and the Problem of Evil* (Oxford: Blackwell, 1986).

Sutherland, J.D., *Fairbairn's Journey into the Interior* (London: Free Association Books, 1989).

Suttie, I.D., *The Origins of Love and Hate* (London: Free Association Books, 1988).

Taylor, C., *Sources of the Self: The Making of Modern Identity* (Cambridge: Cambridge University Press, 1989).

Taylor, V., *Forgiveness and Reconciliation: A Study in New Testament Theology* (London: Macmillan, 2nd edn, 1946).

Telfer, W., *The Forgiveness of Sins: An Essay in the History of Christian Doctrine and Practice* (London: SCM, 1959).

The Mishnah: A New Translation (trans. Jacob Neusner; New Haven: Yale University Press, 1988).

The Tanakh (The Hebrew Bible). A New Translation of the Holy Scriptures (Philadelphia: The Jewish Publication Society of America, 1985).

The Toseftah. Tractate Bava Kamma.

Thoresen, C.E., A.H.S. Harris and F. Luskin, 'Forgiveness and health: An unanswered question', in M.E. McCullough, K.I. Pargament and C.E. Thoresen (eds.), *Forgiveness: Theory, Research and Practice* (New York: The Guilford Press, 2000): pp. 254–280.

Truth and Reconciliation Commission of South Africa, *Final Report* (5 Vols.; Cape Town: Truth and Reconciliation Commission, 1998).

Tutu, D., *No Future without Forgiveness* (London: Rider, 1999).

van der Leeuw, G., *Religion in Essence and Manifestation* (London: Allen and Unwin, 1936).

van Gennep, A., *The Rites of Passage* (London: Routledge, 1960).

Veenstra, G., 'Psychological concepts of forgiveness', *Journal of Psychology and Christianity* 11 (1992), pp. 160–69.

Volf, Miroslav, *Exclusion and Embrace: A Theological Exploration of Identity, Otherness and Reconciliation* (Nashville: Abingdon, 1996).

Wade, N.G. and E.L. Worthington, 'Overcoming interpersonal offences: Is forgiveness the only way to deal with unforgiveness?', *Journal of Counseling and Development* 81 (3) (2003), pp. 343–53.

Wade, S.H., 'Forgiveness scale', *Measures of Religiosity* (Birmingham, Alabama: Religious Education Press, 1989).

Walrond-Skinner, S., 'The function and role of forgiveness in working with couples and families: clearing the ground', *Journal of Family Therapy* 20 (1998), pp. 3–19.

Watts, F., *Theology and Psychology* (Basingstoke: Ashgate, 2002).

—'Shame, sin and guilt', in A. McFadyen and M. Sarot (eds.), *Forgiveness and Truth* (Edinburgh: T&T Clark, 2001): pp. 53–70.

Watts, F., R. Nye and S. Savage, *Psychology for Christian Ministry* (London: Routledge, 2002).

Watts, F. and M. Williams, *The Psychology of Religious Knowing* (Cambridge: Cambridge University Press, 1988).

Weiner, B., 'On sin versus sickness: A theory of perceived responsibility and social motivation', *American Psychologist* 48 (1993), pp. 957–64.

West, W., 'Issues relating to the use of forgiveness in counselling and psychotherapy', *British Journal of Guidance and Counselling* 29 (2001), pp. 415–23.

Wiesenthal, S., *The Sunflower* (New York: Schocken Books, 1976).

Wiesenthal, S. (with a symposium), *The Sunflower: On the Possibilities and Limits of Forgiveness* (New York: Schocken Books, rev. and exp. edn, 1997).

Williams, R., *Open to Judgement. Sermons and Addresses* (London: Darton, Longman and Todd, 1994).

Wilson, R.A., *The Politics of Truth and Reconciliation in South Africa* (Cambridge: Cambridge University Press, 2001).

Winnicott, D.W., *Human Nature* (London: Free Association Books, 1988).

—'The depressive position in normal emotional development' (1954), in D.W. Winnicott, *Through Paediatrics to Psycho-Analysis* (London: The Hogarth

Press: Institute of Psycho-Analysis, 1987): pp. 262–77. (First published London: Tavistock, 1958, this edition first published 1975.)

—'Ego distortion in terms of true and false self' (1960) in D.W. Winnicott, *The Maturational Process and the Facilitation Environment* (New York: International Universities Press, 1965).

—'The development of the capacity for concern' (1963), in D.W. Winnicott, *The Maturational Processes and the Facilitating Environment* (London: Karnac Books and the Institute of Psycho-Analysis, 1990): pp. 73–82. (First published Hogarth Press, 1965.)

Witvliet, C.V.O., T. Ludwig and K. van der Laan, 'Granting forgiveness or harboring grudges: Implications for emotion, physiology and health', *Psychological Science* 121 (2001), pp. 117–23.

Wolfe, D.A., *Child Abuse: Implications for Child Development and Psychopathology* (London: Sage, 1987).

Wolfenstein, M., 'How is mourning possible?', *Psychoanalytic Study of the Child* 2 (1966), pp. 93–123.

Wollaston, I., 'What can and cannot be said', *Journal of Literature and Theology* 6 (1992), pp. 47–56.

Wood, C., *The End of Punishment: Christian perspectives on the crisis in criminal justice* (Edinburgh: St Andrew Press, 1991).

Worthington, E.L., *Dimensions of Forgiveness* (Radnor, Pennsylvania: Templeton Foundation Press, 1998a).

—'An empathy-humility-commitment model of forgiveness applied within family dyads', *Journal of Family Therapy* 20 (1998b), pp. 59–70.

Worthington, E.L., J.W. Berry and L. Parrott, 'Unforgiveness, forgiveness, religion and health', in T.G. Plante and A.C. Sherman (eds.), *Faith and Health* (New York: The Guilford Press, 2001): pp. 107–38.

Worthington, E.L., S.J. Sandage and J.W. Berry, 'Group interventions to promote forgiveness: What researchers and clinicians ought to know', in M.E. McCullough, K.I. Pargament and C.E. Thoresen (eds.), *Forgiveness: Theory, Research and Practice* (New York: Guilford, 2000): pp. 228–53.

Worthington, E.L., T.L. Hight, J.S. Ripley, K.M. Perrone, T.A. Kurusu and D.R. Jones, 'Strategic hope-focused enrichment counseling with individual couples', *Journal of Counseling Psychology* 44 (1997), pp. 381–89.

Worthington, E.L., S.E. Mazzeo and W.L. Kliewer, 'Addictive and eating disorders: Unforgiveness and forgiveness', *Journal of Psychology and Christianity*, 21 (3) (2002), pp. 257–61.

Worthington, E.L. and J.S. Ripley, 'Hope-focused and forgiveness-based group interventions to promote marital enrichment', *Journal of Counseling and Development* 80 (4) (2002), pp. 452–63.

Wuthnow, R., *Meaning and Moral Order* (Cambridge, MA: Harvard University Press, 1987).

Young, F.M., *From Nicea to Chalcedon* (London: SCM, 1985).

Index of Subjects

Important entries are given in bold

Index of Names